Animal Suffering

SCIENCES

Biology, Field Director – Marie-Christine Maurel

Bioethics, Subject Head – Marie-Geneviève Pinsart

Animal Suffering

The Ethics and Politics of Animal Lives

Coordinated by
Florence Burgat
Emilie Dardenne

WILEY

First published 2023 in Great Britain and the United States by ISTE Ltd and John Wiley & Sons, Inc.

ISTE Ltd
27-37 St George's Road
London SW19 4EU
UK

www.iste.co.uk

John Wiley & Sons, Inc.
111 River Street
Hoboken, NJ 07030
USA

www.wiley.com

Any opinions, findings, and conclusions or recommendations expressed in this material are those of the author(s), contributor(s) or editor(s) and do not necessarily reflect the views of ISTE Group.

Library of Congress Control Number: 2022941471

British Library Cataloguing-in-Publication Data
A CIP record for this book is available from the British Library
ISBN 978-1-78945-121-4

ERC code:
LS9 Applied Life Sciences, Biotechnology, and Molecular and Biosystems Engineering
  LS9_3 Applied animal sciences (including animal breeding, veterinary sciences, animal husbandry, animal welfare, aquaculture, fisheries, insect gene drive)
SH5 Cultures and Cultural Production
  SH5_10 Ethics; social and political philosophy

Contents

Introduction

What Does It Mean, to See Animals?

Florence BURGAT

Archives Husserl, Ecole Normale Supérieure, Paris, France

Visibility in thought cannot be superimposed onto that of perception; it may be completely independent of it. Are we not able to see, or have in our perceptive field, such individuals or groups of individuals, injustice or misery, yet not pay attention to what we are seeing? Our eyes become accustomed to everything, our conscience knows how to whiten the dark spots; without forgetting, life would not be possible. All existence feeds on this oblivion, because an acute awareness of all the sufferings present in the world at any time could lead to a prohibition on living. However, there is a big difference between putting the evils that we can do nothing about to one side and perpetuating a good number of them through our behaviors. By revealing the suffering of victims, and their resistance to the treatments inflicted on them, without which it would be easy to consider them as indifferent to their own fate, we encounter the full diversity of sensibilities within a society. Thus, it is likely that the glass abattoir imagined by Jean-Marie Coetzee, in a collection of short stories of the same name (Coetzee 2018, pp. 131–166), would only provoke lasting horror and the impulse for personal change (deciding to stop eating meat, for example), among those who are immediately willing to see, because it is always possible for us to look away and cover our ears. We recall the well-known passage from the *Discourse on the Origin and Basis of Inequality Among Men*: "It is reason that engenders self-love, and reflection that strengthens it; it is reason that makes man shrink into himself; it is reason that makes him keep aloof from everything that can trouble or afflict him: it is philosophy that destroys his connections with other men; it is in consequence of her dictates that he mutters to himself, at the sight of another in

Animal Suffering,
coordinated by Florence BURGAT and Emilie DARDENNE. © ISTE Ltd 2023.

distress: you may perish for aught I care, nothing can hurt me" (Rousseau 1964, p. 156). Is it not often enough for us to adhere to a narrative that reinforces our position of indifference or exteriority? History teaches us this over and over again. It would therefore be naive for us to think that it would be enough to bring to light what has been kept secret, kept in the shadows or never named, to make visible what is not only invisible (materially) but invisibilized (politically), so that the order of values that quietly places animals on the side of goods available for all the uses that please us collapses. (Julien Dugnoille's contribution on the practices observed in the largest "wet market" in South Korea, a market where animals, especially dogs, can be sold while still alive, and then killed on the spot or taken away, alive, by the buyers, seems to confirm this.)

Moral visibility, we might call it, this visibility that owes nothing to any real presence of animals around us. Moreover, this is a presence that we do not want; the history of animals in human societies is largely one of their eradication. Let not the few laws protecting "endangered species" distract us from appreciating things. Indeed, if certain species must be protected, it is because their extermination threatens some of the benefits that their activities offer us; it is not for themselves that they are protected. Moreover, if their protection is too successful, some of them change category and are then declared by lawmakers as "harmful" or, according to the new rhetoric that does not have to realistically imitate what it qualifies, "species likely to cause damage" (French ministerial decree, July 2021). This eradication is more active than ever: directly (targeting animals specifically), indirectly (polluting their habitats or suppressing them) or, paradoxically, by the potentially endless cycle of production, immediately followed by destruction, then new production destined for the same fate, and so on. So it is with the animals we eat, the date of their slaughter conditioning that of their birth – which is why Jacques Derrida judges that the metaphor of genocide should not be overused, "because it is complicated here: the annihilation of species, certainly, would apply, but it [genocide] would pass through the organization and the exploitation of an artificial, infernal, virtually interminable survival" (Derrida 2006, pp. 46–47). The same is true of the wild animals that, in our regions in any case, hunters feed (in the case of wild boars) to encourage their development and justify killing them on the grounds that, because there are too many of them, they ravage the crops, or that they breed (in the case of pheasants) in order to release them on hunting days.

The great divide between "them and us" is accompanied by a radical separation that is both physical and theoretical and which reinforces both sides, an attitude "typical of Western man", according to Canguilhem, while "the mechanization of life, from the theoretical point of view, and the technical use of animals are inseparable" (Canguilhem 1998, p. 111). The industrialization of all fields of activity made possible by the scientific (genetics) and technical (biotechnologies) development, the extraordinary human demographic growth and the resulting urbanization, has had a double consequence: on the one hand, the massive and planned "production" of animals intended to feed a humanity that has become carnivorous in unheard-of proportions, and, on the other hand, in order to "rationalize" this production, the keeping of animals in enclosed spaces on the outskirts of cities or in the countryside.

This invisibility – the not seeing of animals, not hearing them, not suspecting their existence and not knowing anything about the kind of life they lead and the death that follows in the breeding farms, laboratories and slaughterhouses – is partly the result of invisibilization. For, while this stocking, and more precisely this confinement[1], is a response to obvious sanitation reasons, it perhaps responds, above all, to political reasoning. The progressive prohibition of the slaughter of animals in the streets was motivated by hygienic imperatives, but it was also judged to be harmful to social morality, to relations between humans, because of the violence that it exhibited on a daily basis, and therefore trivialized. Neither could laboratories, where experiments are carried out, of which there are infinitely more than at the time of Claude Bernard and which it would be wrong to believe no longer resembled what he himself called vivisections (see Muriel Obriet's contribution on animal experimentation in Europe), be places open to the public. Here again, while there are obvious reasons to generally prohibit public access to laboratories, it is above all a question of not letting anything that takes place there be revealed. How can we fail to note that here it is primarily a question of doing harm to animals (primum nocere), whereas Hippocrates' sermon states that the human medical field is primarily about doing no harm (primum non nocere)? Philippe Devienne's reflections on the ethics of veterinary medicine re-establish the Hippocratic proposition and establish the imperative of treating these patients, which are also animals. With regard to animal experimentation, it seems that public opinion is divided between two beliefs: that of the absolute necessity of resorting to it, failing which we would suffer countless pains and that of incredulity, particularly concerning experiments other than those that fall within the scope of medical research (which nevertheless constitute 70% of procedures). It is true that, unless we choose to be informed, no one can imagine the extent and the cruelty of the practices carried out, in all legality, against animals, whether domestic or wild, terrestrial or aquatic; thus, animal defense associations consider that their first mission is to inform about the reality of animal conditions.

---

1. Animal science uses the term "intensive, confined animal husbandry" and speaks of "keeping" animals in these permanently enclosed and overcrowded places.

The history of sensitivities moves together with that of ideas. The battles here are fought on a ridge line. While ideas have won the first battle – that of recognizing that animals have interests of their own and that it is morally questionable not to take them into account (the discussion concerns the extent of this consideration – see Romain Espinosa's contribution on altruism towards animals in economics) – opponents of this point of view, measuring the mutation of sensitivities, are working to invisibilize the worst treatments. Animal opponents make us forget the real conditions of their exploitation, diverting our attention to supposed "new relationships" that include the mind-boggling idea of a "respectful" killing. Is killing ever respectful? Apart from the case of euthanasia, whose purpose is to shorten intense and incurable suffering, which is not respectful of the individual but rather compassionate, killing will never have anything to do with respect, except in the deviation of the terms according to a tendency that is particularly marked today; do we not talk about the ethics of hunting and of animal experimentation, the protection of animals in slaughterhouses? This is poor ethics and poor protection! (See Tatjana Višak's contribution, which restores their meaning and their significance for the victim itself: suffering, on the one hand, and death, on the other hand.)

By parodying Kant's words, the aim of this soothing rhetoric is to abolish knowledge in order to make room for belief. If everything is hidden from view, if newspeak calls things by their opposite[2], if arguments get involved in their turn, playing on tradition, on cultural foundations, evoking the end of humanity both physically and metaphysically (the things you hear) and if humanity should one day stop breeding animals to eat them, it is easy for all those who do not know, who do not see – and who neither want to see or know – to adhere to the stories thus fomented. These narratives assert that using animals is essential, which prevents the imagination from moving towards other practices and relationships than those that end with the blood of animals; that it is desirable to maintain all forms of use, but avoiding "unnecessary suffering" (as specified in various legislations), which suggests that a good will presides over the organization exploiting and killing; that the "well-being" of animals is, even in situations where its mention seems particularly irrelevant, a constant preoccupation of institutions, which has the consequence of making us forget the reality of genetic modifications that affect the health of animals, of mutilations, of confinement in cages or buildings, of the duration of transport (up to around 50 hours or even days by boat), of slaughter (see Fabien Marchadier's contribution on the legal status of animals in European Union

---

2. For example, "piglet processing" refers to tail docking and castration without anesthesia, "nest balancing" refers to the "slamming" of sick or unhealthy piglets against a wall, "stunning" refers to an electric shock to the head or a gunshot to the skull, and so on.

law). It does not take more than this for us to be able to sleep peacefully because we do not see and do not want to know.

However, animals have acquired visibility in the academic world. What is this about? We must unceasingly remember that questioning the legitimacy of the violence against animals has always, from the beginning, accompanied this violence, splitting humanity into two with the image of the two forces, Eros and Thanatos, which govern all things. A part of humanity tries to protect what the other mistreats, violates and destroys. The scientific interest in the ways of life of animals; the analysis of their status in human societies and the condition that societies reserve to them; the writing of their history with the measurement of these data; the notably moral philosophical questions raised by practices to which animals have been subjected, that have always been restrictive, indifferent to their own interests and very often cruel; the anthropological questions raised, in return, by the institution of humanity's universal hatred of animals, are now undeniably anchored in the field of thought.

In recent decades, the so-called "animal question" has acquired an undeniable visibility in the academic world, and this book is a new example. By way of illustration[3], we can mention the inclusion of the theme "The Animal" in the curriculum of the entrance exam to the grandes écoles for the French general culture test (2020) and in that of the external philosophy agrégation (2012). Recent French baccalaureate exams (series E and S in 2018) have invited students to reflect on the moral problems posed by the violence inflicted on animals. The new curricula explicitly include a reflection on "human and animal", a formulation that is both simple and problematic and that invites reflection from the outset. Moreover, more and more young researchers across various disciplines are choosing to devote their doctoral thesis to a subject related to the animal question. Fortunately, this is no longer a laughing matter in universities. Thus, along the way, from being an anti-notion used to designate the inverse or the negative of the human – a sort of entity deprived of any quality, attribute or disposition, ultimately closer to death than life – "the animal" has become a subject that is debated in universities and schools; it has gradually come to life and has escaped from a singularity that denies the multiplicity of life forms. Before humans, no longer stands this universal void ("the animal", defined by what it lacks and never by the singularity of its wealth), but emerging animals: psychobiological individuals, none of whom is identical to the other, taken in the reefs of a complex existence, made of problems inherent to the fact of

---

3. In order not to turn this illustration into a catalog, we are limiting ourselves to a few French examples.

surviving and living, loaded with affects, a desiring life and therefore always in want.

Academic publications, as well as militant writings, are multiplying in all countries and, with them, different aspects of the animal condition are being echoed through the media; for it is indeed this condition, in the sense that it is imposed by human societies, which must awaken us from our dogmatic sleep. This question cannot, indeed, be confined to abstract questioning of the ways of being-in-the-world of the life forms that are animals. Moreover, since the diffusion of Jakob von Uexküll's work on animal worlds (Uexküll 2010), such a way of proceeding is no longer common. Every being-in-the-world is most concrete, since it is a question of living itself, of situations in which it may, or may not, unfold, both for wild or domesticated animals, for those living on land or in the water (on these situations and conditions of life, see the contributions by Peter Li, Lynne Sneddon and Donald Broom). This volume has therefore not committed the sin of abstraction in giving pride of place to the commodification of animals in order to shed light, in an international perspective, on some of the most important areas of this commodification: the history of captive animals in Europe; the institutionalization of experimentation in the same geographical area; the history and legislation of pig farming in China; the anthropology of the animal condition in South Korea. Apart from this commodification, in the wild, the problems encountered by animals and the ensuing suffering had been overlooked, but are now being taken into account and studied (see the contribution of Oscar Horta). The reflexive disciplines (moral philosophy, veterinary ethics, animal welfare science, law, economics) are, in the course of reading, invited to shed their light on this commodification.

The animal question means referring to the animal as the question, and every real question is troubling. It is not enough to produce knowledge about animals in order to highlight their problems and conditions. It is not so much that biological knowledge is feeding this questioning, but more that the history of science shows that it has, essentially, served to increase the zootechnical and experimental hold through the tailored shaping of individuals. The sciences are applied. The knowledge that describes the habits of animals or their psychology (ethology and animal psychology) is again, in the name of supposed scientific neutrality, rarely put at the service of what makes this question a burning issue. The fear of anthropomorphism, this so-called cardinal sin of ethology and its mortal pitfall, stuns many an ethologist who then opts for a description in the third person and is careful not to take a position on the moral debate on the practices of exploitation of animals, about which they would nevertheless have their say[4]. The ideal of "scientific objectivity" (we would have to have no notion of epistemology to believe in such a thing, especially when it comes to behavior, which necessarily calls for interpretation, since it is itself an interpretation of the world) would thus be achieved at the risk of emptying the object of study of all its substance: in this case, of its psyche. However, certain contemporary ethologists, and not the least of these (think of Jane Goodall, Mark Bekoff and Frans de Waal), are not afraid to think about the theoretical but also practical implications of their discoveries on the complexity of the relational life of animals. They are not afraid to question the image that the mirror, through which our relationships with animals are reflected, displays, as moral philosophy does in a more expected way. It is therefore less the positive knowledge that underpins the animal question than the disciplines that, in essence, invite questions. It is also necessary that the institutional doxa, which ensures the reproduction of ideas and inhibits sideways steps, does not dominate the spirit of research. This growing interest in animals as a question that is asked of us cannot therefore be without a certain moral concern, given that they are, according to the language of the law, subject to the regime of things or goods – two terms here that are synonymous with signifying an owner's absolute right over them: that of destroying them. It is our hope that this volume will contribute to the formulation of the moral problem posed by humanity's treatment of animals and help to clarify it.

References

Canguilhem, G. ([1965] 1998). *La connaissance de la vie*. Vrin, Paris.

Coetzee, J.-M. (2018). *L'abattoir de verre*. Le Seuil, Paris.

Derrida, J. (2006). *L'animal que donc je suis*. Galilée, Paris.

Rousseau J.-J. ([1755] 1964). *Discours sur l'origine et les fondements de l'inégalité parmi les hommes*. Gallimard/Bibliothèque de la Pléiade, Paris.

von Uexküll, J. ([1934] 2010). *A Foray into the Worlds of Animals and Humans, with A Theory of Meaning*, translated by Joseph D. O'Neil. University of Minnesota Press, Minneapolis.

---

4. We would like, by way of illustration, to underline how few ethologists agreed to sign the tribune published in the newspaper *Le Monde* (March 7, 2021, p. 32) under the title "Can the menagerie of the *Jardin des Plantes* boast of possessing Nénette, an orangutan locked up since 1972?" Not only did the researchers of the Muséum National d'Histoire Naturelle, owner of this menagerie, refuse to do so, but also those who had some connection with them then (on the history of this zoo, see the contribution of Violette Pouillard).

1

Extraction and Captive Management of Wild Animals, 18th Century to Present Day

Violette POUILLARD[1,2]
[1] LARHA, CNRS, Lyon, France
[2] Ghent University, Belgium

1.1. Preamble: ancient practices

The keeping of wild animals in captivity dates back to ancient times and has been practiced in many parts of the world. It played not only a food role, with game parks, but also an ornamental and ostentatious role. Animals exhibited during the Roman games bore witness to the splendor of the organizers, to their supremacy over the wild world and to imperial expansion. In the Middle Ages, many aristocrats and ruling elites in Central Europe, the Byzantine Empire or the Umayyad Caliphate in Cordoba maintained ostentatious menageries in addition to game parks. The aristocratic and princely menageries of the modern era showed, in turn, the political power, pomp and culture of their owners, as well as the support given to learned enterprises. Ottoman sultans kept felines, elephants and many other animals in their menageries, and the one belonging to Suleiman the Magnificent in Constantinople included a lion house and a menagerie of pachyderms (Faroqhi 2008; Trinquier 2011; Beck and Guizard 2012; Lesage 2019). In France, the menagerie at Versailles, built by order of Louis XIV in 1664, was the heart of a vast anatomical dissection enterprise that relied on the cadavers of its captive animals (Guerrini 2015). The institution also embodied a shift in sensibilities regarding captivity, which is why animals were mostly kept in outdoor yards. However, this presentation was

Animal Suffering,
coordinated by Florence BURGAT and Emilie DARDENNE. © ISTE Ltd 2023.

primarily for scenographic purposes, as the wings of the flying birds were mutilated in order to keep them on the ground in the yards and to give visitors the illusion of greater freedom. Moreover, animal fights were still in vogue and were featured in a seraglio built at Vincennes on the orders of Louis XIV, completed three years before the menagerie (Sahlins 2017). A democratization of access to wild animals began to take shape in the 18th century, with the princely menageries becoming more open to the public, and also with the development of commercial and fairground menageries, which was made possible by the intensification of animal extraction and circulation (see section 1.3).

1.2. Birth of the modern zoo: new forms of animal captivity

The menagerie at Versailles, whose sumptuous management crystallized criticism, was abolished during the revolutionary period. However, in 1792, Jacques-Henri Bernardin de Saint-Pierre, intendant of Paris' Jardin des Plantes, an institution founded in 1626 as a royal medicinal garden and which had become a center of French natural history, developed the project of establishing a national menagerie that would serve the work of natural history and public instruction (Laissus 1993, pp. 76–82; Spary 2005). The project, established within a turbulent political context, did not materialize immediately, but the Jardin des Plantes menagerie was formed in 1793 by the arrival of show animals seized from the public highway for security reasons and deposited in the Muséum National d'Histoire Naturelle, the former and now nationalized Jardin des Plantes. Seized animals from the stripped princely menageries were added to it, soon followed by acquisitions. The Jardin des Plantes menagerie, often considered by historians as the first zoological garden, quickly became a model, inspiring the creation of the London Zoological Gardens in 1828, which in turn guided the foundation of many other "zoos" (an abbreviation coined at the beginning of the 19th century), in a context of emulation between urban centers and between nations (Laissus 1993; Baratay and Hardouin-Fugier 1998; Mehos 2006).

The first theoreticians of the Jardin des Plantes menagerie insisted on offering the animals a freer captivity, in particular by placing them in parks (e.g. Lacépède 1804, pp. 17–22). However, reconciling captivity with freedom for the animals proved to be a difficult enterprise. The menagerie was part of the Muséum National d'Histoire Naturelle, a public institution whose vocation was, among other things, to mobilize natural history for the utilitarian purposes of agricultural and commercial development. This aim, which was in line with the agricultural programs of the early modern era, was strengthened by the republican project of improving the resources of the nation, within a context marked by food crises. The menagerie was, in particular, called upon to participate in the work of acclimatizing animals from other lands to the local climate and conditions, in order to improve domestic livestock through crossbreeding and by adding new species (Lacépède 1795; Osborne 1994; Spary 2005). This mission reinforced the understanding of animals as resources whose productivity needed to be improved. While the French Revolution was the catalyst for projects to improve the lot of animals, as part of a broader societal renovation which included the abolition of human slavery, animals were not envisaged in any other way than in the service of humans (Spary 2005; Serna 2017). The acclimatization mission became important in Europe, and by extension in the colonial territories, in the 19th century, but it struggled to establish itself over the long term. It was marginalized from the end of the century, in particular due to the difficulties in acclimatizing animals and finding useful functions for the species being acclimatized, especially at a time of developing mechanization and competition from products from the continents of origin, such as ostrich feathers, in a context of imperial expansion (Osborne 1994; Baratay and Hardouin-Fugier 1998, pp. 177–179).

Another function initially envisaged for the menagerie, the study of the behavior of living animals, in the tradition of Buffon, remained subsidiary. It was first carried out with some success by Frédéric Cuvier, head keeper of the menagerie (1803–1838) and brother of the anatomist Georges Cuvier. However, Cuvier did not succeed in giving this function a solid institutional base. After his death, it was marginalized at the menagerie, as well as other European zoos, the difficulties in studying animals with a strongly constrained existence, and surrounded by increasingly large crowds, appearing to be the determining factor. Despite some exceptions, study programs of captive behaviors were preferentially conducted in laboratories from the 20th century, which saw the rise of scientific ethology. In zoos, the studies of behavior remained largely confined to occasional observations, and the empirical knowledge of keepers and employees in charge of the animals, which was often fine and detailed, was rarely called upon beyond the purposes of daily management (Burkhardt 1997, 2010; Baratay and Hardouin-Fugier 1998, p. 162; Hochadel 2005, 2011).

The scientific function of zoological gardens, often asserted from the beginning, was, in the 19th century, much more in line with the naturalist culture of inventory and classification of the world, which had been developing since the work of Linnaeus, and which was invigorated by imperial expansion. This approach encouraged the collection of large numbers of animals belonging to a wide variety of species. Once dead, many captive animals were mobilized for research in taxonomy (classification), comparative anatomy (analysis of the internal structures of animals) and morphology (study of the interactions between animal structures and their functions), the latter disciplines also serving the order of living things. Dead animals and animal parts joined the display cases and drawers of natural history museums, regularly associated with zoos, many of which were created by zoological societies that also had libraries and exhibition spaces. Above all, the display of a wide variety of animals was encouraged by the educational mission of zoos, as well as by their recreational purpose, which required that spectacular animals (such as lions, bears, elephants, giraffes and monkeys) be displayed to crowds. The care taken to attract visitors was particularly strong in the numerically dominant private institutions, whose existence depended on revenues from paid admissions (Baratay and Hardouin-Fugier 1998; Åkerberg 2001; Mehos 2006).

The triple function of zoos – scientific, educational and recreational – rapidly transformed them into living museums or animated encyclopedias. For example, the aim of the managers of London Zoo in the mid-19th century was to "present as many types of [animal] forms as possible, with the view of illustrating the generic variations of the Animal Kingdom". In 1864, they boasted that they had "by far the largest and most complete series of living animals in Europe". By the end of the century, the number of mammals, birds and reptiles alone that could be seen during a visit reached nearly 3,000 animals[1]. This encyclopedic paradigm required wide-ranging animal circulations in order to populate the cages, especially since the number of zoos multiplied throughout the century. The only Western European zoos founded in the 19th century still in operation in 1912, that is, those which escaped the multiple bankruptcies and closures, included, in addition to the Jardin des Plantes menagerie: London (1828), Dublin (1830), Bristol (1835), Manchester (1836), Amsterdam (1838), Antwerp (1843), Berlin (1844), Marseille (1855), Lyon (1857), Rotterdam (1857), Frankfurt (1858), Copenhagen (1859), Paris (the Jardin d'Acclimatation, 1860), Cologne (1860), Dresden (1861), Hamburg (1863), The Hague (1863), Hanover (1864), Karlsruhe (1864), Breslau (1865), Mulhouse (1868), Düsseldorf (1874), Basel (1874), Münster (1875), Posen (1875), Leipzig (1876), Elberfeld (1879), Lisbon (1883), Stockholm (1891), Barcelona (1892) and Königsberg (1896) (Loisel 1912, pp. 432–434). In 1900, there were 32 zoos in the United States, where the first zoological garden was opened in Philadelphia in 1859 (Kisling 1996).

While some zoo animals were born in captivity, either within the zoos themselves or elsewhere, for example, in the menageries of English aristocrats invested in breeding, who then proceeded to transfer animals (Ritvo 1987, p. 239), most were captured in their natural habitat, all the more so as the great diversity of animals and the presence of crowds constrained captive breeding.

---

1. *Report of the Council of the Zoological Society of London 1855*, p. 13, *1864*, p. 18 (citations).

1.3. The rise of the animal trade

In addition to the many animals taken across Europe, the import of captive animals into Europe increased significantly in the early modern era as a consequence of developments in navigation, colonial expansion and scientific exploration. While, in the 16th century, imported animals were mainly ostentatious products that supplied the princely menageries, a dramatic increase in flows occurred in the 18th century, marked by a development of interest in natural history, embodied and encouraged by the popularity of Buffon's *Natural History* and the development of the Linnaean classification. The increased commodification of animals was linked to the development of commercial routes, including those of the slave and colonial trades. The trade in live animals involved thousands of individual, mainly small-sized animals every year (such as passerines, parrots and monkeys), imported from Africa, the Americas, India, Australasia or the Pacific Islands. On board ship, animals kept the sailors and travelers company and then, at the ports of arrival, they served as pets, ostentatious gifts, merchandise to be exchanged for money or as specimens that fed the taste for natural history. The commodification of animals was marked by a democratization similar to that which characterized the economy of other imperial products. Access to animals such as African and South American parrots, once reserved for the powerful, was extended to artisans in large urban centers. The pet culture developed, and, with it, fashion, such as canaries, taken from the Canary Islands since the 15th century and popular for their song, now partially reproduced in captivity, and cardinals, imported from the Americas and prized for their scarlet plumage, particularly after the end of the American Revolution in 1782. While only a fraction of animals arrived alive at their destination, their corpses, dissected, naturalized or petrified in alcohol, supplied the growing number of natural history collections (Hamy 1903; Robbins 2002, pp. 9–36; Baldin 2014).

In the 19th century, wild animals and the products extracted from them became mass consumption items, integrated into the first globalization of goods. Their acquisition achieved democratization as a result of a cluster of factors, including: the extension of the European sphere of influence; the extension of the colonial grip; improvements in means of transportation, including rail and steamboat, and communication technologies, such as the telegraph, which allowed for better coordination of supply and demand; the development of trading companies and international trade and the development of sophisticated hunting weapons (Rothfels 2002; Coote et al. 2017). In Europe and the United States, the demand for dead and live animals reached unprecedented levels with the advent of leisure culture and the development of mass entertainment institutions such as menageries, zoological gardens, circuses, natural history museums, which multiplied and opened to the public, private museums and collections, and international and colonial exhibitions (Brandon-Jones 1997; Nance 2013; Coote et al. 2017).

This exposure of wild animals to crowds in turn reinforced the popular culture of appropriation and domestication of the wild. The possession of pets developed strongly in the 19th century, accompanying the bourgeois withdrawal into private space. New fashions emerged, such as that of aquariums from the middle of the century (Lorenzi 2009; Baldin 2014). The period from 1780 to 1950, that of the "civilization of beasts", marked the peak of the domestic and tame animal presence in Europe, both in rural and urban spaces (Baratay 2008).

The associated thirst for appropriation was fueled by the development and professionalization of trade networks. Stores of naturalized specimens proliferated, supplying museums and private collections (Coote et al. 2017, p. 326). Traders in large live animals operated out of English and German ports (London, Liverpool, Bristol, Hamburg) (Flint 1996; Hanson 2002, pp. 71–84; Rothfels 2002, pp. 45–59). Among them, Carl Hagenbeck, based in Hamburg, developed a merchant empire made up of sprawling networks of collectors, mainly in Africa and Asia. In March 1910 alone, his collectors sent him 20 lions, two cheetahs, six hyenas, 300 monkeys, four rhinoceroses, an elephant, a giraffe, a buffalo, 12 antelopes, 17 Grevy's zebras, warthogs, four dromedaries, eight horses, 40 ostriches, as well as many "small animals" from Africa, and tigers, leopards, several hundred monkeys, six elephants, antelopes and eight zebus from India (Loisel 1912, p. 327). Hagenbeck opened a Tierpark in 1874, then a zoo in Stellingen, in the suburbs of Hamburg, in 1907. These zoos served as animal storage facilities, training centers, and places for exhibiting animals, and also humans. Thus, in his Tierpark, Hagenbeck exhibited, among others, a family of Sami with reindeer, Sudanese people with horses and camels, "eskimos" with sled dogs, Sri Lankans with elephants, as well as Cameroonians, after the conquest in 1886. He thus contributed to popularizing the exhibition of exoticized humans[2], which is age old, but which became commonplace in zoos and colonial exhibitions from the end of the 19th century, to manifest the claims of conquest, "civilization" and domestication of the world extended to humans, themselves thus rejected to the outer limits of humanity with the racist support of physical anthropology (Bancel et al. 2002; Ames 2008; Blanchard et al. 2011; Bruce 2017, pp. 57–96, pp. 137–144).

Several other private zoological gardens invested in commercial policies to increase their financial incomes. This was the case with the Jardin d'Acclimatation

---

2. "Exoticism" refers to a form of cultural apprehension and appropriation, largely modeled on imperial geography, that related to distant, strange and fascinating otherness, which one enjoys appropriating, staging and domesticating (Staszak 2008).

in the Bois de Boulogne (1860), where Hagenbeck also presented human exhibits, and the Antwerp Zoological Garden (1843), both of which played an important role in the commodification of animals. According to an account from 1906, at the Antwerp Zoo, "[in] August of each year, for example, the aviaries and reserve stores often contain 50,000 to 60,000 small exotic passerines that are then purchased by dealers and hobbyists" (Loisel 1912, pp. 290–291). World War I brought a halt to the international animal trade and was a near-fatal shock to the Hagenbeck empire (Ames 2008, pp. 223–224). However, zoos, other animal-based industries and developing animal experimentation quickly spurred the resumption of trade. In 1927, the British animal dealer Chapman employed about 20 collectors, 14 of whom were based on the African continent, three in Asia, and others in Oceania and South America[3]. The appropriation of animals did not rely solely on the professionals of their trade.

1.4. A collective appropriation of wildlife

Political and economic elites in Africa and Asia regularly resorted to capturing wild animals for ostentatious or diplomatic purposes, by using them as gifts or medium of exchange. The practice was reinvigorated by the asymmetric negotiations accompanying European colonial expansion (Bodson 1998; Ringmar 2006; Buquet 2012; Simons 2019). In India, many rulers and notables owned rich menageries, a tradition that partly survived the British occupation. These collections were notably supplied by the port of Calcutta, an important center for animal trade (Brandon-Jones 1997). The injection of a growing number of animals into globalizing transfer networks was thus the result of a complex intertwining of local and global dynamics, political negotiations and colonial servitudes.

The taste for the company of wild animals and for private menageries and natural history collections encouraged an appropriation of animals that was often directly operated by amateurs. Amateur collecting developed considerably in colonial lands, where hunting seemed inseparable from conquest: supported by technological aids, in particular increasingly sophisticated firearms, it participated in the violent mastery of territories, with the big game hunter being "the archetype of imperial man" (MacKenzie 1997; Arzel 2014; Gissibl 2016, pp. 73–79 (citation p. 74), 88–89). Many military personnel, "explorers", missionaries, colonial administrators and settlers owned naturalistic collections and small menageries out of a hunting and naturalist infatuation, to stave off boredom, to interact with local residents and to maintain ties with the metropolis, where specimens were often brought back or

---

3. "A world-wide industry," *Chapman's Monthly Notes*, 16, April–May 1927, pp. 1–2; also "Now is the time," *Chapman's Monthly Notes*, 18, October 1927, p. 3.

shipped. Collections offered "an illusion of cognitive control" over the colonial experience and environments, while the scholarly veneer conferred on these endeavors served to justify colonial conquest and control (Breckenridge 1989, pp. 209–211 (citation); Bonneuil 1999, pp. 161–165; Arzel 2018, pp. 200–206).

In the colonized territories, captures, operated by a multitude of actors, became a collective appropriation. In addition to their official activities, some settlers engaged in hunting and capture themselves, often in a subsidiary capacity. However, the collections of dead and live animals were mostly supplied by collecting, bartering and buying from rural populations possessing the ethological and technological knowledge necessary for the capture of these resources. Similarly, Western collectors and hunters sent by museums, zoos and traders bought or bartered from rural populations much more than they hunted themselves. Their work consisted mainly of inciting the surrounding populations to engage in mass collection, and then in selecting the captures and grouping those chosen into compounds before shipping them out together. This collective appropriation of animals, with marked environmental effects, whose flows were partially absorbed and redirected by animal traders, reached an unprecedented dimension from the interwar period, a time of territorial apogee that was accompanied by a growth in the European presence in the colonies. Colonial authorities supervised and encouraged appropriation. They regularly took charge of it themselves when it came to the animals most protected by colonial law, which did not so much protect the animals as the new colonial uses that were made of them. Among these, exhibitions in the cages and showcases of the zoos and museums of Western cities occupied pride of place, since they playfully demonstrated to crowds the extent of the conquest, mastery and domestication of the territories, underpinned by an increasingly well-oiled machine (Pouillard 2019).

The claims of efficient colonial management could not, however, hide the deadly economy on which exports were based. On the one hand, many of the young captured were by-products of hunting, recovered near to slaughtered animals. On the other hand, the specific quest for young animals, which were easier to handle and more amenable to human control, set in motion an enterprise of deliberate destruction of adults, especially mammals. For example, the official killings of Eastern gorillas carried out by the Belgian colonial authorities in 1948–1949 in Eastern Congo, by an official Capture Group led by a hunting officer who relied on local labor, resulted in the slaughter of a minimum of 21–28 gorillas for the capture of 12 young gorillas (Pouillard 2015).

The animals that survived the capture operations experienced a period of waiting in captivity compounds and places of deposit and transit, where a new wave of mortality would mow down the individuals most weakened by the social and environmental changes imposed by their extraction. The distances to the ports of departure were sometimes considerable and the means of transport in the 19th century were crude, with the construction of railroads developing gradually in the second half of the century. Carl Hagenbeck, referring to the transportation of animals captured in the Egyptian Sudan by his suppliers to the Red Sea ports, noted that "in spite of the care given to them, many [...] succumb on the way" (Hagenbeck 1951 [1908], p. 153). The animals then underwent a sea voyage from Asia or Africa to European ports, which, at the beginning of the 19th century, took several months. Mostly they were taken on board ships chartered for purposes other than animal trade, and thus followed the sometimes extended routes of scientific missions, human migration and trade, including the routes of the slave trade until its effective abolition in the second half of the century (Robbins 2002, pp. 12–17, pp. 27–29, p. 32). While advances in navigation, particularly the development of steam-powered ocean-going vessels, gradually reduced crossing times, these remained difficult times for the animals. According to the testimony of animal trader Josef Menges (1876), who worked for Hagenbeck, losses during transportation regularly reached one-third and sometimes up to two-thirds of the captured animals (Rothfels 2002:57). In 1870, the director of the Jardin d'Acclimatation, Albert Geoffroy Saint-Hilaire, wrote:

> When one has, as we have, the opportunity to frequently see newly landed animals and the cages in which they have undergone a journey sometimes several months long, one can understand the incredible levels of mortality that often occur during transportation, despite the most assiduous care (Geoffroy 1870, pp. 1–18).

The figures for animals arriving alive at Western urban zoos in the 19th century and during the first half of the 20th century, of the order of several hundred to thousands of individuals per year, for each institution (Pouillard 2019, pp. 236–238), therefore only tell a minor part of the appropriation orchestrated by the zoos, largely based on a colonial extraction with elusive networks, in terms of their extent and ramifications. The dead collections of museums were likewise based on wide ranging extractive processes: the zoological collections of the Paris Muséum National d'Histoire Naturelle alone included, all origins combined, 650,000 specimens in 1858 and 8.5 million in 1921 (Bonneuil 1999, pp. 151–152).

1.5. The confinement of wild animals

In the 19th century and during the first half of the 20th century, zoological gardens housed livestock that varied constantly according to the arrivals in two types of installations. Parks, already present in many previous aristocratic menageries, were designed to allow the animals to move more freely and to allow visitors to better observe their movements, but the device caused mutilations to the flying birds. However, several renowned zoos developed large aviaries from the end of the 19th century, such as the one in the Jardin des Plantes menagerie (1888): 12 meters high, 37 meters long, 25 meters wide, dimensions considered "colossal" at the time, exceeding "all those that exist", and allowing trees to be included[4]. In contrast, so-called "ferocious" animals, and those that could not withstand the temperate climate, in other words, the majority of the livestock, were kept in cages in buildings often equipped with heating systems. These buildings were expensive, therefore rarely replaced, and not very adaptable to accommodate a large, diversified and highly variable herd.

This situation created conditions of close proximity of the animals to each other and to the public. The resulting contagious transmissions, aggressions between animals, visitor violence towards animals and the inefficiency and technical failures of the heating systems, as well as various sanitary problems, led to significant mortality. A statistical study shows that the average longevity in captivity of primates that entered and died at London Zoo from 1865, the date of the opening of a new dedicated building, to 1926, the year of the destruction of the building, that is, 6,043 individuals, was 433 days, or around one year and two months[5], whereas the age of entry of these animals was usually low, since they were generally imported as juveniles (Pouillard 2019). The level of imports is thus also explained by the fact that the zoo was "a place of perpetual death" (Flack 2018, p. 98).

The creation of the Stellingen Zoo by Carl Hagenbeck in 1907 has long been considered a turning point in the history of animal captivity. The site included several panoramas featuring animals in landscapes of painted concrete and concealing their captivity by replacing the bars with moats. The large panorama at Stellingen allowed visitors to look out over a pond, with a multitude of birds, and then over an African steppe, in the background of which was a lion's rock, itself overhung by large rocks populated by mountain herbivores whose silhouettes stood out against the horizon. The sensation of immersion in distant landscapes and the illusion of animal consent offered by the panoramas met with immense popular success. Stellingen in turn became a model, imitated in most European and American zoos, many of which opened infrastructures directly inspired by

---

4. National Archives, Pierrefitte-sur-Seine, AJ/15/845, A. Milne-Edwards, *Rapport sur l'état actuel de la Ménagerie...* [1891].

5. From Zoological Society of London Archives, GB0814 QAA. *Daily Occurrences 1865–2000.*

Hagenbeck's installations (African plains, monkey rocks and so on) (Rothfels 2002; Ames 2008; Pouillard 2019).

However, at Stellingen, and later in other zoos, while the panoramas were attracting the attention of visitors, most of the animals were living in encyclopedic structures lining the cages. Panoramas, on the contrary, required the formation of groups of animals, often abruptly put together, according to transfers and arrivals, sometimes by placing phylogenetically related but geographically distant species together, as in the case of the herbivores from different regions of the world in the large panorama at Stellingen (Rothfels 2002, pp. 173–174). The artificial character of the groupings and the illusion of latitude offered to the animals regularly imposed new constraints on them: mutilations of birds to prevent their flight; training of big cats; placement in narrow lodges, mostly hidden from the view of visitors, at night or for management reasons (Loisel 1912, p. 318, p. 323; Baratay and Hardouin-Fugier 1998, pp. 250–253).

While the change offered by Hagenbeck at Stellingen with the panoramas was therefore largely a matter of spectacle and illusion rather than of the improvement of the condition of the captives, its influence was also marked in terms of health management. Hagenbeck valued the placement of animals in the open air in all weathers, while the confinement of animals from warm climates in facilities that were regularly stifling or too cold was the dominant model. The idea was promoted in other European zoos, in particular London Zoo, under the influence of scientists and pathologists who reached managerial positions at the beginning of the 20th century, and it fell into the emerging hygienist movement. The aim was to revitalize animal bodies degenerated by confinement, deformed by rickets and osteomalacia (softening of the bones), eaten away by parasites or consumed by tuberculosis, by giving them access to air and light. The placing of animals in the open air operated at a slow pace, and its effects were regularly fatal in cold weather in the absence of shelter and heated areas. It also remained uneven, being mostly granted to mammals and birds, right up to the present day (Pouillard 2019, pp. 179–184). However, an increasing number of individuals avoided permanent indoor confinement.

The body revitalization program encompassed many other aspects, such as improved nutrition, cage disinfection and veterinary care. All of this led to a gradual decrease in mortality in the best managed zoos from the beginning of the interwar period (Pouillard 2019). This clinical turn was accompanied, however, by a denudation of captive structures: many cages were bare spaces, lined with tiles and other materials ensuring a watertight environment and facilitating sanitation. The sight of destitute animals in empty cages brought about a resurgence in criticism, as old as captivity itself, from visitors.

1.6. Zoo ethics

The founders of the Jardin des Plantes menagerie intended to reconcile the exploitation and the liberation of animals. To solve this contradiction, they had represented the menagerie as a place of harmony between humans and animals, under the benevolent but firm grip of humans. However, beyond the intentions expressed in the founding texts, in front of the narrow, often unhealthy cages of the nascent menagerie, a number of visitors expressed strong criticism. The context was one of a development, since the 18th century, of sensitivities towards animals, under the influence of various factors, such as the rise of the relations of proximity with the pets and the "cult of tender-heartedness", which, for humans, claimed the abolition of slavery and sentences of torture (Foucault 1975; Thomas 1985 (citation p. 229)). During the early decades, critics of captivity regularly used the vocabulary of imprisonment and slavery to describe the fate of animals (example: Jauffret 1798, p. 76, p. 84).

Throughout the history of zoos, reproaches have mostly focused on the modalities of captivity. Thus, it was that, in the 19th century and during the early decades of the 20th century, complaints about the parks were less frequent, except during the cold or humid months, when their occupants faced the bite of temperatures, without heating, or being bogged down in unsuitable soil. Criticism of the captivity of wild animals per se, which was long-standing and expressed, in particular, in philosophical and literary texts such as those of Montaigne or Rousseau, remained marginal (Rousseau 1969 [1755], pp. 111–112; Montaigne 2009 [1572–1580], p. 155).

The first animal protection organizations were established at the beginning of the 19th century. The most important of these, by reputation and number of members, such as the first protective society, the Society for the Prevention of Cruelty to Animals (1824) in England, or the Société Protectrice des Animaux (1845) in France, did not condemn captivity. Indeed, captivity corresponded with the ideal of animal acclimatization promoted by these associations in the 19th century, as well as the desire for proximity and physical contact with animals, including wild animals. From the 19th century to the present day, the activities of these associations have therefore focused on the modalities of captivity, drawing an evolving line distinguishing between "good" and "bad" zoos and calling for the latter to be closed or reformed, with the support of zoos placed in the former category (Baratay and Hardouin-Fugier 1998, pp. 208–210; Pouillard 2019).

However, beyond what separated the various critical expressions around captivity, most were formed in response to human perceptions of suffering expressed by animals, both physical and mental (Baratay 2011). Certain animal behaviors polarized attention. At the beginning of the 19th century, a serval in the Jardin des Plantes menagerie had "not a moment's rest", made "prodigious jumps" and swung in a "peculiar manner [...] when not jumping"; he killed himself by hitting the ceiling of its cage. The polar bears of the institution had "a singular and perpetual movement of the head and neck, from top to bottom and from bottom to top". Contemporaries, when questioning the causes of these behaviors, linked them to the conditions of captivity. Thus, polar bears must have "acquired this habit because the cage in which they spent their first year was too narrow" (Anonymous 1801, pp. 17–18; Cuvier n.d., p. 7).

From the middle of the 20th century onwards, within the context of the development of zoo psychology, and under the influence of the frequency of these so-called stereotypical behaviors and of the large proportion of individuals affected, research programs on the subject were set up. The insights provided confirmed the intuitions and empirical observations made by visitors and keepers from the very establishment of the zoo, while refining the established causalities. The zoologist and specialist in stereotypical behaviors Georgia Mason defines these as repetitive behaviors, devoid of apparent function, invariable and taking various forms depending on the species concerned (pacing, rhythmic rocking, self-mutilation, over-grooming, regurgitation and re-ingestion of food, licking of objects or supports and so on). They are caused by internal states associated with deficiencies in captive conditions, particularly frustration, fear, stress or lack of comfort. These internal states trigger persistent behavioral responses that are interpreted as deriving from attempts to replace a behavior that is impossible to perform under captive conditions, to escape confinement or more broadly to mitigate the difficulties of captive life. For example, pacing is regularly linked to unsuccessful attempts to escape (Mason et al. 2007, pp. 163–172).

The frequency of stereotypical behaviors, their striking character, especially in the most acute forms, such as self-mutilation, as well as the interpretation of lay people, which polarizes attention on the shortcomings of captivity conditions, prompted the cessation of the exhibition of certain species (such as gorillas and bears) in certain zoos from the last decades of the 20th century, as well as adaptations in captivity conditions (Flack 2016; Pouillard 2019). Beginning in the late 1970s, within a context of rising criticism of zoos (see section 1.7), staff at many institutions set out to develop and institutionalize "enrichment" programs, a term coined in 1978 to describe "any change to an animal's environment that is implemented to improve the animal's physical fitness and mental well-being". The primary goals of enrichment "are to stimulate species-specific behavior, to increase activity, and prevent stereotypies" (Hosey et al. 2013, p. 251, p. 255). Enrichment programs focus on developing occupational devices, including environmental, dietary, olfactory, auditory and tactile, for at least the most popular animals, often mammals, whose sufferings also appear most visible. While the most acute forms of stereotypical behaviors have disappeared in European zoos and the frequency and occurrence of these behaviors are decreasing, they remain endemic in captivity for a number of species (Mason et al. 2007, pp. 166–168; Birkett and Newton-Fisher 2011).

However, reforms aimed at diversifying the behavior of captive animals and the increasing attention paid to captive conditions were also a response to the desire to promote their reproduction, while criticism of their capture was increasingly strong.

1.7. Captive breeding

A cluster of factors promoted the deployment of criticism of zoos from the 1960s and 1970s. This was the time when colonial domination was being called into question, ecologist movements were on the rise, confinement in prisons or psychiatric clinics was being criticized, and the status of animals was being more vigorously questioned, supported by the publication of *Animal Liberation* by the Australian philosopher Peter Singer in 1975. Studies of "animal psychiatry" and reports on captive animals testified to the extent of their disorders. These visions contrasted with images of wild animal life in nature disseminated through the popularization of field research on animal behavior and the trivialization of wildlife documentaries (Baratay and Hardouin-Fugier 1998, pp. 236–237; Kean 1998, pp. 197–203; Traïni 2011, pp. 193–201; Singer 2015 [1975]).

At the same time, the number of private zoos was increasing, and with it the number of "bad" zoos decried by protection associations and traditional zoos. In 1969, the managers of the Zoological Society of London, the institution responsible for the London and Whipsnade Zoos, spoke of the proliferation of zoos, many of which were guilty of "neglect"[6]. The number of zoos in the British Isles had then increased from 65 to 95 in three years. In 1990, France had 324 animal parks, vivariums and butterfly greenhouses, many of which were created during the 30 years following the end of World War II (*Les Trente Glorieuses*). This increase in the number of private zoos was a direct result of the increase in the commodification of wild animals, to which it, in turn, contributed (Pouillard 2019, pp. 289–290).

In 1952, the rate of import of wild animals into Europe, mainly for animal traders and animal testing, was such, as was the harm done to the animals being

---

6. Zoological Society of London, *Annual Report 1969*, p. 16.

transported, that the Royal Society for the Prevention of Cruelty to Animals opened a facility at London Heathrow Airport to care for animals before they reached their final destination. In the early 1960s, this facility handled approximately 720,000 animals per year. The numbers increased in subsequent years, and, by 1977, the association had handled more than 16 million animals at this one entry point. In the 1970s and 1980s, the written press regularly published contributions on the traffic, especially during the arrival of dying individuals at airports. In Belgium, one of the European hubs of the wildlife trade in the 1970s and 1980s, campaigns led by animal protection associations and journalistic investigations made it possible to read and see photographs of dead and dying masses of animals left at Zaventem Airport, near the capital. Articles periodically questioned zoos, and certain animal protection associations were formed around this opposition to zoos and animal trafficking, such as France's Ligue Française des Droits de l'Animal (LFDA) (1977), which leaned towards abolishing the captivity of wild animals (Pouillard 2019, pp. 290–302).

The industrial commodification of animals also gave rise to an international legal response, aimed at regulating the trade, but not stopping it. The Convention on International Trade in Endangered Species of Fauna and Flora (CITES), or Washington Convention, which came into force in 1975, and which was transcribed into law in the United Kingdom in 1976, in France in 1978, and in Belgium later (1984), is a commercial regulatory instrument which governs the trade of species listed in its appendices through the granting of import and export licenses, which are only required for those species considered most threatened (Boisson de Chazournes et al. 2005, pp. 105–113). CITES, as well as other legal instruments regulating the import of wild animals, does, however, grant exemptions to zoos for the transfer of animals. Many zoos, especially those on the animals' continents of origin, served as a cover for the illegal trafficking of animals and became centers for laundering the captured, for example, by lying about the wild or captive origin of the animals. Some European zoos, including the most prestigious, at the same time continued to obtain supplies by occasionally resorting to poaching (Domalain 1975).

In spite of these flaws, the legal corpus encouraged a change in practices, motivated by the rise in criticism. A number of managers invested in a reform of the animal economy of their institution, enabled and encouraged by the increase in average longevity, itself supported by several factors, such as hygiene measures, nutritional improvements and advances in veterinary medicine for zoo animals. Captive breeding programs were developed, with increased attention paid to animal social organizations. Several buildings built from the 1960s and 1970s onwards for primates thus exposed a smaller number of species to allow the formation of pairs, then social groups aiming to imitate the social structures of the species. Management programs increasingly took into account the effects of social stress, in particular to counteract the numerous maternal rejections and infanticides. For example, the role of conspecific rearing of young in developing social learning, and thus in providing the animals with the conditions to raise their own young, which had been demonstrated in primates since at least the early 1960s (Kortlandt and Kooij 1963), was gradually being taken into account in management procedures. Integrating animals into social structures that mimic their own, which decreases social stress, remains to this day "one of the most important, but most difficult tasks, to achieve in captivity" (Hosey et al. 2013, pp. 197–201, citation p. 199).

The development of captive breeding has also been based on the increase in the circulation of animals between zoos: exchanges have served to find internally, without recourse to capture, individuals that could best be matched according to elementary criteria of species and sex, and then increasingly refined criteria, guided by genetic determinants. Breeding loans, practiced since the 19th century, thus reached unprecedented dimensions from the second half of the 20th century. This intensification of transfers was based on the development of regional and international bodies bringing together zoos and zoo directors. It mobilized management tools such as studbooks, genealogical registers of animals used since the end of the 18th century for domestic animals. Studbooks became cardinal instruments for the transfer of zoo animals, especially when they became computerized from the 1980s to facilitate their demographic and genetic analysis in order to improve animal movements on this basis (Olney 2001). Studbooks in turn contributed to the establishment of regional and international captive breeding programs, which were started in the 1970s. Antwerp Zoo, for example, has, since 1977, been developing an exchange and breeding plan for okapi, a species for which it holds the studbook (Pouillard 2011).

The aims of captive breeding are, first, to ensure reproduction in captivity, but second to avoid inbreeding and to maintain a high level of genetic diversity over a long period of time – the classic goal of breeding programs is to maintain 90%–95% genetic diversity in a demographically stable population for 200 years (Hosey et al. 2013, p. 296). Some animals with genes deemed particularly interesting are therefore subject to regular transfers between zoos. Despite the care that accompanies these transfers, they partially replicate the social breakdowns previously inflicted by capture: in addition to being stressful for the animals, including socially, they may dislocate learning processes when conducted at an age younger than weaning, or when imposed on animals that do not experience separation in the wild, such as female elephants, who normally do not leave their mother or their natal group (Latham and Mason 2008, p. 85).

Captive breeding programs go hand in hand with redeployments of the control exercised over the animals through transfers and the use of medically assisted reproduction, developed with the help of reproductive sciences, and through procedures aimed at maximizing reproduction, which regularly involve invasive manipulations, such as blood sampling, laparotomies, endoscopies, sexing operations and monitoring of reproductive cycles and pregnancies. For the species for which reproduction is achieved, it is still a question of obtaining the desired size and composition of the herds, according to genetic, demographic or scenographic criteria. Birth control operates through contraception, sterilization, and more rarely through management culling, the slaughter of healthy individuals (Richardson 2003; Pouillard 2019, pp. 311–314, pp. 390–392).

The development of captive breeding, as well as the progressive decrease in the number of species presented in zoos, allowed a gradual but marked reduction in the number of specimens taken from the wild, starting in the 1950s and 1960s for mammals and birds, and a few decades later for reptiles and amphibians. Removal from the wild continues for less popular species that cannot be reproduced in captivity, which is the case for many fish (Pouillard 2019).

1.8. Capture and conservation

Captive breeding programs serve the development of a new function that zoos have endorsed since the 1960s: species conservation, which initially involved producing new captive animals from other, already captive animals in order to reinject them into the wild through reintroduction operations. However, reintroductions have remained marginal in terms of the number of species and individuals concerned, due to the difficulties of implementation. The conservation function of zoos was however institutionalized by the main international wildlife protection organizations, such as the International Union for the Protection of Nature (formed in 1948, renamed International Union for Conservation of Nature in 1956) or the World Wildlife Fund (1961, renamed World Wide Fund for Nature in 1986), who both participated in the definition of wildlife protection policies characterized by a close management of protected species and areas, with regularly invasive implications. This interventionist paradigm, which was crystallized at the end of the 19th century, particularly in the colonial field, led to animals being considered as parts (of species), then sums (of genes), rather than as individuals. The constraints imposed on captive animals have thus been justified in the name of safeguarding the whole to which they belong or the parts that constitute them, in other words, the greater good that should result for biodiversity (Pouillard 2019).

Such a program requires new catches, however sporadic. On the one hand, breeding programs need to be established. Among several examples: in 1970, the Zoological Society of London purchased 20 white rhinos from the Natal Game Department, captured from the Umfolozi Game Reserve in order to be installed at Whipsnade Zoo, a project financed by the World Wildlife Fund (Adams 2004, p. 135, p. 201; Pouillard 2019, pp. 366–367); in 2007, 15 crocodiles from the Philippines were imported to Europe to establish a captive breeding program aimed at their rescue[7]. On the other hand, the issue is to maintain sufficient genetic diversity in captive populations. Conservation biologists, particularly those specializing in population management of zoo collections, note that "immigrants from the wild should periodically be incorporated into the captive population if possible" (Ballou et al. 2012, citations p. 238). This is especially the case if the number of founders (animals captured from the wild, unrelated to each other, and who have reproduced) is small.

Despite the disengagement encouraged by critics, the conservationist programs themselves, increasingly globalized in scope after World War II due to the actions of international wildlife protection organizations, remain profoundly shaped by an understanding of animals marked by extraction and management under close human supervision, with deep historical roots.

1.9. References

Adams, W.M. (2004). *Against Extinction. The Story of Conservation*. Earthscan/Fauna & Flora International, London.

Åkerberg, S. (2001). *Knowledge and Pleasure at Regent's Park. The Gardens of the Zoological Society of London during the Ninenteenth Century*. Umea University, Umea.

Ames, E. (2008). *Carl Hagenbeck's Empire of Entertainments*. University of Washington Press, Seattle/London.

Anonyme (1801). *Notice des animaux vivants actuellement à la Ménagerie du Muséum…* Imprimeur Patris, Paris.

Arzel, L. (2014). À la guerre comme à la chasse ? Une anthropologie historique de la violence coloniale dans l'État Indépendant du Congo (1885–1908). In *L'Afrique belge aux XIXᵉ et XXᵉ siècles. Nouvelles recherches et perspectives en histoire coloniale*, Van Schuylenbergh, P., Plasman, P.-L., Lanneau C. (eds). P.I.E/Peter Lang, Brussels.

---

7. Zoological Society of London, *Annual Report 2007–2008*, pp. 12–13.

Arzel, L. (2018). Chasser, récolter, exposer. Des bagages des collecteurs à la mise en musée, le parcours des objets naturalistes au Congo colonial des années 1880 aux années 1910. In *Le spécimen et le collecteur. Savoirs naturalistes, pouvoirs* et altérités *(XVIIIe–XXe siècles)*, Juhé-Beaulaton, D. and Leblan, V. (eds). Muséum national d'Histoire naturelle, Paris.

Baldin, D. (2014). *Histoire des animaux domestiques. XIXe–XXe siècle.* Éditions du Seuil, Paris.

Ballou, J.D., Lees, C., Faust, L.J., Long, S., Lynch, C., Bingaman Lackey, L., Foose, T.J. (2012). Demographic and genetic management of captive populations. In *Wild Mammals in Captivity. Principles & Techniques for Zoo Management*, Kleiman, D.G., Thompson, K.V., Baer, C.K. (eds). University of Chicago Press, Chicago.

Bancel, N., Blanchard, P., Boëtsch, G., Deroo, E., Lemaire, S. (eds) (2002). *Zoos humains. De la vénus hottentote aux* reality shows. La Découverte, Paris.

Baratay, É. (2008). *Bêtes de somme. Des animaux au service des hommes.* La Martinière, Paris.

Baratay, É. (2011). La souffrance animale, face masquée de la protection aux XIXe–XXe siècles. *Revue québécoise de droit international*, 24(1), 217–236.

Baratay, É. and Hardouin-Fugier, É. (1998). *Zoos. Histoire des jardins zoologiques en Occident (XVIe–XXe siècle).* La Découverte, Paris.

Beck, C. and Guizard, F. (eds) (2012). *La bête captive au Moyen Âge et à l'Époque moderne.* Encrage Édition, Amiens.

Birkett, L.P. and Newton-Fisher, N.E. (2011). How abnormal is the behaviour of captive, zoo-living chimpanzees? *PloS ONE*, 6(6), 1–7.

Blanchard, P., Boëtsch, G., Jacomijn Snoep, N. (eds) (2011). *Exhibitions. L'invention du sauvage*. Actes Sud/Musée du quai Branly, Arles/Paris.

Bodson, L. (ed.) (1998). *Les animaux exotiques dans les relations internationales : espèces, fonctions, significations*. Université de Liège, Liège.

Boisson de Chazournes, L., Desgagné, R., Mbengue, M.M., Romano, C. (2005). *Protection internationale de l'environnement*. A. Pedone, Paris.

Bonneuil, C. (1999). Le Muséum national d'histoire naturelle et l'expansion coloniale de la Troisième République. *Revue française d'histoire d'outre-mer*, 86(322–323), 143–169.

Brandon-Jones, C. (1997). Edward Blyth, Charles Darwin, and the animal trade in nineteenth-century India and Britain. *Journal of the History of Biology*, 30(2), 145–178.

Breckenridge, C.A. (1989). The aesthetics and politics of colonial collecting: India at world fairs. *Comparative Studies in Society and History*, 31(2), 195–216.

Bruce, G. (2017). *Through the Lion Gate. A History of the Berlin Zoo.* Oxford University Press, Oxford.

Buquet, T. (2012). La belle captive. La girafe dans les ménageries princières au Moyen Âge. In *La bête captive au Moyen Âge et à l'époque moderne*, Beck, C. and Guizard, F. (eds). Encrage Édition, Amiens.

Burkhardt, R.W. (1997). La Ménagerie et la vie du Muséum. In *Le Muséum au premier siècle de son histoire*, Blanckaert, C., Cohen, C., Corsi, P., Fischer, J.-L. (eds). MNHN, Paris.

Burkhardt, R.W. (2001). A man and his menagerie. *Natural History*, 110(1), 62–69.

Coote, A., Haynes, A., Philp, J., Ville, S. (2017). When commerce, science, and leisure collaborated: The nineteenth-century global trade boom in natural history collections. *Journal of Global History*, 12, 319–339.

Cuvier, G. (n.d.). Le Serval. In *La Ménagerie du Muséum national d'Histoire naturelle ou les animaux vivants*, de Lacépède and Cuvier, G. (eds). Patris, Paris.

Domalain, J.Y. (1975). *L'adieu aux bêtes. J'ai été trafiquant d'animaux sauvages*. Arthaud, Paris.

Faroqhi, S. (2008). Exotic animals at the sultan's court. In *Another Mirror for Princes: The Public Image of the Ottoman Sultans and Its Reception*, Faroqhi, S. (ed.). Isis Press, Istanbul.

Flack, A. (2016). "In Sight, Insane": Animal agency, captivity and the frozen wilderness in the late-twentieth century. *Environment and History*, 22(4), 629–652.

Flack, A. (2018). *The Wild Within. Histories of a Landmark British Zoo*. University of Virginia Press, Charlottesville/London.

Flint, R.W. (1996). American showmen and European dealers. Commerce in wild animals in nineteenth-century America. In *New Worlds, New Animals. From Menagerie to Zoological Park in the Nineteenth Century*, Hoage, R.J. and Deiss, W.A. (eds). The Johns Hopkins University Press, Baltimore.

Foucault, M. (1975). *Surveiller et punir. Naissance de la prison*. Gallimard, Paris.

Geoffroy Saint-Hilaire, A. (1870). Note sur le transport des animaux vivants. *Bulletin mensuel de la Société zoologique d'acclimatation*, 1–18.

Gissibl, B. (2016). *The Nature of German Imperialism: Conservation and the Politics of Wildlife in Colonial East Africa*. Berghahn Books, New York/Oxford.

Guerrini, A. (2015). *The Courtier's Anatomists. Animals and Humans in Louis XIV's Paris*. University of Chicago Press, Chicago.

Hagenbeck, C. (1951 [1908]). *Cages sans barreaux*. Nouvelles Éditions de Paris, Paris.

Hamy, E.-T. (1903). Le commerce des animaux exotiques à Marseille à la fin du XVIe siècle. *Bulletin du Muséum d'Histoire Naturelle*, 7, 316–318.

Hanson, E. (2002). *Animal Attractions. Nature on Display in American Zoos*. Princeton University Press, Princeton/Oxford.

Hochadel, O. (2005). Science in the 19th century zoo. *Endeavour*, 29(1), 38–42.

Hochadel, O. (2011). Watching exotic animals next door: "Scientific" observations at the Zoo (ca. 1870–1910). *Science in Context*, 24(2), 183–214.

Hosey, G., Melfi, V., Pankhurst, S. (2013). *Zoo Animals. Behaviour, Management, and Welfare*. Oxford University Press, Oxford.

Jauffret, L. (1798). *Voyage au Jardin des plantes…* C. Houel, Paris.

Kean, H. (1998). *Animal Rights. Political and Social Change in Britain since 1800*. Reaktion Books, London.

Kisling, V.N. (1996). The origin and development of American zoological parks to 1899. In *New Worlds, New Animals. From Menagerie to Zoological Park in the Nineteenth Century*, Hoage, R.J. and Deiss, W.A. (eds). The Johns Hopkins University Press, Baltimore.

Kortlandt, A. and Kooij, M. (1963). Protohominid behaviour in primates. In *The Primates*, Napier, J. and Barnicot, N.A. (eds). Zoological Society of London, London.

Lacépède (1795). Lettre relative aux établissemens publics destinés à renfermer des animaux vivans, et connus sous le nom de Ménageries. *La Décade philosophique, littéraire et politique*, 59, 449–462.

Lacépède (1804). Introduction. In *La Ménagerie du Muséum national d'Histoire naturelle…* Lacépède, Cuvier, G., Geoffroy, É. (eds). Renouard, Paris.

Laissus, Y. (1993). Les animaux du Jardin des plantes, 1793–1934. In *Les animaux du Muséum, 1793–1993*, Laissus, Y. and Petter, J.-J. (eds). MNHN/Imprimerie Nationale Éditions, Paris.

Latham, N.R. and Mason, G.J. (2008). Maternal deprivation and the development of stereotypic behaviour. *Applied Animal Behaviour Science*, 110, 84–108.

Lesage, A. (2019). "Je ne scay quelle grande voix il fait". Faire parler l'hippopotame décrit par Pierre Belon. In *Aux sources de l'histoire animale*, Baratay, É. (ed.). Éditions de la Sorbonne, Paris.

Loisel, G. (1912). *Histoire des ménageries de l'Antiquité à nos jours 3. Époque contemporaine (XIXe et XXe siècles)*. Doin et fils, Paris.

Lorenzi, C. (2009). L'engouement pour l'aquarium en France (1855–1870). *Sociétés & Représentations*, 28(2), 253–271.

MacKenzie, J.M. (1997 [1988]). *The Empire of Nature. Hunting, Conservation and British Imperialism*. Manchester University Press, Manchester.

Mason, G., Clubb, R., Latham, N., Vickery, S. (2007). Why and how should we use environmental enrichment to tackle stereotypic behaviour? *Applied Animal Behaviour Science*, 102, 163–188.

Mehos, D.C. (2006). *Science and Culture for Members Only. The Amsterdam Zoo Artis in the Nineteenth Century*. Amsterdam University Press, Amsterdam.

de Montaigne, M. (2009 [1572–1580]). *Essais 2*. Gallimard, Paris.

Nance, S. (2013). *Entertaining Elephants. Animal Agency and the Business of the American Circus*. The Johns Hopkins University Press, Baltimore.

Olney, P.J.S. (2001). Studbooks. In *Encyclopedia of the World's Zoos 3*, Bell, C.E. (ed.). Fitzroy Dearborn Publishers, Chicago.

Osborne, M.A. (1994). *Nature, the Exotic, and the Science of French Colonialism*. Indiana University Press, Bloomington/Indianapolis.

Pouillard, V. (2011). Le jardin zoologique et le rapport à la faune sauvage : gestion des "collections zoologiques" au zoo d'Anvers (1843–vers 2000). *Revue belge de Philologie et d'Histoire*, 89(3–4), 1193–1232.

Pouillard, V. (2015). Vie et mort des gorilles de l'Est (*Gorilla beringei*) dans les jardins zoologiques occidentaux (1923–2011). *Revue de synthèse*, 136, 375–402.

Pouillard, V. (2019). *Histoire des zoos par les animaux. Impérialisme, contrôle, conservation*. Champ Vallon, Seyssel.

Richardson, D.M. (2003). Is management euthanasia a necessary tool for realising an institutional or a regional collection plan? In *Proceedings EAZA Conference 2001*, Hiddinga, B. (ed.). EAZA, Amsterdam.

Ringmar, E. (2006). Audience for a giraffe: European expansionism and the quest for the exotic. *Journal of World History*, 17(4), 375–397.

Ritvo, H. (1987). *The Animal Estate. The English and Other Creatures in the Victorian Age*. Harvard University Press, Cambridge.

Robbins, L.E. (2002). *Elephant Slaves and Pampered Parrots. Animals in Eighteenth-Century Paris*. The Johns Hopkins University Press, Baltimore/London.

Rothfels, N. (2002). *Savages and Beasts. The Birth of the Modern Zoo*. The Johns Hopkins University Press, Baltimore/London.

Rousseau, J.-J. (1969 [1755]). *Discours sur l'origine et les fondements de l'inégalité parmi les hommes*. Gallimard, Paris.

Sahlins, P. (2017). *1668. The Year of the Animal in France*. Zone Books, New York.

Serna, P. (2017). *Comme des bêtes. Histoire politique de l'animal en Révolution (1750–1840)*. Fayard, Paris.

Simons, J. (2019). *Obaysch. A Hippopotamus in Victorian London*. Sydney University Press, Sydney.

Singer, P. (2015 [1975]). *Animal Liberation*. The Bodley Head, London.

Spary, E.C. (2005). *Le jardin d'utopie. L'histoire naturelle en France de l'Ancien Régime à la Révolution*. MNHN, Paris.

Staszak, J.-F. (2008). Qu'est-ce que l'exotisme ? *Le Globe*, 148, 7–30.

Thomas, K. (1985). *Dans le Jardin de la nature. La mutation des sensibilités en Angleterre à l'époque moderne (1500–1800)*. Gallimard, Paris.

Traïni, C. (2011). *La cause animale (1820–1980). Essai de sociologie historique*. Presses universitaires de France, Paris.

Trinquier, J. (2011). Les prédateurs dans l'arène : gibier traqué ou combattants valeureux ? In *Prédateurs dans tous leurs états. Évolution, biodiversité, interactions, mythes, symboles. XXXIe rencontres internationales d'archéologie et d'histoire d'Antibes*, Brugal, J.-P., Gardeisen, A., Zucker, A. (eds). APDCA, Antibes.

2

Pig Welfare in China

Peter J. Lı

University of Houston-Downtown, USA

2.1. Introduction

The Covid-19 pandemic (SARS-CoV-2) has been a global public health crisis. As of the writing of this chapter, the pandemic is still ravaging the world. By mid-May 2021, over 161 million people worldwide have been infected with the virus. Over 3.3 million have died.[1] The pandemic should be a wake-up call on the global public health danger of intensive animal farming. As the epicenter of the pandemic, China surprised its own citizens and critics when the National People's Congress (NPC), its national legislature, imposed a complete ban on February 24, 2020 on the trade and eating of wild animals (NPC 2020). The country's wildlife farming operation has been criticized for years by the Chinese public for its shocking welfare problems (see, for example, Si 2011). In contrast to this Chinese recognition of the public health threat from animal cruelty on the country's wildlife farms, China is yet to connect the public health risks with industrialized livestock production. Paradoxically, it was building amid the Covid-19 pandemic perhaps the world's biggest pig breeding campus with multistory buildings in Central China's Henan Province (Patton 2020). Making this so-called high-tech farming facility more out of place was the fact that China was still combating the African Swine Fever (ASF) that had in 2018–2019 created a fatal welfare crisis to 39% of the country's pigs (Mackenzie 2019). Shouldn't China give more attention to the welfare conditions on its livestock farms?

---

1. See www.worldometers.info/coronavirus/ for the worldwide updates on the Covid-19 information.

Animal Suffering,
coordinated by Florence BURGAT and Emilie DARDENNE. © ISTE Ltd 2023.

This chapter focuses on China's pig farming. It is important to point out that China's livestock production as a whole has undergone great changes in the last four decades. Its pig farming in the last 72 years (since 1949) has shown consistent government attention on productivity, though for different purposes, and an equally consistent lack of attention on the welfare conditions on the farms. A review of the government policies in the pre-reform (1949–1978) and reform (1978 and the present) eras is designed to highlight the political objective of pig farming to the Chinese government and why pig welfare was never a consideration.

2.2. Pig farming: an overview

China leads the world in pig farming and livestock production in general. While the country has 19% of the world's population, it produces more than 23% of the world's meat.[2] As the world's biggest pig farming nation, China slaughtered 703 million pigs in 2018, half of the slaughter number in the world (FAOSTAT 2021). Pork is a daily food choice of the country's 1.4 billion people. A fluctuation in the supply of pork has social stability implications. What has mostly preoccupied the Chinese government, particularly the local authorities, is therefore productivity of livestock production, not the farming conditions. While farming conditions did not constitute a major issue in ancient China, its neglect in the contemporary can have fateful consequences.

2.2.1. *History*

China is one of the earliest civilizations that domesticated pigs. Archaeological findings in the 20th century revealed that pigs and their wild cousins were part of the survival struggles of the Chinese ancestors since the pre-historical era. The discovery in Zhoukoudian near Beijing of the Peking Men (the Beijing hominids) who were believed to have inhabited what is now North China between 700,000 to 300,000 years ago brought archaeologist attention on the food sources of the ancient humans. Inside the caves of the ancient Peking Men, archaeologists found bony fossils of wild boar (*Sus lydekkeri*) besides the biggest amount of bones from deer and other wild animals (Zhang 1976; Binford and Ho 1985). Seven to five thousand years ago, China's Yangshao Neolithic culture emerged in the country's Yellow River areas. A large quantity of pig bones, the biggest amount of all animal bones, were unearthed in its archaeological sites, suggesting the prevalence of pig farming

2. In 2019, the world's meat output total was 336.6 million tons while that of China was 78 million, accounting for 22.99% of the world's total output. The data was retrieved April 28, 2021 from the UN Food and Agriculture Organization (FAOSTAT) database.

at that time (Zhang 1976). Pig domestication was believed to have taken place 9,000 years ago, or 2,000–3,000 years before the rise of the Yangshao culture. And domestication of pigs did not just happen in one location. It happened separately in North and South China (Luo and Zhang 2008; Yuan 2010). Pig farming as an agricultural production began some 6,000 years ago (Zhang 1976). The fact that pigs were part of the early human agricultural development and part of human efforts to survive the harsh environment warrants human gratefulness by giving pigs an enriched environment on the farm.

In ancient China, the well-being of pigs was not a burning issue largely because pig farms where a large number of pigs were crowded into a small space did not exist. Ancient Chinese attention was more on farming techniques. In their study of livestock production in ancient China, scholars have found a plethora of classics addressing a wide range of measures, solutions and remedies to the problems found in pig farming. Chinese ancestors not only domesticated pigs but also made efforts to improve the breeding stock, with the aim of producing a breed that was more productive. Breed selection was further developed in the Han dynasty (202 BC–220 AD). Ancient breed selection was best summarized in 齐民要术 (*The Qi Min Yao Shu* or Essential Techniques for the People's Livelihood), a collection of ancient Chinese agricultural texts, written by Jia Sixie, a Northern Wei Dynasty (386–398) scholar. In the succeeding dynasties, breed selection was also discussed in 农桑辑要 (A Collection of Essays on Grain and Animal Farming) of the Yuan Dynasty (1273), 农政全书 (A Complete Collection of Agricultural Production) of the Ming Dynasty (1639) and 三农纪 (A Collection of Books on Agriculture, 1760) of the Qing Dynasty. These works introduced in great details what a good breeding pig should look like (Zhang 1976). These classical works did discuss techniques on piglet care, fattening, neutering and remedies for pig diseases. Legend has it that castration was performed on pigs in the era of the Yellow Emperor (2,698–2,598 BC). And traditional Chinese veterinary prescriptions were included in Han Dynasty medicine books (Zhang 1976).

To ancient Chinese, pigs were more a means of production than a source of meat. The Chinese character for home, that is, 家, is composed of two parts. The part of 宀 means roof of a house while 豕 means pig. Therefore, a Chinese household will not be complete without farming a pig. Although pig farming was never a major productive activity, the fact that every household farmed one or more pigs perhaps made ancient China the world's leader in pig farming. Pigs were fed food leftovers, grain brans, vegetables and wild plants. They did not compete for food with humans. Raising a pig produced fertilizer to the farmland that never lay fallow. Its contribution to agriculture as a source of fertilizer was often greater than as food. Despite the fact that only one or two pigs were raised per each household in China's dynastic past and pork was the most favored meat, the Chinese diet was dominated with plant-based foods (Xu 2009). The country's traditional plant-based diet, an outgrowth of limited agricultural productivity, served to reinforce religious belief that vegetarianism was a more peaceful, merciful, moral and a less destructive lifestyle. The level of cruelty to pigs in ancient times was considerably lower than it is today to pigs raised in crowded conditions. The state policy of slaughter suspension in ancient China also served to discourage livestock farming as a major agricultural endeavor (Mang 2005).

2.2.2. Contemporary China

The welfare conditions of pig farming in contemporary China have become a salient problem. China since 1949 can be divided into two phases: the pre-reform era (1949–1978) and the reform era (1978 and present). The two eras have distinctive policies, political objectives and animal welfare consequences.

2.2.2.1. The pre-reform era

Pig farming in the pre-reform era (1949–1978) went through three phases. The first phase covered the first seven years following the founding of the People's Republic of China (PRC). In 1949, the country had 58 million pigs in inventory, a drop of 26.5% compared with 1936, the best year in history. Per capita meat output in 1949 was only 4.1 kilograms from the total meat output of 2.2 million tons (Xu et al. 2011). Raising pigs to supply meat to the markets received more attention from the Chinese government. "Private ownership and private farming with state support" was the official policy for boosting pig farming in the early 1950s (Xiao et al. 2009). Like the country's dynastic rulers, the Chinese Communist government continued to see pig farming as a source of fertilizer, important to boost grain output per acreage (State Council 1952). In 1959, the Chinese government warned against pig production decline as a result of peasant resistance to the government's collectivization efforts. The top concern of the decline to the authorities was not meat supply but fertilizer shortage (Sun 2010). Pig farming and pigs were all an instrument for the achievement of the state's political objectives.

The second phase, that is, 1958–1960, was a most disruptive period in the history of the People's Republic of China. In this period, an unknown number of 10,000-pig farms were built, yet without a single case of success. In fact, most of these so-called 10,000-pig farms, a potential animal welfare disaster, existed in name only. In 1961, as a result of the failure of the agricultural production in general, pork output did not even reach 1/3 of the output in 1958 (Chen 2009). The number of pigs in inventory went down to 76 million, a drop of 48.2% compared with that in 1957 (Xu et al. 2011). A food security crisis, also called the Great Chinese Famine (1959–1962), broke out. By 1962, more than 30 million peasants had starved to death (Yang 2012). There is no reason to believe that pigs were properly fed when people starved to death massively during the famine. The well-being of the pigs at that time was completely overshadowed by the humanity's worst starvation.

The third phase started in 1962 and lasted until 1978, two years after the death of Mao Zedong. In 1965, the number of pigs in inventory reached 167 million, an increase of 67% over that of 1962. Famine was over but food scarcity persisted (Xu et al. 2011). Overall, peasants were able to provide better care to their livestock. Agricultural production grew modestly in the final years of Mao's rule (Chen 2009). Pig farming, despite Mao's passion for collective farming, had remained the only "private" production during his rule. In 1978, the last year of the pre-reform era, China produced 8 million tons of pork, averaged to about 8.2 kilograms of meat per person annually (FAOSTAT 2021). This output was the fruit of labor of the hundreds of millions of the Chinese peasants who raised one or two pigs a year. Except for the small number of state-owned pig farms, most vices of modern livestock production such as fighting and bar biting caused by over-crowding and confinement were not present in peasant pig farming operation.

Pig farming in ancient times and the pre-reform era shared some characteristics. Livestock production was private peasant operation. Pig farming was a small and peasant household backyard operation. Productivity was low. Besides vaccination and use of modern veterinary drugs, breeding, farming, fattening and slaughter were all traditional. Commercial feed was non-existent. Trans-provincial pig transport was limited to destinations such as Shanghai and Hong Kong. Pig slaughter was largely done at the backyard of the peasant households, a practice that desensitized most of the Chinese to livestock slaughter. Most other vices associated with intensive animal production did not exist.

2.2.3. *The reform era (1978–the present)*

Since 1978, the industry has expanded exponentially thanks to strong government support. Following the party's decision in November 1978 to allow a diversified rural production that balanced food grain production with the production of cash crops, livestock and fisheries, peasants took the first major step to increase livestock production. In 1979, meat output, 17% higher in amount than the previous year, was a direct result of the policy change. Much of the increase came from pig farming that made up 80% of the livestock industry (FAOSTAT 2021). Pig farming has always fluctuated with food grain production. The output of meat and pork total in 1985 went up to 19.5 million and 17 million tons, respectively, as a result of the increase in food grain production (FAOSTAT 2021).

Unlike the pre-reform era, the Chinese government in the reform era has seen pig farming primarily as a source of meat. It initiated the "food basket program" in 1988, a state guided effort to ensure a steady supply of non-staple food items to the country's urban residents. In 1991, China overtook the US as the world's leading livestock producer thanks largely to the explosive growth of pig farming. The final decade of the 20th century witnessed a continuous expansion of pig farming. In 1997, pork output reached 36 million tons, a 58% increase over that of 1990. This output volume was reflected in the new record of 30 kilograms of per capita pork consumption for the country's 1.2 billion people (FAOSTAT 2021). The livestock industry made a new record in 2014 when 745 million pigs were slaughtered and 57 million tons of pork was produced (FAOSTAT 2021). Contributing to the exponential growth of the country's pig farming are factors ranging from the state's strong policy support, a change of production model, use of modern technology, and massive adoption of Western farming tools and practices that have unavoidable animal welfare side effects.

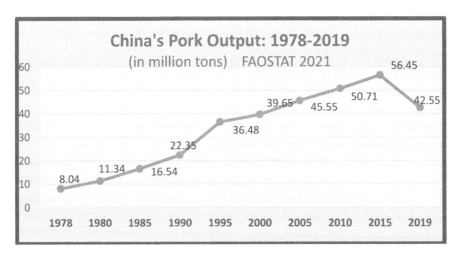

Figure 2.1. *China's pork production: 1978–2019*

The expansion of livestock production has helped improve the country's food supply. In the pre-reform era, the average Chinese rarely saw animal products in their diet and they had no access to protein from plant-based products either. The daily supply of calories for an average Chinese had never exceeded 2,000 kcals (OWID 2021). Today, food shortage is history. Improvement of food supply has led to the increase of the daily intake of calories, in 2013, for example, to 3,108 kcal for the Chinese in excess of the world's average (OWID 2021). In 2016, the level of per capita meat supply in China exceeded most countries. It was closer to the level of meat supply in the most developed countries (OWID 2021). By the end of 2017, malnutrition as a contributing factor of death in China had also become history. Pig farming has contributed to China's phenomenal food security accomplishment.

2.2.4. Pig farming with Chinese characteristics

In the last four decades, the Chinese government has faced two seemingly irreconcilable contradictions when it is pushing for greater livestock production. On the one hand, the authorities hope to see a higher level of intensification in pig farming. The Chinese government believes that production of scale has the advantages of higher productivity, better disease prevention and better policy compliance. On the other hand, the authorities, particularly local governments, are aware of the fact that production of scale does not help rural employment. What has emerged is pig farming with Chinese characteristics. Pig production has been dominated by small- and medium-sized farms that have enthusiastically embraced Western farming techniques, tools and practices. China's pig farms are not necessarily Western in mode of production; yet they are Western or modern in farming practices.

2.2.4.1. Production intensification

In 1983, the Party called for rural production to be ready for "two transformations," i.e., transformation from a self-sufficiency economy to commercial production of scale and from traditional farming to modern intensive production (Central Document Research Institute 1983). To the Chinese authorities, a new production model and adoption of new practices were necessary to push livestock production to a higher level. For this purpose, the government adopted policies to allow peasants to have the right of farmland use or of its transfer, to work in non-rural jobs, to open their own non-agriculture businesses; to produce free from state-imposed procurement; and to engage in autonomous productive activities of new products (Shi and Zhang 2018). The more entrepreneurial of the peasants began to specialize in livestock and pig farming as their main production activity. When a larger number of pigs were farmed, the farmers had to resort to practices that could maximize space use and generate an output within the shortest time. Peasant household-based operations have since swept across the country. In 2003, peasant farms raising between 1 and 49 pigs, a small operation, were owned by 107 million households. They accounted for 94% of all the pig farms in the country. These small farms produced 99% of the pork (China Animal Husbandry Yearbook Compilation Committee 2005). Thanks to government's policy incentives, intensification of pig farming continued. By the end of the 1990s, some 30% of the Chinese peasants who raised between 1 and 49 pigs had stopped pig farming. In 2012, the total number of peasant household-based pig farms dropped to 54.7 million. In 2013, it went down further to 51 million (China Animal Husbandry Yearbook Compilation Committee 2014). These are no longer traditional farming, although they are still predominantly peasant household-based operations. Productivity has also been improved. But, small operations, in the eyes of the Chinese authorities, are still behind production of scale in productivity. Besides, they are also believed to be a source of pollution.

In the new century, livestock production has been tasked for sustainable expansion. Through its Ministry of Agriculture, Ministry of Finance, National Standards Bureau, and National Environmental Agency, the Chinese government (State Council) endorsed 51 policy documents in order to launch the industry on a new path of continuous growth. These included the Waste Discharge Standard in Livestock Production (2001), Technical Specifications for the Harmless Disposal of Pollutants from the Livestock Production (2006), Directive of the State Council on the Promotion of Sustained and Healthy Development of the Livestock Industry (2007) and the State Council Directive on the Strengthening of the Work Related to the Prevention and Control of African Swine Fever (2019). While most of these policies touch on the well-being of pigs, the Chinese government is paradoxically more determined to push for a higher level of intensive operation as a solution to farm disease outbreaks, illegal discharge and unlawful disposal of farm mortality. The authorities believe that farms of scale are more likely to comply with laws and policies because of unbearable penalties for violations (Tang and Wang 2020).

To encourage further intensification of production, the Chinese government has come up with different funding programs. In 2011, Baoji City in Shaanxi Province deployed state funding to support farming operations of scale. The target recipients were farms that raised between 500 and 999 pigs, 1,000 and 1,999 pigs, 2,000 and 3,000 pigs and 10,000+ pigs. Farms of these four operation scales were qualified for the funding of 250,000 yuan ($38.225), 500,000 yuan ($76,450), 700,000 yuan ($107,031) and 800,000 yuan ($122,321). Besides, production scale, employing standardized farming procedures, and joint operation by 50 peasant households or more were also eligible for a government subsidy of 500,000 yuan (Baoji News 2011). Through state funding, the authorities aimed to phase out small farms. In July 2011, the national Chinese government promised to earmark 2.5 billion yuan to be used to support standardized farming operations of scale and the building of exclusive farming areas (Li 2011). Other funding efforts included provision of subsidies to the farmers in insurance coverage for breeding sows (Chongqing

Agriculture Committee 2010), for fattening pigs (China Animal Husbandry Information 2011), for compulsory vaccination, for compensating farmers in situations of pig culls and mortality disposal, for supporting breed refinement and for rewarding farms that sell pigs to markets outside their respective localities (Farmers Daily 2016; MOF 2016).

The above information on the state funding of the livestock production is not a complete overview of all the funding programs. These funding examples showcase the Chinese authorities' effort to encourage production of scale for better productivity, disease prevention and other policy compliance by the producers. The government's efforts paid off. In 2017, the total number of pig farms went down further to 38 million (MOA 2018). While most of these farms remain small- and medium-sized operations (36 million raising 1–49 pigs, 1.2 million raising 50–99 pigs, 603,091 farms raising 100–499 pigs, for example) (MOA 2018), they are using modern and Western farming practices.

2.2.4.2. Rural employment

China's surplus rural labor can check the further intensification of pig farming. In fact, the pig farming industry experimented in the early 1980s operations of scale with farming equipment imported from the U.S. and other countries in the suburbs of major urban centers. Yet, these farms, towards the end of the 1980s, had not been successful. If China's livestock production were to be replaced by production of scale like those in North America, a considerable number of the rural laborers would lose jobs on the pig farms, for example. The Chinese authorities are also facing the challenging of rural employment. Livestock farmers are expected to help retain the rural labor force in agricultural production. To the Chinese authorities, livestock production not only brings income to the rural families and relieves rural employment pressure but also helps stabilize the rural labor force for food grain and other crop farming. China has in the last four decades experienced a breathtaking urbanization process. In 2018, rural population dropped to 40.42% from 82.08% in 1978 (National Bureau of Statistics of China 2019). Peasant household-based small-scale food grain production is largely non-profitable and is not attractive to the peasants (Jiang 2017). The agricultural labor force had gone down to 314 million as of the end of 2016 (Chen and Hu 2020). The Chinese government vowed to "protect and mobilize rural labor force for food grain production" (The State Council Information Office 2019). Side-line productions in livestock, fruits, vegetables and other cash crops serve to retain the farmers in food grain production.

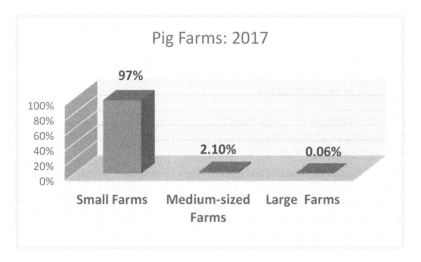

Figure 2.2. *Pig farms by scale of production: 2017. Source:*
China Animal Husbandry and Veterinary Yearbook (2018)

The preceding discussion hopes to show that productivity and employment occupy the authorities' attention. By encouraging intensification of production, the Chinese government paid little attention to its side effects. Employment, as Premier Li said, is the foundation of economic growth and a matter of great importance (Chinanews 2021). Provinces with a sizable livestock industry such as Shandong, Henan and Guangxi have all disclosed their employment targets for 2021. Henan and Shandong hope to increase employment by 1.1 million whereas Sichuan expects 8.5 million to be employed in 2021 (Twenty-first Century Economy 2021). The consolidation of employment in livestock production serves the employment objectives of the local authorities. Local authorities have been pulled in two opposite directions. On the one hand, they want to see further intensification of livestock production in their respective regions out of a concern for productivity and, falsely, for disease control. On the other hand, they are pressured to achieve full employment of the rural labor that can better be fulfilled by small-scale farming operations. This dilemma is likely to continue for the foreseeable future. It is the employment value of pig farming and livestock production in general that has perhaps underlain local government tolerance of problems such as pollution, animal welfare, epidemics, drug abuse and others.

2.3. Animal welfare

Factory farming in all its forms or adaptations has unavoidable consequences in animal welfare. China's livestock industry has since the early 1980s enthusiastically embraced the Western factory farming model and its associated technologies, tools and practices (Shi et al. 1987; Li 2021, pp. 179–215). The use of the Western modern farming practices and tools have given rise to welfare problems that did not exist in China's past and have exacerbated or triggered new welfare problems unique to China's pig production.

2.3.1. *A new challenge*

Pig farming in the pre-reform era was traditional in mode of production. Besides vaccination against common swine diseases and use of veterinary drugs when necessary, peasants used no other modern instruments for farming purposes. Pigs were occasionally allowed to roam in the fields, on the hills, and along the streams to feed on wild plants and vegetable roots. Their feed was composed of raw vegetables, potatoes or cooked vegetables mixed with brans and other grain by-products. Industrial feed was non-existent. While one or two pigs per peasant household lived a short life in generally squalid sheds with poor sanitation and straw-bedded floors, there was no such thing as over-crowding, tail biting or fighting, the common vices of concentrated animal feeding operations. Swine diseases did not occur as often as they do today. Welfare problems in the pre-reform era were typically seen in feed shortage, poor housing and regional practices that undercut the well-being of pigs such as the building of pigsties under roadside public toilets in a northern province, subjecting the pigs to disease dangers besides other concerns (Li 2009). The massive introduction of Western farming tools and practices has created conditions for the rise of more serious welfare problems in pig farming.

2.3.1.1. *Welfare concerns*

Welfare problems in China's pig production do not concentrate in farms of scale. The majority of China's pig farms are small operations. But they employ factory farming practices and tools. It is important to point out that animal welfare problems can be amplified both by the scale of operation and by the adoption of Western farming practices. Pigs in a small farm that used gestation crates, commercial feed, indoor housing without straw beddings, etc. could suffer similar welfare problems as pigs in operations of scale (Li 2009). They are prevalent in small farms. Over-crowding is prevalent in most farms. Fighting is common. Barren environment, concrete floors, and limited climate control are features of most small- and medium-sized operations (Jiang and Gao 2006; Zhan et al. 2011). Suppression of natural behaviors is an intrinsic problem with modern pig farming. Sows and even boars for breeding purposes are confined in crates. The use of industrial feed has been popularized in even the smallest farms in the country. Pigs are deprived of the ability to root and to chew on fiber-rich vegetables and wild plants. Confinement in crates denies the sows and boars the ability to move around and to exercise, causing mental and physical agony. Artificial insemination has been adopted by most, if not all, breeding farms. Not only are the boars deprived of their natural mating behavior, they are sometimes coerced and abused in the course of semen collection (Zhang 2017). Abuse of feed additives and use of banned substances such as clenbuterol, are a huge problem. One of the welfare issues impacting pigs fed clenbuterol is that these pigs are believed to be more susceptible to cardiovascular problems on the farms and during transport besides reduced immunity (Jiang and Gao 2006).

2.3.2. Breeding sow welfare

Intensive breeding farms are stressful to the breeding sows. In a recent study in a span of four years on the health and welfare of a major breeding farm, Chinese researchers found that death on the farm was caused by five major health issues: abdominal bloating (21.5%), sudden death (21.2%), various illnesses (19.6%), uterine prolapse (11.6%) and paralysis (8.3%) (Yang and Li 2017). Each one of these mortality factors can be triggered or exacerbated by the compromised welfare conditions on the farm. For example, one of the triggers of paralysis is leg problems which are common on the country's breeding farms. In a 2009 study, sows on some Chinese breeding farms were reportedly confined in sow crates for much longer than their counterparts in other countries (Li 2009). Sows confined for too long in gestation and farrowing crates and having a crushing weight on their hind legs are known to develop foot problems leading to paralysis. Sow crates have been enthusiastically embraced by the Chinese pig farmers. In China, foot or lameness problems with the breeding sows in large facilities are also common in small- and medium-sized farms as long as sow crates are used. To the farmers, culling was really a reluctant last measure, not necessarily to end suffering but to stop economic loss. Sow crate use is a major contributor to most welfare issues on the breeding farms. What is disturbing is that breeding boars are sometimes kept inside crates on some farms for maximizing space use and for better collecting semen (Zhang 2017).

Sow crates are not an invention of China. They were an introduced "foreign gadget". However, sow crates are a most popular farming instrument. Farm visits by this author in 2005, 2006, 2014 and 2018 in China confirmed the continuous popularity of this tool to the farmers. Sow crates have been uniformly adopted in breeding operations of different scales of operation. Other welfare problems brought about by the crates are quite similar. Sham chewing and bar biting are common. As a stressor, crates frustrate sows' ability to express their natural behaviors and cause psychological reactions similar to depression among humans. Lack of movement is known to affect the immunity of the sows and vitality of the piglets (Quan 2019).

The welfare of newborn piglets has not attracted much attention as in recent years. Typical of concentrated farming operations are practices that undercut the well-being of the piglets. Early weaning is unnatural and traumatic to both the sows and piglets. Early weaning in some cases has gone from 28 days to as short as 14 days, undercutting the physical and psychological well-being of the pigs (Zhan et al. 2011; Quan 2019). Ear-tagging, teeth-cutting, tail docking, castration and transport to fattening facilities are all part of the welfare problems impacting the piglets. Take castration as an example; China's pig farming standard requires that castration of male piglets must be done with the help of anesthetic seven days after their birth (Zhang et al. 2017). It is an open question if all breeders are in compliance with this requirement.

2.3.3. *Live transport*

To control pollution from livestock production, the Chinese government started towards the end of the 1990s a nationwide effort to move animal farming out of the suburban areas of major urban centers and regions of high population density. Pig farms, for example, were closed outside Shanghai or were moved to nearby Jiangsu and Zhejiang Provinces. In 2016, the Chinese government released the National Pig Production and Development Plan: 2016–2020, putting forward the expected direction of the pig farming industry for the 13th Five-Year Plan period. The plan aims to encourage the concentration of livestock production in seven provinces (Hebei, Shandong, Henan, Chongqing, Guangxi, Sichuan and Hainan), the so-called "national pig farming key area," in eight other provinces (Jiangsu, Zhejiang, Fujian, Anhui, Jiangxi, Hunan and Guangdong), that is, the restricted region, and in still other six provinces (Liaoning, Jilin, Heilongjiang, Yunnan and Guizhou), a region with potentials of future growth (MOA 2016). The 13th Five-Year Plan further strengthened the trend of concentration of livestock production in regions of food grain production in North, Southwest and Northeast China. While this distribution of the livestock production was aimed at reducing pollution to population centers and the country's main water systems in eastern, central and southern parts of the country, the proposal has the animal welfare implications that the authorities did not take into account. Live transport connecting the centers of production and centers of consumption will be busier and more stressful for the animals concerned.

China has some of the longest live transport routes in the world. While slaughter operations and refrigeration facilities are yet to be established close to the farms, long-distance and trans-provincial transport send billions of livestock animals on the highways, on the train, on the boats and in other forms of transportation. Over-crowding is common. Pigs in transport are often denied rest, feed and water. Reports of accidents involving pig trucks described brutal injuries to the pigs when they were thrown to the hard road surface because of collision or other violent crashes (Han 2018). Long-distance transport has made forced watering of pigs a "necessity" to make up the lost weight (Jiangsu Broadcasting General Station 2019). The welfare problems associated with live transport are certainly intrinsic to modern animal farming. Forced watering, a form of torture, is driven by a crude quest for profit. Since the 1990s, the Chinese government has issued numerous directives banning forced watering of the pigs in an effort to stop this act (MOA 2020). Pigs suffer both from cruelty intrinsic to live transport and from forced watering inflicted by the transporters.

2.3.4. Culling and slaughter

Frequency of animal diseases is indicative of poor welfare on livestock farms. A search on pig farm disease situation through a Chinese official website has confirmed a high frequency of disease outbreaks on Chinese pig farms.[3] In the government database, diseases that include swine fever, pig blue ear disease, Cysticercosis, anthrax, swine erysipelas and brucellosis happen in most farming provinces and on a yearly basis. For example, in 2010, 134,699 pigs died or were culled because of these diseases. In the next seven years, the mortality number for each year fluctuated from as low as 32,272 pigs in 2017 to 110,515 in 2014. In 2018, only the first 6 months' number (19,945) was reported partly because of the outbreak of the African Swine Fever. These mortality figures from a Chinese government database can only be used as a reference because it does showcase most farm diseases that occur on the farms. Their accuracy in the number of instances of diseases and mortality rates may be a far cry from the real situation. While it might be unfair to criticize China's national government for releasing inaccurate info, it would not be too remote from the fact if we point out that the inaccurate data was a result of gross under-reporting by the farmers and local authorities. The reality is that China slaughters close to 700 million pigs a year and has 400 million in stock. Some 90 million pigs die or are culled each year mostly from diseases (Si 2020). These 90 million pigs either die a brutal death caused by diseases or are culled in inhumane ways.

---

3. A search was conducted in February 2021 on pig disease outbreaks between 2010 and 2019 on the website of China's Central People's Government at www.gov.cn.

In the new century, welfare crises exacerbated by disease outbreaks on pig farms have intensified. Farm diseases ranging from the foot-and-mouth disease, blue-ear disease in 2007, to SADS (swine acute diarrhea syndrome) in 2016, and most recently the African Swine Fever (ASF) have brutalized tens of millions of pigs. In 2018–2019, ASF, a highly infectious and deadly virus, swept across Africa, Europe and Asia. Its outbreak in China was most rapacious and devastating, causing enormous suffering to the pigs before their death or culling. By September 2019, China reportedly had seen a 39% reduction in hog head, causing supply decline and pork price hikes in the country. The culling of a staggering number of the impacted pigs was admittedly an animal welfare disaster. In one report, 1.38 million pigs in a number of provinces were culled by the end of July 2019 (Dxumu (Great Livestock Industry) 2019). Reports of live burials in isolated cases and other shocking practices sent a gruesome image to the public (Suo 2019). While the country was emerging from the pandemic, ASF was detected in early 2021 among a small number of pigs in several provinces, causing the country's Ministry of Agriculture to issue a warning to the producers to stick to the government's orders and regulations regarding epidemic control and prevention (MOA 2021). ASF would continue to brutalize the pigs and undermine their welfare for some time.

Just like confining boars in crates next to breeding sows creates a stressful situation to the former, allowing pigs to see the slaughter of other pigs was brutal (Zhang 2017). Slaughtering pigs in front of others waiting for their turn is yet to arouse the awareness of the majority of the slaughterhouse workers to the mental trauma suffered by the pigs. Conversations between this author and a slaughterhouse worker confirmed that most of the latter saw the call to insulate the pigs waiting to be slaughtered from those that are being killed as "weird sentimentalism". To the slaughterhouse workers, pigs are to die anyway. "Preventing pigs from seeing slaughter is nothing but hypocrisy."[4] Chinese slaughterhouse workers are as much of a roadblock to humane slaughter as the lack of serious interest from the authorities. "Don't eat pork if you don't want them killed" is an answer they would always give when asked if humane slaughter, such as ways that make the slaughter quick and least traumatic to the pigs, should be considered and practiced. In 2007, China started a training program on humane slaughter in Henan, the country's top pig production province (Chinese Economy 2007). Humane slaughter is yet to be introduced nationwide. Small and illegal slaughter operations, despite government crackdown, are often beyond the state regulatory reach. Not only were sick, dying and even dead pigs slaughtered and processed in these illegal facilities, pigs were also more likely to subject to rough handling, physical abuse and practices such as forced watering.

---

4. Conversation with a slaughterhouse worker in November 2020.

2.4. Conclusion

Pig farming and livestock production in general serve the political objective of the post-Mao reformist state. Livestock production was a target sector of the state's economic modernization program initiated in 1978. The expansion of livestock production and the exponential growth in meat output was closely linked to the state's reform policies. As a strategic production, pig farming is linked to food security and regime legitimacy. In China's historical periods between the founding of the Western Han dynasty in 206 BCE and 1911, the year China's last imperial empire collapsed, there were 2,117 years. As many as 2,073 famines took placed in 826 years, 39% of the 2,117 years (Teng et al. 2014). The high frequency of the famines in China's history explained political instability and violent dynastic changes. The state support of the deployment of Western factory farming practices and tools, provision of policy incentives, state input of financial assistance to the farmers and infrastructure construction are all part of the leaders' efforts to stabilize the existing ruling order eroded by the ultra-Leftist economic policy of the pre-reform era. While this policy objective did serve the well-being of the Chinese people, its over-emphasis on productivity has unavoidable animal welfare consequences.

Like the rest of the world, China's animal agriculture and pig farming in particular are a costly source of food. Industrialized animal farming and use of modern farming tools have welfare problems that are not common in traditional livestock farming. The welfare problems on China's pig farms are symptomatic of those in concentrated animal feeding operations in other countries. China's pig farming has Chinese characteristics. It is still dominated by small operations of some 37 million farms. While the level of intensification cannot be compared to those in North America and elsewhere, Chinese small pig farms are "Western" and no less modern in that they have embraced sow crates, early weaning, ear-tagging, tail docking, high farming density, concrete floors, industrial feed, artificial insemination, drug use and abuse, additive use and live transport. There are also practices and problems unique to China such as extensive live transport, frequent farm disease outbreaks, forced watering, placing of breeding boars in crates, rough handling and illegal slaughter.

Pig welfare problems will continue in China. Instead of acknowledging the animal welfare, environmental and epidemic outbreak risks of intensive animal production, the Chinese government has mistakenly placed its hope on further concentration of pig farming. The Covid-19 pandemic should serve as a wake-up call. Intensive animal production is no asset but a huge liability. China has exceeded Japan in meat consumption. European and North American meat consumption is not an example for China to follow. Hunger is history and proteins from plant-based produce are abundant on the Chinese market. It is time that China reconsiders its food security strategy in the interest of public health, global safety, environmental justice and animal welfare.

The frequency of farm epidemics is one indicator of the welfare problems on the pig farms. China's traditional pig farming had its welfare problems. Pigs were fed table scraps and vegetables. Inadequate feed was a constant problem. Pig farming in the reform era has been dominated by small producers of less than 50 pigs. Yet even this scale of operation has been intensified. Western factory farming practices and tools have been fully employed. To increase productivity, the farmers have resorted to tools and practices ranging from sow crates, tail docking, teeth cutting, early weaning, artificial insemination, use and sometimes abuse of antibiotic drugs and growth promoters. These tools and practices were not Chinese in origin and had no precedent in China's dynastic past although the Chinese were one of the first peoples who domesticated pigs. The problems with the well-being of the pigs have a lot to do with the farming model and its associated practices. Traditionally, pigs were slaughtered in the backyard of the peasant households. The building of centralized slaughter operations has ushered in long-distance live transport sending millions of pigs on excruciating journeys to their death. Forced watering of pigs, a practice outlawed in ancient China, was revived. The massive farm mortality, the illegal disposal of pigs to rivers and other forbidden areas, and the contamination of rivers and farmland by livestock waste can all be attributed to the phenomenal expansion of the country's livestock production, an expansion made possible by China's adoption of the Western farming model and practices.

Are there solutions to the many problems caused by pig production and the animal husbandry industry in general? To the pessimists, no solutions are acceptable as long as farm animals are raised to be destroyed for food for humans. However, animal liberation starts with concrete steps to reduce suffering. Reduction of meat and dairy consumption is no doubt a first step towards a higher level of humane consumption. In China, meatless campaigns have been stonewalled. Most, if not all, of the public question the intention of the campaigners who call for a reduction of meat consumption. "You would agree with us if you had lived through the days of food deprivation in the pre-reform era," commented a retiree I interviewed in 2014 when I asked if China was ready to reduce meat consumption. He was not wrong that people had lived on starvation rations during the Mao era. What he and policy-makers in China have failed to realize is that China today is producing a staggering number of products that generate plant-based protein, whereas in Mao's years, there was a general collapse in the production of all kinds of produce. China's traditional diet was plant based with diversified food ingredients (Zhao 2006). In

Mao's China, the diet of the average Chinese lost balance and was dominated by leafy vegetables and food grains. China's agricultural production can ensure a balanced diet today more than any other eras in history.

China and the rest of the world have come to a crossroads. It is time that the intensive animal farming model be placed under a microscope to see its potential as a breeding ground for future pandemics. One contributing factor, as the World Health Organization and scientists involved in the investigation of the origin of Covid-19 pandemic have pointed out, is captive breeding of wild animals in conditions very similar to livestock production. The fact that pig farming and other livestock production are a source of zoonoses calls for a new look at the cost of industrialized animal farming. It is time for the world to come up with a strategy to counter another ticking time bomb.

2.5. References

Baoji, N. (2011). Pig farms can receive up to 800,000 yuan in subsidy in Baoji. Baoji News, March 22 [Online]. Available at: http://www.cschenxin.com/zhu/news/910339. shtml [Accessed 12 December 2020].

Becker, J. (1998). *Hungry Ghosts: Mao's Secret Famine*. Henry Holt and Company, New York.

Binford, L.R. and Ho, C.K. (1985). Taphonomy at a distance: Zhoukoudian, "The Cave Home of Beijing Man"? *Current Anthropology*, 26(4), 413.

Central Document Research Institute (1983). Party central committee notice on releasing the "several questions of current rural policies" [Online]. Available at: http://www. reformdata.org/1983/0102/7467.shtml [Accessed 8 March 2021].

Central Document Research Institute (2004). *The Chronicle of Deng Xiaoping's Life*. Vol. 1, The Party Central Documentary Press, 238(380), 450–451.

Chen, R. (2009). An analysis of the fluctuation cycles of our country's pig production. *Journal of Technology and Economics of Agriculture*, 3, 83.

Chen, H. and Hu, J.H. (2020). China has additional room for food grain production increase by at least 180 million tons pending the removal of three bottlenecks, a Yicai story of August 23 [Online]. Available at: https://www.yicai.com/news/100744696.html [Accessed 8 March 2021].

China Animal Husbandry Information (2011). Hunan's fattening pigs have insurance coverage and 20% of the premium is paid by state finance [Online]. Available at: http://www.agronet.com.cn/tech/461841.html [Accessed 12 November 2019].

China Animal Husbandry Yearbook Compilation Committee (2005). Pig farms by number of pigs raised. *China Animal Husbandry Yearbook: 2005*. China Agriculture Press, Beijing.

China Animal Husbandry Yearbook Compilation Committee (2014). Pig farms by number of pigs raised. *China Animal Husbandry and Veterinary Yearbook: 2014* and *2015*, China Agriculture Press, Beijing, 186 (2014), 184 (2015).

China Economic Network (2010). Document 1 of 1985: Ten policies for further enlivening rural economy. *A China Economic Network Story of February 1* [Online]. Available at: http://finance.sina.com.cn/g/20100201/13387346448.shtml.

Chinese Economy (2007). Why do we need to push for humane slaughter? *Chinese Economy*, December [Online]. Available at: http://www.ce.cn/cysc/sp/info/200712/19/t20071219_13969184.shtml [Accessed 19 March 2020].

Chinanews (2021). Li Keqiang: Employment is a matter of great importance to the country and to the family. *Chinanews.com*, 11 March [Online]. Available at: https://www.chinanews.com/gn/2021/03-11/9430059.shtml [Accessed 8 April 2021].

Chongqing Agriculture Committee (2010). An explanation of Chongqing city government insurance policy regarding breeding sows [Online]. Available at: https://www.ppxmw.com/yangzhi/2437.html.

Dxumu (Great Livestock Industry) (2019). A collection of data on the African Swine Fever in China (as of 31 July of 2019) [Online]. Available at: https://www.dxumu.com/16790.html [Accessed 18 January 2020].

FAOSTAT (2021). Livestock primary [Online]. Available at: http://www.fao.org/faostat/en/#data/QL [Accessed 23 December 2020].

Farmers Daily (2016). Government's policy measures in support of a further development of livestock production. *Farmers Daily*, April 6 [Online]. Available at: http://www.tlddjt.com/shuju/nr_xx.asp?bh=1061 [Accessed 18 September 2019].

Han, C.L. (2018). Traffic police worked for 10 hours to help and process a highway accident in Dongguan involving 136 pigs. *Nanfang Metropolitan News*, February 24 [Online]. Available at: https://m.mp.oeeee.com/a/BAAFRD00002018022468455.html [Accessed 5 December 2020].

Jiang, H.L. (2017). The importance of a desirable level of production of scale from the perspective of food security and profitability of food grain production. *Farmers Daily*, September 19 [Online]. Available at: http://news.cau.edu.cn/art/2017/9/19/art_8779_531310.html [Accessed 7 January 2021].

Jiang, X.H. and Gao, F.X. (2006). The major animal welfare problems in China's livestock production. *China Animal Health*, 12, 13–14.

Li, P. (2009). Exponential growth, animal welfare, environmental and food safety impact: The case of China's livestock production. *Journal of Agricultural and Environmental Ethics*, 22, 217–240.

Li, J. (2011). The national government advanced five measures to stabilize meat price and earmarked 2.5 billion yuan to support pig farming, a Xinjing News story of July 14 [Online]. Available at: https://finance.qq.com/a/20110714/000823.htm.

Li, P. (2021). *Animal Welfare in China*. Sydney University Press, Sydney.

Luo, Y.B. and Zhang, J.Z. (2008). A new study of the pig bones unearthed from the Jia Hu relics in Wuyang county of Henan. *Chinese Archaeological Studies*, 1, 90–96.

Mackenzie, D. (2019). A quarter of all pigs have died this year due to African swine fever. *New Scientist*, 5 November [Online]. Available at: https://www.newscientist. com/article/2222501-a-quarter-of-all-pigs-have-died-this-year-due-to-african-swine-fever/ [Accessed 28 March 2021].

Mang, P. (2005). *The World of the Interrelated Self and Other: Chinese Beliefs, Lives and Views of Animals*. China University of Law and Politics Press, Beijing.

MOA (2016). The general trend of livestock production for the next five years is emerging. *Guangdong Livestock and Veterinary Science*, 41(5), 51.

MOA (2018). *The Livestock and Veterinary Statistical Year*. Beijing.

MOA (2020). The Ministry of Agriculture and Rural Affairs general office directive on the launch of a targeted campaign cracking down upon criminal acts in pig slaughter. *MOA*, Document 57, December 8 [Online]. Available at: http://www.gov.cn/zhengce/zhengceku/ 2020-12/10/content_5568626.htm [Accessed 12 January 2021].

MOA (2021). Emergence implementation measures for preventing and controlling African swine fever. *MOA*, March [Online]. Available at: https://new.qq.com/omn/20210505/ 20210505A00M1F00.html [Accessed 7 April 2021].

MOF (Ministry of Finance) (2016). The varieties and amounts of state policy subsidies to the country's pig farmers [Online]. Available at: https://wenku.baidu.com/view/66e02381 ba1aa8114431d9c7.html [Accessed 12 November 2019].

National Bureau of Statistics of China (2019). China Statistical Yearbook of 2019 [Online]. Available at: http://www.stats.gov.cn/tjsj/ndsj/2019/indexch.htm [Accessed 12 December 2020].

NPC (National People's Congress) (2020). Decision of the standing committee of the National People's Congress on a complete ban of illegal wildlife trade and the elimination of the unhealthy habit of indiscriminate wild animal meat consumption for the protection of human life and health. *NPC*, 24 February [Online]. Available at: http://www.npc. gov.cn/englishnpc/lawsoftheprc/202003/e31e4fac9a9b4df693d0e2340d016dcd.shtml [Accessed 23 March 2021].

OWID (Our World in Data) (2021). Food supply [Online]. Available at: https:// ourworldindata.org/food-supply [Accessed 23 February 2021].

Patton, D. (2020). Flush with cash, Chinese hog producer builds world's largest pig farm. *Reuters*, December 7 [Online]. Available at: https://www.reuters.com/article/us-china-swinefever-muyuanfoods-change-s/flush-with-cash-chinese-hog-producer-builds-worlds-largest-pig-farm-idUSKBN28H0MU [Accessed 15 February 2021].

Quan, D.S. (2019). The impact of sow crate confinement time on the welfare of breeding pigs. *Contemporary Animal Husbandry Technology*, 11(59), 8–12.

Shi, W. and Zhang, F.Y. (2018). A synopsis of 20 party central committee document one. *A Farmers Daily*, 7 December [Online]. Available at: http://www.farmer.com. cn/zt2018/ncgg/bwzg/201812/t20181207_1420983.html [Accessed 7 July 2020].

Shi, P.R., Lian, Y.P., Liu, X.F., Li, Y. (1987). A preliminary analysis of the current state and future direction of China's factory farming in pig production. *Journal of Agricultural Engineering*, 2, 2–16.

Si, M. (2011). Fighting for China's battery bears. *China Dialogue*, 14 March [Online]. Available at: https://chinadialogue.net/en/nature/4162-fighting-for-china-s-battery-bears/ [Accessed 12 August 2016].

Si, R.S. (2020). Risk perception, environmental regulation and research on farmers' dead pig harmless disposal behavior. Dissertation, Northwest China University of Agriculture and Forestry, Xianyang.

Sun, H.B., Zhou, D.X., Hu, D.H. (2010). A review and analysis of the policies for the promotion of production of scale for pig farming in China: A historical evaluation of the intensification of peasant household farming operations. *Journal of Agricultural and Economic Issues*, Supplementary issue, 26, 29.

Suo, H.X. (2019). Swine fever is disastrous for the big farmers who resort to live burial to cull the diseased pigs. *A China Management*, 5 September [Online]. Available at: https://news.sina.cn/2019-09-05/detail-iicezueu3533281.d.html?from=wap [Accessed 4 November 2020].

The State Council (1952). The state council decision on agriculture production in 1952 [Online]. Available at: http://www.sz148.net/gwy/news/xzfg/fg/19520226/8093.html [Accessed 19 November 2019].

The State Council Information Office (2019). Food security in China [Online]. Available at: http://www.gov.cn/zhengce/2019-10/14/content_5439410.htm [Accessed 8 March 2021].

Tang, L. and Wang, M.L. (2020). The development, policy analysis and realistic constraints of China's pig farming. *World Agriculture*, 499(113), 115–116.

Teng, J.C., Su, J., Fang, X. (2014). An analysis and reconstruction of the chronicle of the famines and their characteristics between West Han and Qing Dynasty. *Journal of Chinese History and Geography*, 4, 26–32.

Twenty-first Century Economy (2021). Twenty-nine provinces have released their "employment plan" with Jiangxu, Guangdong, Shandong and Henan hoping to have more than a million new jobs. *21st Century Economy*, February 3rd [Online]. Available at: https://m.21jingji.com/article/20210203/herald/4250934e8847fac1ed90e31 d9a0979e5_zaker.html [Accessed 21 April 2021].

Xiao, H.B., Pu, H., Wang, J.M. (2009). A review of history and an analysis of the current state of China's pig farming. *Market Perspective*, 45(16), 8.

Xu, W.S. (2009). *A History of Pig Farming in China*. China Agriculture Press, Beijing.

Xu, X.G., Chen, J., Li, J. (2011). The evolution and features of China's livestock production. *Market Perspective*, 47(20), 14.

Yang, J.S. (2012). *Tombstone: The Untold Story of Mao's Great Famine*. Cosmos Books, Hong Kong.

Yang, D.W. and Li, T.K. (2017). An analysis of the causes of mortality on a large breeding farm and measures for mortality prevention. *PIGS Today*, March, 86–88.

Yuan, J. (2010). An archaeological study of domesticated animals in ancient China. *Quaternary Sciences*, 30(2), 301.

Zhan, J.Y., Zhang, B., Wang, Z.L. (2011). The animal welfare problems in our country's livestock production. *Hunan Feed*, 4, 35–37.

Zhang, C.G. (1976). China's history of pig farming. *Acta Zoological Sinica*, 22(1), 14.

Zhang, S. (2017a). Resistance to the antibiotic of last resort is silently spreading. *The Atlantic*, January 12, 37–40 [Online]. Available at: https://www.theatlantic.com/health/archive/2017/01/colistin-resistance-spread/512705/ [Accessed 3 January 2021].

Zhang, Z.L. (2017b). An analysis of the welfare conditions of breeding boars. *Husbandry and Forage*, 2, 59–62.

Zhang, Z.L., Li, Y.L., Xue, Z., Sun, P., Xu, H.F. (2017). The welfare problems of China's pig breeding farms of scale and recommended solutions. *Journal of the Ecology of Livestock Production*, 38(9), 83–86.

Zhao, R.G. (2006). *A History of China's Food Culture*. Shanghai People's Publishing House, Shanghai.

3

Dogs "Outside the Law": An Ethnographic Look at Animal Lives in South Korea

Julien DUGNOILLE
University of Exeter, UK

3.1. Introduction

This chapter proposes to compare the official discourses on the treatment of animals within South Korean "animal welfare" legislation with the practices observed in the largest "wet market" (understood here as a market where animals can be sold while still alive and then killed on the spot or taken away, alive, by buyers) in South Korea (also known as the Republic of Korea, and henceforth referred to as "Korea"). An initial ethnographic field survey conducted in 2012–2013 on the consumption of dog meat will be the reference point for this comparison, which aims to show that there is a distinction between what these official discourses hope to establish and observable animal lives on the ground, that is, within the context of this book, the suffering, damage and mistreatment to which the animals sold, traded and/or consumed in this type of market are subjected, and particularly with regard to species whose slaughter is not regulated by Korean law.

First, the example of dog meat will be used to shed light on the practical difficulty of what is known as the "welfarist" approach to animal commodification in Korea. On the international scene, this approach (animal welfare), the aim of which is to make the living conditions of animals intended for consumption "better",

Animal Suffering,
coordinated by Florence BURGAT and Emilie DARDENNE. © ISTE Ltd 2023.

is often contrasted with an "abolitionist" approach, which seeks to prohibit all animal commodification by means, in particular, of establishing fundamental rights for animals (Regan 2004; Deckha 2008; Francione and Garner 2010). However, the welfarist approach, in the case of Korean society, does not appear to be consistent with many of the often complex social, moral and cultural principles that govern day-to-day interactions between humans and non-humans. For example, certain groups within the Korean population, committed to perceived traditional animal commodification practices and principles, view the manner in which animal bodies of certain species are to be prepared prior to killing and consumption quite differently from Western-influenced animal welfare principles as articulated in Korean law, since the suffering of the animals put to death is sometimes an integral part of the dishes sought by these consumers. That said, the abolitionist approach, often promulgated in Korea by Western activists, usually Americans visiting Korea for a few years, also only rarely takes into consideration the imperialist nature of the stances it posits as universal with respect to human–non-human interactions. This is particularly evident when these Western groups make the abolition of the dog meat trade their special mission, claiming, without contextualizing the place of the dog in Korean and/or Euro-American history and culture, that dogs should not belong to the category of livestock. In this sense, Korean civil society generally views with disfavor the application of Western discourses on animal welfare, and even more so on abolitionism, to its society. For this reason, Korean animal rights NGOs are trying to establish a "Korean-style" approach to human–non-human interactions, drawing on historical and cultural sources to establish the Korean basis for the moral principles they are promoting in their campaigns to raise awareness of the condition and welfare of Korean animals (Dugnoille 2021). The subject is complex, since, within this context, considerations of welfarism or abolitionism are sometimes relegated to the background by these NGOs themselves, so as not to jeopardize certain values and/or practices perceived as intrinsically Korean, such as the consumption of dog meat as a symbol of cultural and national identity. For this reason, in the second part, I will explore why the protection of certain species whose consumption is linked to a discourse of identity must also be accompanied by an acute understanding of the postcolonial conditions that govern contemporary Korean society. Finally, in the third part, I will attempt to explain how the roaming of species whose consumption is both unregulated and which carries a strong symbolic value, such as dogs, constitutes a sad privilege compared with the condition of animals whose consumption is strictly regulated, in Korea as elsewhere, and whose killing and commodification are largely normalized.

3.2. Talking about South Korean dogs in order to talk about animal lives

The consumption of dog meat is taken in this chapter as a special case in a broader discussion on animal lives and welfarism. Indeed, although dogs are consumed by the millions each year in Korea, the (anti-)imperialist and (post-) colonialist positions associated with their consumption, as well as the legal loophole that allows for their commodification (see section 1.3.2.2), mean that they are the beneficiaries of both cruelties and privileges that are quite unique compared with other species more commonly consumed in Korean society. The anthropological analysis of this practice is further complicated by the fact that, according to historical and archaeological studies on this subject (Joo 2000; Cwiertka and Walraven 2001; Chu 2002, 2004; Pettid 2008; Kim 2011; Yun and Gi-Bong 2015; Byington 2016), Koreans share a long history of friendship with dogs, and their ambivalent relationship with this species, which navigates between intimacy/friendship and functionality (i.e. as a source of food), perpetuates in contemporary Korean society. Moreover, it is also important to understand that discourses according to which types of dogs are meant to be eaten and others to be seen as pets, often "served up" to foreigners in order to avoid cultural confrontation, are often too rigid to adequately represent what happens in practice. As I show in my book dedicated to this subject (Dugnoille 2021), many dogs initially kept as pets or guard dogs are then sent for slaughter and "recycled" as food. In some cases, they are even eaten by their own keepers. However, this is only one possible trajectory among many other, often very complex "cultural biographies" (Kopytoff 2013). Some dogs pass from being pets to livestock, or vice versa, until they become real family members. These opposite processes, which could be described as commodification, in the first case, and singularization in the second, are never linear, however, and Korean dogs wander in both directions along this long cultural continuum. They are thus "itinerant animals" (Dugnoille 2021), since they navigate throughout their individual lives within a system of exchange which they never really leave.

3.2.1. *The socio-cultural context of dog meat consumption*

In the run-up to the 1988 Olympic Games in Seoul, the Korean government banned the sale of dog meat in the capital's wet markets and asked restaurant owners specializing in dog food dishes to remove dog carcasses from their displays (Derr 2004, p. 26) to avoid offending foreign sensitivities, especially in major urban centers that were more likely to be frequented by tourists from around the world. At the time, this veil thrown over the practice was widely criticized by a section of Korean civil society, which saw in this a new wave of cultural imperialism. Indeed, this episode reminded some of the Japanese domination from 1910 to 1945, during which many Korean cultural traditions were erased and designated as retrograde (Moon 2018). This wave of protest thus revived feelings of national pride and protectionism towards dog meat consumption, and also unleashed discourses advocating a form of cultural relativism, judging the condemnation of dog meat consumption as an imperialist attack on Korean society. Moreover, this reaction was reflected nationally in a renewed interest, after the 1988 Olympic Games, in dog meat dishes (Kim 1994). However, this wave of protest during the 1988 Olympics was relatively mild compared with the reactions during the 2002 FIFA World Cup, co-hosted by Korea, where not only the general public but also influential Korean public figures and politicians took a stand in favor of dog meat, painting it as a national cultural symbol in response to the accusations of "barbarism" publicly stated by foreign, and especially French, personalities such as Brigitte Bardot (Cwiertka and Walraven 2001; Chu 2002; Kim 2008; Oh and Jackson 2011; Yoon, 2016).

Since then, the consumption of dog meat has fundamentally divided Korean society, as evidenced by a survey published in 2018 in the *Korea Herald*, which revealed that about half of Koreans surveyed are radically opposed to prohibiting this practice, while the other half see it as a shameful and outdated tradition (Yonhap 2018). Moreover, tensions have been reignited in the run-up to the 2018 Winter Olympics, held in P'yŏngch'ang, where it seems that the practice of hiding dog meat restaurants has, once again, been introduced by the government. Indeed, animal activists claim that Kangwŏn provincial authorities have offered about 3,000,000 won (around US$3,000) to 18 dog meat restaurants in P'yŏngch'ang and Kangnŭng in order for them to conceal or change the titles of their establishments mentioning the term "dog meat" (Koreandogs.org 2017). If this practice has the same effect on the general public as that used during the 1988 Summer Olympics, then we may see a further upsurge in the consumption of dog meat dishes in Korea in the coming years.

In practice, as Kim (2008) indicates, dog meat is the fourth most consumed meat in Korea, after pork, beef and chicken. Kim adds that the total quantity of dog meat eaten each year is about 100,000 tonnes (2008, p. 202), a figure that includes dogs slaughtered for the production of *kaesoju*, an alcoholic beverage that mixes dog meat and *soju* (Korean alcohol, traditionally made from rice), and which is used as a health tonic to regulate body temperature and increase sexual stamina (see the ethnographic analysis of this practice later in this chapter). Studies conducted by KAPS indicate that the annual value of the industry is approximately US$2 billion, with approximately 6,000 registered restaurants in 2007, plus an additional 14,000 establishments that are not listed as specialty restaurants but which nevertheless sell dog food and related products (Kim 2008). Adult dogs are usually served as *posint'ang*, that is, as a stew, or soup (*t'ang*), but they can also be boiled and served in slices (*suyuk*), fried (*turuch'igi*) or even in fondue (*chŏn'gol*). Since a single serving only requires 100–200 g of meat, a single dog can therefore feed several individuals over several meals. Note, however, that dog meat is not consumed as often as other types of meat in Korea; one of the reasons for this is that dog meat stew is a much more expensive dish than an equivalent dish containing, for example, beef, pork, duck or chicken, with a dog usually costing the restaurant owner around US$180. It should also be noted that puppies are also destined for the butcher's shop: they are used to make soups or stews, as a puppy is usually only large enough for one or two individual portions. In the markets, only the healthiest dogs are kept alive in cages, while the others are killed, kept in the refrigerator and then sold to customers at a lower price than live animals, which is also the case for chickens, ducks, fish or shellfish.

Along with the rise in popularity of dog meat, a civil movement in Korea is advocating for the trade to end or be legalized. This movement corresponds to a generational renewal. Government surveys conducted in the 2000s indeed revealed a growing opposition to dog meat consumption among the younger generations (Jeffreys in Oh and Jackson 2011). This has resulted in a steady decline in the industry, following the renewed interest in this meat following the 1988 Olympics, which seems to have accelerated since the beginning of the 2000s: whereas in 2002, the number of dogs slaughtered for food in Korea was 3 million per year (Jeffreys in Oh and Jackson 2011), in the early 2010s, KARA ([자료첨부] 길고양이 케어테이커 워크숍 후기입니다) ([KARA] Report of the seminar on the protection of stray cats (note that this report also deals with the consumption of dog meat, although its name does not indicate this), 2012) and Ann (2010) estimated that "barely" 1–2 million dogs were consumed each year (note, however, that any reference to Ann's work must be taken with caution, since this Korean researcher is known for his very biased approach in favor of the consumption of dog meat). These figures also match those collected by protection groups on animals such as KAPS (in Kim 2008). In 2020, KARA estimated the number of dogs consumed every year at a little under a million ([기자회견문] 대법원의 '개 전기도살 사건 유죄 판결'은 되돌릴 수 없는 시대정신의 반영이다!) ([Press conference] The Supreme Court's condemnation of dog slaughter reflects an irreversible change in mentality! (2020)), that is, a third of what it was almost 20 years earlier. However, when observed ethnographically, the practice is far from having disappeared, and its strongest support remains the large influx of customers from wet markets and restaurants, which exerts enormous pressure on canine food merchants to prepare the requested meat "correctly" (we will see what "correctly" means later in this chapter). Such pressure is a heavy burden for dog meat sellers to bear, as the legal status of this trade is highly ambiguous and subject to interpretation.

3.2.2. "Animal welfare" in Korean legislation

The legal status of Korean animals does not recognize or reflect the hybridity that exists between the most extreme forms of singularization and commodification applied to certain species in contemporary society, and in particular to dogs. In 1991, it was legally established that "animals" (*tongmul*) were to be protected by the Animal Protection Act (동물보호법 (Animal Protection Act) 2020; English translation: *South Korea's Animal Protection Law*, 1991), the aim of which was to "ensure adequate protection and management of animals by preventing their mistreatment" and requiring Korean citizens to treat them with care and respect (see Article 1.1). In the same year, it was also established that the term "animal" should be understood to mean "cattle, horses, pigs, dogs, cats, rabbits, chickens, ducks, goats, sheep, deer, foxes, mink and other species designated by the Minister of Agriculture and Forestry" (Article 2.1). One of the main principles of this 1991 Act was that "every person who owns an animal shall recognize the dignity and value of that animal and shall try, as far as possible, to provide it with the opportunity to exercise its natural behaviors in order to guarantee it a normal life" (Article 3.1). The problem with this initial, Western welfarist-influenced formulation is that some parts of the Act, such as those referring to the "natural behaviors" of animals or to the need to "ensure a normal life" for them, were formulated in a way that left room for interpretation. As a result, over the next 16 years, some animal welfare groups called for more specific prohibitions, reflecting certain considered traditional practices, such as the use of violence in the killing of certain species in wet markets and specialist restaurants. Some groups, such as International Aid for Korean Animals (IAKA), even suggested that the 1991 Act was deliberately evasive in order to both reinforce Korea's image as a modern society on the international scene and to preserve the status quo regarding abusive dog meat consumption practices in the interests of the Korean economy (South Korea's Animal Protection Laws n.d.). Indeed, banning certain controversial forms[1] of killing that were popular with consumers could have serious consequences for this section of the Korean economy, as many consumers sought the added value associated with such killings in their

1. The moral justifications for certain controversial forms of killing offered by some of my participants fit into a moral paradigm that does not align with the one I adhere to as a European anthropologist. The participants' paradigm places the disrespect for commensality and intergenerational cooking practices as a more important moral issue than any consideration for animal suffering. Thus, from the perspective of some Korean consumers, I have spoken to, this is not cruelty but the perpetuation of a traditional practice that is more important than the individual lives that are sacrificed in the process. I explore these issues in more detail in a forthcoming article on ethical engagement within ethnographic practices that attempt to explore the perspective of nonhuman as well as human actors ("multi-species ethnography").

consumption of dog meat, based on the belief that dogs that die in pain carry therapeutic properties in their flesh (see next section).

Thus, it was due to pressure from these NGOs on the government that, in 2007, amendments to specifically prohibit uncontrolled slaughter and commodification practices were added to the 1991 Act (동물보호법; English translation: *South Korea's Animal Protection Law* 2007):

> No person shall commit the following acts against animals: Act of killing in public or in the presence of another animal [...]. Extracting bodily fluids or installing devices to extract bodily fluids from the living animal [...]. The owner or keeper of an animal shall not abandon [or kill] the animal in a brutal manner, for example, by hanging it by the neck (Article 7.1-7, my translation).

Note that the reference to body fluid extraction devices is specifically intended to prohibit trade in bear bile, extracted through a catheter placed on the live bear. The reference to killing "in a brutal manner by hanging the animal by the neck" is directly targeted at the requests made by some consumers of dog meat. In addition, from a welfarist perspective, the government also specified legal modes of killing, in that it was established that animals killed in any context must be, if not stunned, then at least asphyxiated in such a way as to "minimize their suffering" (Article 11.1). These 2007 amendments to the Animal Welfare Act were also accompanied by the development of a mandatory registration system for companion animals (Kim 2008). In this sense, Korea has, on this occasion, attempted to establish a welfarist discourse within its legal framework, reminiscent of that established in many post-domestic societies (i.e. societies in which the distinction between the consumer and the consumed is so mediated that the consumer often forgets the individual animal they are consuming and sees animal flesh as an inanimate substance), and which aims to normalize a different approach between livestock and pets. Finally, under Article 8.1.4 of the Animal Welfare Act, animals recognized as "livestock" were to be treated humanely, and could not be slaughtered outside the framework of being sent to slaughter without a "justifiable" reason, for example, for medical reasons or to prevent epidemics. The question of whether dogs were or were not understood to be included in the category of livestock remains unanswered to this day, as the separation of pets from food sources is part of a largely Western paradigm, which does not correspond to the fluid way in which dogs are perceived in Korea. This Western paradigm is also conceptual in the sense that it does not apply systematically to all animals in Western contexts (think of the status of the rabbit or the horse in France, for example). Moreover, not only does the reinforcement of a division between pet and livestock not correspond to Korean culture and history, but neither is it probably in the interest of Korean dogs, since the more their consumption is normalized, the more anonymous their lives become, and the more easily they are conceived as inanimate merchandise. I will return to this point in my third and final section.

Regardless of the legal advances of a welfarist nature, it should be noted that the legislation in place rarely punishes those who fail to implement these measures in practice. In particular, tolerance seems to be the norm for restaurants whose owners keep animals alive until they are slaughtered in the adjacent aisles, without supervision, in order to turn them into culinary dishes or traditional medicines. The consumption of fish, chickens, ducks and shellfish requires the slaughter of individuals in front of their fellow animals, also destined for consumption, which compromises enforcement of the Act.

On the contrary, as we will see in the next section, for species such as dogs, even more violent methods are often used and, also, rarely reprimanded. These unsupervised killings are facilitated by the fact that dogs are not included in the 1962 Farm Animal Treatment Act and thus are not recognized as a source of meat or as "livestock" (Kim 2008). However, since it is not explicitly stated anywhere in Korean law that the breeding and slaughter of dogs for food is prohibited (as is the case in the legislation of many countries where the consumption of this species is not or no longer standardized), according to animal law experts, the slaughter of dogs (and as far as I have been able to observe, also of cats, see (Dugnoille 2021)) is "outside the law" as it is neither legal nor illegal, as long as it does not violate the current Animal Protection Act (APA) (Kim 2008; Czajkowski 2014). I might add that the penalty linked to the infraction of this law is rarely applied, because its application is the responsibility of the local authorities, whose members, often indifferent to animal welfare, are moreover rarely trained in these issues, and thus little disposed to actively sanction a practice whose cultural and identity resonances have such a magnitude for civil society.

However, as Kim notes, the Animal Welfare Act of 2007 also contains a clause to train inspectors in this regard, so that they become agents of the law (Kim 2008, p. 219). They could, in theory, seize abused animals and turn them over to animal welfare organizations. In any event, animal law experts (Kim 2008; Czajkowski 2014) argue that the status quo related to dog meat consumption is maintained nationally because it allows the government to maintain a neutral position, in which the dog meat trade remains a pseudo-legal activity, without having to decide on the issue of animal welfare and, in particular, the legal and cultural issues of the status of dogs in Korea. This status quo also allows the Korean government to make no decisions in either direction, so as not to alienate any part of Korean society.

Finally, this legal no-man's-land places significant pressure on shopkeepers, who feel they must use the methods requested by their customers, or risk losing their business and being forced to close. If filmed in the act and reported to the police, however, these vendors face a fine of up to US$10,000 and up to one year in jail. Nevertheless, some consumers see certain killing methods as a way to perpetuate a tradition of commensality that goes beyond considerations of suffering, sentience, and conscience of the animals being commodified. The moral imperative mobilized by these consumers is thus, above all, to ensure the continuity of the practice through several generations.

3.3. Animal lives in markets

3.3.1. *Introducing Moran Market*

Let us now turn to these killings in order to explore not only the experiences of consumers and producers, but also those of the animals involved. To do so, I will take Korea's largest wet market as my ethnographic backdrop. The Moran Market has long been the largest market in Korea, where dogs could be bought and prepared as food, and so is a temple of dog meat consumption. The *Korea Herald* reported that, in 2015, this market alone sold more than 80,000 dead or living dogs annually and provided one-third of the country's consumed dog meat (Kim 2016). Nevertheless, in late 2016, following pressure from civil society and some animal protection groups, the district government of the city of Sŏngnam (where Moran Market is located) announced that all dog slaughter would be banned within its jurisdiction and that, as a result, all dog meat shopkeepers would be requested to dismantle their slaughter equipment as soon as possible. Despite this decision, the ban was slow to take effect and, as of March 2017, dog slaughter could still be observed at Moran Market. In May 2017, the slaughterhouses at 21 of the 22 outlets were permanently removed, but one adamant vendor nonetheless brought his slaughter equipment back to the market. Moreover, in 2018, many nearby restaurants and stores were still selling dog meat, indicating that it will be some time before all shopkeepers, restaurant owners and dealers in the jurisdiction completely stop engaging in the dog meat trade. After shutting down dog meat stalls at Moran Market, Seoul city authorities then announced that, from 2019, there would be no more dog slaughter at Kyŏngdong Market in Tongdaemun (a northeastern district of Seoul). Outside of the Seoul area, the large Kup'o Market in Pusan (in the south of the country) is now facing similar pressure from civil society as local residents have complained of noises and smells that point to illegal slaughter methods.

For opponents of dog meat consumption, the abolition of dog slaughter at the Moran Market was a huge success, since it was a symbol of national identity with strong emotional connotations and therefore, a priori, difficult to dismantle. In fact, according to the city's official tourism page, the market was built in 1962, in other words, after the Japanese colonization of 1910–1945. This is important to note, because many so-called "traditional" markets across the country, such as Namdaemun Market and Noryangjin Fish Market, were developed under Japanese administration and their infrastructure and general organization have remained unchanged since then. This is not the case with Moran Market, which is perceived as inherently "Korean", selling a wide variety of products, including live and dead animals such as dogs, cats, chickens, ducks and rabbits. The fact that these traditional markets have withstood the influence of the Japanese administrative infrastructure adds to the fact that they are perceived as important havens of cultural and national independence. However, here I must place the advent of dog meat consumption as a national symbol within its historical context. It was only as a result of successive episodes of cultural imperialism during the course of the 20th century, first by the Japanese and then by the Americans, that the image of the "good pet dog" came to challenge the ambiguous but nonetheless unproblematic dog-human relationship in Korea. In the 1920s and 1930s, dogs (mainly, but not exclusively, German Shepherds) had been used as weapons of war in Korea by the Japanese armed forces to maintain order through threat and terror (Skabelund 2011). At the same time, the Japanese imperial forces in Korea had also promoted and imported the image of the Japanese war dog, responding to the commands of its "master", as an illustration of Japan's civilizational achievement (compared with Korea), an image of progress itself inherited from Victorian England and its tradition of dog breeding and dog keeping as an emblem of modernity (Ritvo 1987). Then, in the 1950s, after the Korean War, the Americans exported many aspects of their culture to Korea, establishing them as necessary conditions for the modernization of Korean society (Cwiertka 2013; Dugnoille 2021). Within this context, the idea that dogs should be seen as pets and not as sources of food was strongly promoted. That the concept of the pet dog has been associated with colonialism in Korea for the past hundred years is therefore not really surprising. Hence, even today, some Koreans have great difficulty in accepting the Euro-American perspective that dogs should be seen as pets; the question of their legal status divides Korean society more than ever before, not only because it is a cultural symbol, but also because it is a symbol of resistance to past and present imperialism. In this sense, the freedom to buy and consume dogs in such traditional markets takes on a special magnitude and significance for many Korean consumers and producers, a point to which I will return in the next section.

On the contrary, it should be noted that, for many consumers, examining live animals (cats, dogs and also chickens, ducks or rabbits) before eating them is of great importance. This is to determine if a potential meal will come from a product that is healthy and good quality at the time of slaughter. In this sense, as mentioned above, some restaurants offer dishes made from animals in cages on the storefront of their premises (*ttŭnjang*) to attract their customers. As a result, brief encounters between humans and their meat are improvised.

3.3.2. *Ethnographic overview*

At the time when I began my research (2012), Moran Market was the largest dog meat market in South Korea. A variety of other products were available for sale there, including flowers, fruits, vegetables and spices, and also live animals such as chickens, ducks, rabbits or cats. In this market, dogs had a status very similar to that of animals more commonly consumed for the same therapeutic purposes, such as chickens. Indeed, in Korea, chickens are sometimes consumed as *samgyet'ang* for the same purpose as dogs, namely, in the hope of regulating body temperature during hot weather. However, dogs and chickens are not only eaten during the summer. Indeed, it became evident during my fieldwork that dog meat was served month after month, all year round. While the frequency of dog meat consumption varied among individuals, the majority of consumers I met mentioned eating dog meat dishes two to three times a year. At the time, I observed that the recipes requiring dog meat in the vast majority of stalls included *t'ang* or *posint'ang* (soup), *suyuk* (boiled in water) and *much'im* (fried with seasoning). *Chn'gol* (stew), *turuch'igi* (boiled, then lightly roasted with spices) and *soju* (alcoholic juice) were less common. The main seasonings served with these dog meat recipes were soybean paste, vinegar, *tadaegi* (a mixture of red bell pepper, ginger, garlic, onion and black pepper), pepper, salt, onion, ginger, garlic and mustard. The side dishes were most often Chinese cabbage, leek salad and *kimch'i*. The wide variety of dog meat dishes indicates that this culinary practice is much more diverse than a simple summer dish, as previous studies (such as Podberscek 2009) and non-ethnographic and shorter studies on the subject had suggested.

In the course of my research, it further became apparent that some consumers believed that dog meat was particularly effective in maximizing endurance (especially sexual). Others believed that it regulated bodily strength and energy, or even that if dogs died of fright, the level of adrenaline in their blood would give their meat special energetic qualities, which were then passed on to the person eating it. This explains why these clients demanded that their meat be "tenderized", that is, that the dogs be hung and/or beaten to death. My interviewees often associated their talk of adrenaline and stamina with the so-called "ideal" virtues as explored in the *Tongŭi pogam*, a classic text dating from the 17th century in which the consumption of dog meat is presented as being particularly good for body temperature regulation, for sexual stamina (usually for men but not exclusively) and for digestion (Hŏ 1977; Hŏ et al. 2009). The *Tongŭi pogam* refers to different parts of a dog's body to cure all kinds of afflictions, including epilepsy, obstinacy in children, difficult childbirth, anger, depression, poor digestion or even fatigue.

During my research (from 2012 to the present), the main consumers of dog meat turned out to be groups of generally older men (in their 50s or older) who were taking the meat in hopes of maximizing their virility. This is in keeping with the dominant cultural paradigm of Korean patriarchy (Han 2016). Through social activities, these groups of men seek to exert power and force over other groups that are structurally and culturally subordinate to them, including, of course, women, children and animals. Violence against dogs, a particularly controversial aspect of the dog meat trade, is often blamed on the shopkeepers, but more often comes from the customers. While the particularly violent killings they demand are practices that shopkeepers and restaurant owners could do without, it is not uncommon for them to be asked to slaughter dogs by hanging them with ropes, beating them with a stick, or boiling them alive.

At the time of my initial research (2012–2013), most market stalls were associated with a family name and displayed signs showing the longevity of their business as a guarantee of quality. These family businesses were sometimes connected to other stalls in adjacent rows where live animals, often smaller ones, could be purchased. These stalls were usually run by older family members, often women, who sold live juvenile dogs or puppies alongside live ducks, rabbits, and young and adult cats. Juyun, for example, one of the female shopkeepers I met at the time, began working in the dog meat business when she married her husband in 1977. Her husband inherited the Moran Market stall from his father, so he and Juyun took over the family business once the patriarch became too old to handle it. By 2012, Juyun and her husband were buying their dogs from various farms across the country, including in greater Seoul. Reluctantly, Juyun often had to hang her dogs by ropes at the request of customers fond of the so-called adrenaline content of the dogs suffering during their killing. She was often afraid that dogs would escape or struggle, and she preferred her husband to do the job for her, but the demand was often such that she had to comply when her husband was busy with other tasks. She had to catch the dog selected by the client with a sort of wire ring attached to the end of a metal stick, which closed around the dog's neck as it tried to struggle. The dog was then dragged to the back of the store, a rope was put around its neck and was passed through a hook that was more or less fixed to the ceiling, and the rope was pulled until the dog was lifted, struggled, and finally died, strangled and exhausted.

According to the request, there were also times when Juyun had to beat some dogs to death with a metal bar, a baseball bat, or any other metal or wooden stick at her disposal. After that, the fur and skin of the dog had to be burned with a kind of blowtorch and then the dead dog had to be boiled in a pressure cooker and then cut into pieces. During these operations, the customers waited patiently around small tables attached to the stalls, talking among themselves. They sometimes asked to be served specific parts of the dog's body, each of which was supposed to cure a particular affliction. Once again, these conceptions loosely mirror those described in the *Tonguĭ pogam* about the five vital organs (arteries, bones, joints, stomach/liver and intestines). Teeth were sometimes requested "to take away" since they were meant for capricious or temperamental children. The heart was thought to regulate the temperament of particularly aggressive and angry adults, with mood swings and/or deep depression. Some clients thought that the stomach was good for women who were breastfeeding a newborn, that the bile could cure eye problems, the kidney for kidney problems, the penis for impotence and so on. In any case, preparing the dogs was an exhausting task and a great psychological burden for the shopkeepers. Indeed, Juyun sometimes spoke of the agony of the animals she had to beat. She also told me that she resented the customers for making her bear such a burden, but that she knew only too well that she could not truly escape the demands of these older men, a group at the very top of Korean society, in which gender and class relations are influenced by a particularly strong Confucian and patriarchal heritage (Kim 2012; Han 2016).

As this ethnographic vignette indicates, the condition of animals is the very source of some of the trade in certain species. Dogs are valued as suffering commodities. It is precisely because they are capable of suffering, and their suffering is "outside the law", that their consumption continues to attract a steady stream of customers. Moreover, the pain of these dogs is not only valued as a vector of energetic qualities but also as a symbol of national resistance. Indeed, the Korean term *han* was often used by my interviewees to justify the abuse of dogs in the trade. *Han* is seen as the anger of Koreans towards the hardships encountered throughout their history, especially their contemporary history. Moreover, *han* is both what triggers civil society movements with a sense of vengeful anger, and also the resignation of members of that society to their fate. In Abelmann's terms (1996, p. 37), *han* thus facilitates both resistance and non-resistance. It is thus a question of being indignant about the power in place and of being resigned to it at the same time. It is a double movement, considered by many of my interviewees as "typically Korean" and which is also expressed in the face of past struggles. Thus, the connection to Japanese and American colonialism and imperialism resurfaces when *han* is mobilized in discourses around the consumption of dog meat: by consuming members of a species particularly valued by two former colonial forces as a pet and as an instrument of modernization and terror, some consumers engage in a form of resistance against an imperialist past that has sought to damage Korean culture. The dogs' anger is thus consumed in order to compensate for the anger of the Koreans themselves in the face of difficult episodes from history and, at the same time, to strengthen certain individuals psychically and physically. When we understand this, it is not surprising to see an upsurge in the consumption of dog meat following international condemnations of the practice at the sporting events described at the beginning of this chapter.

Of course, dogs are the first to suffer from this symbolic burden, but there is a glimmer of hope: since this suffering is only made possible by the legal status quo around their consumption, their commodification is therefore unregulated and, in fact, some individuals manage to escape being killed even after entering the system of their commercialization, thanks to some animal rights advocates, who facilitate their singularization as pets or as symbols of a fight against violence and Korean patriarchy (see Dugnoille (2014) for an example of singularization). Thus, it is also a sad privilege that members of this species enjoy. The following section explores this idea in more detail.

3.4. On the condition of the dogs

An ethnographic approach to the consumption of dog meat in Korea highlights the fact that any attempt to regulate the trade must be informed by two considerations: first, that those who produce and consume dog meat construct their cultural and/or national identity around the practice, and, second, that the impact that these identity constructions have on the experiences of the dogs themselves is considerable, particularly when they are subjected to violent practices. As I noted above, from a consumer perspective, the suffering of dogs is not really in question, as it feeds into an argument in favor of the trade. Indeed, even among those who are at the heart of their commercialization, the passage from life to carcass has never been equated with the simple negation of the sentience of these individual animals. On the contrary, dogs have a special value among Korean consumers precisely because, not being subject to welfarist regulations, their sentience can potentially be passed on to the products they produce. The anger and fear that these animals feel during their killing is supposed to remain in their flesh once they are transformed into a dish, and thus be transferred in turn to consumers. Sometimes consumers believe that they are being transferred not so much the adrenaline that remains in the flesh of the dogs, but the very fear and anger of the animal being killed. Some consumers reported to me that they have felt the animals' sensitivity, fear and anger in the form of fever, guilt or anxiety after consumption (Dugnoille 2021). In all cases, it is the very fact that dogs are considered sentient beings that has led them to be transformed into commodities. Thus, from the consumer's perspective, this commodification of sentience can only take place through the cultural and legal limbo in which dogs are currently held. Regulating the trade to give dogs the same status accorded to any so-called "livestock" animal would greatly diminish their value as products.

Of course, the regulation of the dog meat trade is even more complex when we consider the perspective of the dogs themselves, and when we consider this in comparison to animals categorized as livestock. For example, maintaining the current legal status means that dogs continue to suffer from direct (physical) violence, as their killing remains unsupervised, and also from what Galtung calls "structural" and "cultural" forms of violence (1990). "Structural violence" is a form of violence in which a social structure or institution prevents a group from accessing the same rights as others based on a specific characteristic (1990), such as in the case of discrimination based on gender, age and race. In the case of both livestock and non-livestock animals, each member of these two groups suffers from a form of structural violence, since, on the basis of their belonging to a specific species, they are considered "good to kill" while other animal species are seen as "sacrificeable" (Haraway 2008, p. 80); that is, because their species status is less culturally related to human beings, their death is less "grievable" (Butler 2009) than that of pets, for instance. In societies with animal protection legislation, structural violence is made possible by laws that normalize the direct violence necessary for their commodification. However, even though animals classified as "livestock" are discriminated against on the basis of their species, they cannot simply be killed without rules. In the case of Korean dogs, the law that might normalize their status as "good to kill" animals remains deliberately vague. The fact remains that, with or without the legal status of livestock, millions of dogs are consumed every year in Korea, which means that, in practice, they are effectively treated as livestock. However, they are neither just "livestock" nor just "pets": they are both killable and expendable.

Because of this flaw, dogs also suffer from the fact that their fear and anger at the killing is an integral part of the product sought and consumed. Thus, not only do dogs suffer from "structural violence" and direct (physical) violence, but also from what Galtung calls "cultural violence", that is, the way culture is used to legitimize physical (direct) and/or structural violence against them. As he points out, cultural violence thus makes other forms of violence look, or even feel, right (1990, p. 291). The constant roaming of dogs along the commodification–singularization continuum is thus culturally normalized, and their dual status as livestock and pet allows them to suffer this triple violence. Only a regulation of the trade could put an end to this; therefore, from a welfarist perspective, the dog meat trade should be regulated. From this point of view, the roaming of dogs makes them worse off than animals classified as livestock only.

Conversely, an abolitionist approach that would fight for a total ban on the dog meat trade before addressing other, broader issues of animal commodification raises some questions. It is true that if a goal is more easily achieved in the short term, the tangible possibility of achieving that goal would make it a priority. On the contrary, it could be argued that if the abolition of a practice seems achievable, it is because the animal species in question already enjoys a certain privilege over other species whose killing is normalized. If this is the case, we might question why the human and financial resources mobilized for the abolition of the trade in the already privileged species should not go to those whose death is commonplace. It is therefore difficult to decide the question of moral priority between unregulated and mass commodification.

3.5. Conclusion

In any case, in light of my research on the postcolonial resonance taken on by that debates around the abolition and/or regularization of dog meat consumption in Korea, it should first be recognized that any willingness to intervene in these debates must be informed by an in depth understanding of how those who produce and consume dog meat in Korea construct their identities around this practice. Nevertheless, since the focus of this book is on animal lives, it is also appropriate to offer conclusions that take into consideration the perspective of Korean animals who are, of course, directly affected by these debates. My findings reveal that some dogs originally destined to be commodified were fortunate enough to be singled out, suggesting at least a small chance that dogs could be rescued from this trade. I would therefore argue that, in the event that abolition of the practice is impossible, the status quo should, for the time being, be maintained, precisely because of the dangers inherent in regulating the legal status of dogs as "livestock". As Vialles and Pachirat have shown, regulating the animal trade is often accompanied by a mechanism of invisibility, in which deaths associated with the production of meat and other animal products are kept away from urban centers, out of sight of consumers, often in the interest of so-called public health and hygiene. Indeed, a number of the dog slaughterhouses that have begun to be established in Korea are being built farther and farther away from urban centers, thereby reducing the visibility of the killing of these dogs. In other words, a form of legal and social indeterminacy of dogs means that they are not yet trapped in what Vialles calls "the spiral of avoidance" (1987), a cultural and structural process in which the blame for the killing of animals is shifted from consumers to producers to traders to slaughterhouse workers (and from slaughterhouse workers to each other, from the person who stuns the animals to the person who cuts their throats and so on). Furthermore, increasing the physical and legal distance between the consumer and the consumed, by dissociating the individual animal from the mere substance ingested, may lead to an increased demand for this food product (Vialles 1987; Wilkie 2010; Pachirat 2013; Buller and Roe 2018). Increasing the distinction between dogs, as individuals, and dog-based products could lead to a higher domestic demand and even create an international market for these products. Thus, while the roaming of dogs is problematic in many ways because it allows for unsupervised slaughter and thus some degree of violence, it is difficult, at least in my view, to argue for the recognition of dogs as "livestock", because as such, such regulation would likely increase their commodification and lead to more normalized violence on a much larger scale.

Nevertheless, while utilitarian and anti-speciesist considerations should also be given some weight, the priority of banning the dog meat trade must also be considered in the context of other animal liberation issues, because, as I mentioned above, far fewer dogs are consumed than any member of the three species more commonly traded in Korea (pigs, cows and chickens). Moreover, dogs, unlike these three species, still have a chance to be singled out, at least temporarily. In this sense, it must be concluded that the itinerancy of dogs, compared to the fixed status of other livestock species in Korea, as elsewhere, is a sad privilege, and also a fate whose visibility might help to raise awareness among some human populations from post-domestic societies about the prevailing normalization of the commodification of other species whose death is almost universally perceived as less "grievable" than that of man's best friend.

3.6. References

Ann, Y.-G. (2010). The effect of dogmeat eating on sanitation and food waste consumption. *Korean Journal of Food & Nutrition*, 23(1), 124–133.

Buller, H. and Roe, E. (2018). *Food and Animal Welfare*. Bloomsbury Academic, London.

Butler, J. (2009). *Frames of War: When Is Life Grievable?* London, Verso.

Byington, M.E. (2016). *The Ancient State of Puyŏ in Northeast Asia: Archaeology and Historical Memory*. Harvard University Asia Center. doi: 10.2307/j.ctv47w4dm.

Chu, K. (2002). *Kaegogi wa munhwa chegukchuŭi: Irŭnba munmyŏng kwa yaman e kwanhayŏ.* Ch'op'an, Chungang M & B, Sŏul-si.

Chu, K. (2004). *Uri munhwa ŭi susukkekki.* K'ŏrŏ kaejŏngp'an, Han'gyŏre Sinmunsa, Sŏul-si.

Cwiertka, K.J. (2013). *Cuisine, Colonialism and Cold War: Food in Twentieth-Century Korea.* Reaktion Books, London [Online]. Available at: https://public.ebookcentral. proquest.com/choice/publicfullrecord.aspx?p=1550747 [Accessed 27 April 2020].

Cwiertka, K.J. and Walraven, B. (eds) (2001). *Asian Food: The Global and the Local.* University of Hawai'i Press, Honolulu.

Czajkowski, C. (2014). Dog meat trade in South Korea: A report on the current state of the trade and efforts to eliminate it. *Animal Law*, 21(1), 29–64.

Deckha, M. (2008). Disturbing images: PETA and the feminist ethics of animal advocacy. *Ethics and the Environment*, 13(2), 35–76.

Derr, M. (2004). *Dog's Best Friend: Annals of the Dog-Human Relationship.* University of Chicago Press, Chicago.

Dugnoille, J. (2014). From plate to pet: Promotion of trans-species companionship by Korean animal activists. *Anthropology Today*, 30(6), 3–7. doi: 10.1111/1467-8322.12140.

Dugnoille, J. (2021). *Itinerant Animals: Cultural Biographies of Cats and Dogs in South Korea.* Purdue University Press, West Lafayette.

Francione, G.L. and Garner, R. (2010). *The Animal Rights Debate: Abolition or Regulation?* Columbia University Press, New York.

Galtung, J. (1990). Cultural violence. *Journal of Peace Research*, 27(3), 291–305.

Han, G.S. (2016). Nouveau-riche nationalism and multiculturalism in Korea [Online]. Available at: http://search.ebscohost.com/login.aspx?direct=true&scope=site&db=nlebk& db=nlabk&AN=1061367 [Accessed 7 September 2018].

Hŏ, C. (1977). *Tongŭi pogam : Kugyŏk chŭngbo (The Precious Mirror of Korean Medicine).* Namsangdang, Seoul.

Hŏ, C. (2009). *How to Read Donguibogam Easily.* National Government Publication, Seoul.

Joo, Y. (2000). 음식전쟁, 문화전쟁 *(Food War Cultural War).* 사계절출판사 (한국문화총서, 10), Seoul.

Kim, K.O. (1994). Production of food and consumption of culture: Survey. *Han'guk Munhwa Illyukak (Korean Cultural Anthropology)*, 26, 7–50.

Kim, R.E. (2008). Dog meat in Korea: A socio-legal challenge. *Animal Law*, 14, 201–236.

Kim, G.S. (2011). 우리나라 유적 출토 개 유체 고찰 (A study of dog-remains from archaeological sites in Korea). 호남고고학보, 37(0), 5–25.

Kim, J. (2012). *A History of Korea: From "Land of the Morning Calm" to States in Conflict.* Bloomington, Indiana University Press.

Kim, D.S. (2016). Illegal dog slaughter to be banned in Moran Market [Online]. Available at: http://m.koreaherald.com/view.php?ud=20161213000847#cb [Accessed 14 December 2016].

Kopytoff, I. (2013). The cultural biography of things: Commoditization as process. In *The Social Life of Things: Commodities in Cultural Perspective*, Appadurai, A. (ed.). Cambridge University Press, Cambridge.

Koreandogs.org (2017). Pyeongchang's project to hide the dog meat restaurants from Olympic visitors! [Online]. Available at: https://koreandogs.org/pc2018-sign-project/ [Accessed 30 April 2020].

Moon, H. (2018). Fictions of liberation: A paradoxical "palimpsest of colonial identity" of *Chŏng* (*Jeong*). *Journal of Pastoral Theology*, 28(3), 160–174. doi: 10.1080/10649867. 2018.1547959.

Oh, M. and Jackson, J. (2011). Animal rights vs. cultural rights: Exploring the dog meat debate in South Korea from a world polity perspective. *Journal of Intercultural Studies*, 32(1), 31–56. doi: 10.1080/07256868.2010.491272.

Pachirat, T. (2013). *Every Twelve Seconds: Industrialized Slaughter and the Politics of Sight.* Yale University Press, New Haven.

Pettid, M.J. (2008). *Korean Cuisine: An Illustrated History*. Reaktion Books, London.

Podberscek, A.L. (2009). Good to pet and eat: The keeping and consuming of dogs and cats in South Korea. *Journal of Social Issues*, 65(3), 615–632. doi: 10.1111/j.1540-4560.2009. 01616.x.

Regan, T. (2004). *The Case for Animal Rights*, Updated with a new foreword. University of California Press, Berkeley.

Ritvo, H. (1987). *The Animal Estate: The English and Other Creatures in the Victorian Age.* Harvard University Press, Cambridge, MA.

Skabelund, A.H. (2011). *Empire of Dogs: Canines, Japan, and the Making of the Modern Imperial World*. Cornell University Press, Ithaca.

South Korea's Animal Protection Law (1991). Animal Protection Law 1991 [Online]. Available at: http://koreananimals.org/animal-protection-law-1991/.

South Korea's Animal Protection Law (2007). Animal Protection Laws 2007 [Online]. Available at: http://koreananimals.org/animal-protection-law-2007/ [Accessed 14 March 2017].

South Korea's Animal Protection Laws (n.d.). International Aid for Korean Animals (IAKA) [Online]. Available at: http://koreananimals.org/south-koreas-animal-protection-laws/ [Accessed 28 April 2020].

Vialles, N. (1987). *Le sang et la chair : les abattoirs des pays de l'Adour*. Editions de la Maison des sciences de l'homme, Paris.

Wilkie, R. (2010). *Livestock/deadstock: Working with Farm Animals from Birth to Slaughter*. Temple University Press, Philadelphia.

Yonhap (2018). Poll shows Koreans evenly divided over legal ban on dog slaughter. *Korea Herald* [Online]. Available at: http://www.koreaherald.com/view.php?ud=201811230003 85&ACE_SEARCH=1 [Accessed 18 May 2020].

Yoon, H. (2016). Disappearing bitches: Canine affect and postcolonial bioethics. *Configurations*, 24(3), 351–374. doi: 10.1353/con.2016.0022.

Yun, J.J. and Gi-Bong, Y. (2015). An attitude survey of religious believers on Korean culinary culture taking canine flesh – Focusing on the case of Daesoonjinrihoe. *Journal of the Korean Academy of New Religions*, 32(32), 25–62. doi: 10.22245/jkanr.2015.32. 32.25.

[기자회견문] 대법원의 '개 전기도살 사건 유죄 판결'은 되돌릴 수 없는 시대정신의 반영이다! (2020). Available at: https://www.ekara.org/activity/against/read/12892 [Accessed 24 April 2020].

동물보호법 (2020). Korean law available here in Korean: https://ko.wikisource.org/ wiki/동물보호법_(제8852호) and http://www.law.go.kr/법령/동물보호법.

[자료첨부] 길고양이 케어테이커 워크숍 후기입니다. (2012). *카라 (KARA)*. Available at: https://ekara.org/activity/cat/read/2123.

4

The Legal Status of Animals in European Law

Fabien MARCHADIER

Equipe de recherche en droit privé (ERDP), Université de Poitiers, France

4.1. Introduction

4.1.1. *Emergence of a legal protection of the animal by the European Union*

Although its founding treaties did not give the European Union jurisdiction to work for the protection of animals, it could not ignore the fact that, among the economic activities governed by its standards, some involve animals to which a great deal of harm can be done (animal husbandry[1], transportation[2], slaughter[3],

---

1. Council Directive 98/58/EC of July 20, 1998 concerning the protection of animals kept for farming purposes; Council Directive 1999/74/EC of July 19, 1999 establishing minimum standards for the protection of laying hens; Council Directive 2007/43/EC of June 28, 2007 laying down minimum regulations for the protection of chickens kept for meat production; Council Directive 2008/119/EC of December 18, 2008 laying down minimum standards for the protection of calves; Council Directive 2008/120/EC of December 18, 2008 laying down minimum standards for the protection of pigs.
2. Council Regulation (EC) No. 1/2005 of December 22, 2004 on the protection of animals during transport and related operations.
3. Council Regulation (EC) No. 1099/2009 of September 24, 2009 on the protection of animals at the time of killing, in particular Cons. 2.

Animal Suffering,
coordinated by Florence BURGAT and Emilie DARDENNE. © ISTE Ltd 2023.

experimentation[4]). In addition, several of its members, including France, which adopted a system to protect domestic animals in the middle of the 19th century[5], had embarked on the path of legal protection for animals. The Council of Europe, through its parliamentary assembly, had emphasized that treating animals with humanity and benevolence was a civilization issue[6]. The commitment of Member States in favor of the protection of the animals through evolving legislation and their ratification of the conventions of the Council of Europe could only encourage the European Union to address the problem. For that, it was able to take advantage of the powers granted to it, in particular for the establishment and the operation of the internal market, or for the development and the implementation of the common agricultural policy[7]. The institutional context of the construction of Europe did not make it possible to reasonably envisage the development of a status of animals. The protection of animals is not in itself the object of any policy of the Union, but it first appeared opportune[8], then it became a "Community value"[9], a "basic objective"[10] to be carried out. The approach is therefore sectoral. Consideration for animals is diffuse and influences the elaboration of norms relating to killing, international transportation, scientific experimentation, breeding, trade in furs and cosmetics, hunting techniques or the evaluation of the toxicity of products. Thus, under the guise of completion of the internal market, the alignment of national laws through directives, or the standardization of rules through regulations, are no longer aimed solely at avoiding distortions of competition between Member States. These directives and regulations are the instrument of a policy led by the European

---

4. Directive 2010/63/EU of the European Parliament and of the Council of September 22, 2010 on the protection of animals used for scientific purposes.

5. The Grammont Act of July 2, 1850 on the mistreatment of domestic animals: official journal, August 20, 1944, page 299.

6. Consultative Assembly of the Council of Europe, Recommendation 287 (1961) of September 22, 1961 on the international transport of animals. Comp. European Parliament Res. December 12, 2012 on the protection of animals during transport, point A: "The protection of animals in the 21st century is an expression of humanity and a challenge facing European civilization and culture."

7. Art. 37 of the EEC Treaty is specifically mentioned in the Council Directive 2008/120/EC of December 18, 2008 laying down minimum standards for the protection of pigs and the Council Directive 2007/43/EC of June 28, 2007 laying down minimum regulations for the protection of chickens kept for meat production.

8. Cons. 2 of the Council Directive 74/577/EEC of November 18, 1974 on the stunning of animals before slaughter (repealed) stressing that "the Community should also take action to avoid in general all forms of cruelty to animals".

9. Cons. 4, Regulation No. 1099/2009 "Protection of animals at the time of killing".

10. Cons. 7, Directive No. 2007/43/EC "Protection of chickens kept for meat production".

Commission and Parliament seeking to achieve a high level of animal protection[11]. This aim goes hand in hand with the proper functioning of the market, which should come first, but which is sometimes relegated to the background[12]. The results, at least according to European institutions, are generally positive. In a 2018 report[13], the European Court of Auditors noted that it is widely accepted that the EU's animal welfare standards are among the highest in the world. While weaknesses persist, the Court does not fail to commend the Commission's efforts to enforce these standards in its Member States, who, it is pointed out, have a major role to play in ensuring their effectiveness.

The European Union wanted to develop an ambitious program, but it seems to have come up against realism, that other synonym for capitulation. In 1974, it wished to "take action to avoid in general all forms of cruelty to animals"[14], but the first achievements were rather modest and will remain so. It is simply a matter of ensuring that, at the time of slaughter, animals are only subject to "absolutely unavoidable suffering". Then, in 1993[15], the adverb disappeared and the wording evolved. Pain was added to suffering and the new rules were intended to spare animals from avoidable suffering[16]. As for the fight against cruelty, there is little or nothing left of it. Protection is no longer based on benevolence and compassion, but on cold economic rationality. Protection consists of "ensuring rational development

---

11. See, for example, the structure of point 5 of the preamble to the Council Directive 77/489/EEC of July 18, 1977 on the protection of animals during international transport (repealed).

12. Comp. Cons. 1 and 2 of the Council Directive 74/577/EEC of November 18, 1974 on the stunning of animals before slaughter (repealed) and Directive on the protection of laying hens (1999/74/EC, Cons. 5 & 6), Directive on the protection of chickens kept for meat production (2007/43/EC, Cons. 1 & 6) or Directive on the protection of laboratory animals (2010/63/EU).

13. Special Report No. 31/2018, *Animal welfare in the EU: closing the gap between ambitious goals and practical implementation*. Comp. Resolution No. 493 AN of November 1, 2020 on the protection of animal welfare in the European Union, "considering that the problem of implementation of standards remains the central issue of European animal welfare policies".

14. This is to be compared with the much more modest objectives of the Council of Europe as they appear in the Convention of December 13, 1968 on the Protection of Animals during International Transport. This first achievement is not part of any general project to fight against animal suffering. If it is to be avoided, it is only "as far as possible", as the preamble states. Above all, the Member States affirm their conviction that "the requirements of international animal transport are not incompatible with animal welfare".

15. Council Directive 93/119/EC of December 22, 1993 on the protection of animals at the time of slaughter or killing (repealed).

16. Cons. 5.

of production and to facilitate the completion of the internal market in animals and animal products"[17]. In 2010, it aims to achieve the abolition of procedures applied to animals for scientific and educational purposes[18]. However, the newly adopted directive is only one step in a project that is constantly being postponed[19]. There is no mention of removing animals from the legal category of things. They remain in some respects a commodity, an agricultural product, susceptible to appropriation, circulation (transportation, notably to places of slaughter) and marketing (sale – import/export). The Union's action in favor of animals does not aim to break the chains of animal exploitation, the necessity of which is continually emphasized (particularly from a food and agricultural perspective, at least for a certain type of food – meat – and a certain type of agriculture, that which aims to control the biological cycle of domesticated species). It is therefore not a question of changing the model, but of making it acceptable (for whom: the animals or the humans who benefit from it?)[20].

4.1.2. Realization of the legal protection of animals by the European Union: the concept of welfare

Legally protecting animals does not mean granting them a specific legal status, but rather preserving their welfare regardless of their legal status and qualification. To this end, the Union requires its institutions and Member States, when formulating and implementing EU policy in defined areas, to take full account of the welfare requirements of animals as sentient beings and not as commodities or agricultural products[21] (Marguénaud 2009, p. 13; Hervouet 2015, p. 211; Sowery 2018); thus, it is the intrinsic value of the animal that is considered, not its utility value (Dubos

---

17. Cons. 4.

18. See Cons. No. 10, Directive No. 2010/63 "Animal Experiments".

19. See the Commission Communication of June 3, 2015 (C(2015) 3773 final) on the European Citizens' Initiative "Stop Vivisection". However, this objective has been achieved in cosmetics (Regulation (EC) No. 1223/2009 of the European Parliament and of the Council of November 30, 2009 on cosmetic products, art. 18, section 2, b).

20. The Council of Europe's work on animal protection is based on the same philosophy. The five conventions drawn up under the impetus of the Parliamentary Assembly (Protection of Animals during International Transport (1968, ETS 65), Protection of Animals kept for Farming Purposes (1976, ETS 87), Protection of Animals for Slaughter (1979, ETS 102), Protection of Vertebrate Animals used for Experimental and other Scientific Purposes (1986, ETS 123) and Protection of Pet Animals (1987, ETS 125)) reflect the idea that humans may and sometimes must use animals, but have a moral obligation to ensure, within reasonable limits, that, in each case, the health and welfare of the animal is not unnecessarily threatened.

21. Article 13 of the Treaty on the Functioning of the European Union – hereinafter, TFEU.

2017, p. 13; Sowery 2018). The notion of welfare structures all of the EU's sectoral actions and gives them coherence. The effectiveness of the injunction contained in Article 13 TFEU will be commensurate with the identification of its requirements. However, it comes up against two pitfalls: the first concerns its scope and the second is related to its indeterminacy.

The consideration of the welfare requirements of animals, as sentient beings, is not general. It is only required for certain policies: agriculture, fisheries, transport, the internal market, research and technological development and space. For other policies, if there is no ban, there is no obligation. This means that in areas as essential as health and the environment, consideration of animal welfare is only a mere possibility. If welfare is a measure of how well a being adapts to its environment and living conditions (Broom 2001, p. 148), then environmental policy is crucial from the perspective of wild animal welfare. Above all, whatever the policy concerned, animal welfare can be lawfully ignored for the sake of religious rites, cultural traditions and regional heritage. The indeterminacy of these "rites, transitions and heritage" (to use the terms of Art. 13 TFEU) is as problematic as the indeterminacy of the requirements that the Union and its Member States must take into account.

There is no precise rule defining animal welfare[22]. It is constantly quoted alongside a rather weak guarantee of physical integrity. The animal must not experience any pain, suffering or injury that would be unnecessary or avoidable; that is, certain pain, suffering and injury is, if not useful, then at least inevitable. This usefulness or necessity of suffering is not thought with a view to preserving the animals, but a certain model of relationship between human beings and animals. The utility and necessity are the same as the realization of the requirements of animal welfare. Ultimately, animal welfare is only a vague guideline that can be assessed in different, or even very different, ways. The texts in which it is mentioned are accompanied by annexes detailing the spaces, times and procedures that can be lawfully applied to animals. The purpose of these technical standards seems to be less to guarantee a high level (at least as high as can be imagined in the context of breeding, transportation, experimentation or slaughter) of well-being, than to establish the amount of suffering inflicted on animals that is deemed acceptable by producers, breeders and consumers, all of whom are showing, in varying degrees

---

22. See, however, the definition proposed by the World Organization for Animal Health (OIE): "An animal experiences good welfare if the animal is healthy, comfortable, well nourished, safe, is not suffering from unpleasant states such as pain, fear and distress, and is able to express behaviors that are important for its physical and mental state."

and according to varying behaviors, an increasing concern about the treatment of animals[23].

The protection thus offered to animals is ambiguous (Marchadier 2018). The use of a soothing vocabulary, the content of standards, the delimitation of their field of application and the derogations that are tolerated organize a system which, far from banning violence towards animals, defines the conditions for its exercise. All these texts form a code of exploitation of animals institutionalizing the suffering inflicted on them. The notion of welfare covers this suffering with a discreet veil, but the very principle of this suffering is solidly entrenched (see section 5.2) and its implementation meticulously regulated (see section 5.3).

4.2. Institutionalized suffering

The promotion of animal welfare is the European Union's response to the issue of the suffering of animals as sentient beings. It is tempting to make the ironic claim that animal welfare is more important than human welfare; however, it is not humans who are crammed together for fattening and consumption. They are not the ones who are subjected to forced swimming tests to reproduce the state of resignation characteristic of depression in order to test a new molecule designed to combat this illness. The concern for animal well-being is a reflection of the harm inflicted on them, and, paradoxically, the way in which animal welfare is guaranteed institutionalizes their suffering. Consideration for animal welfare lacks generality: it does not erase animal suffering, but incorporates it by postulating that, in some form and to some extent, it is unavoidable (see section 5.2.1). Even if it seems avoidable, it is, in other contexts, justifiable (see section 5.2.2).

4.2.1. Inevitable suffering

The protection of the animal, of its physical integrity and its sensitivity, has always been singular. The Grammont Act of July 2, 1850 did not punish all mistreatment of animals, but only those that were publicly and abusively inflicted. The notion of abuse has disappeared from the legislation, but not the idea behind it. There are situations in which the exercise of violence towards animals is lawful, even if they may appear to be increasingly less frequent. Now, it is necessity that justifies mistreating an animal or voluntarily harming its life, and that, for a time and

---

23. See, in particular, Special Eurobarometer No. 442, *Attitudes of Europeans towards Animal Welfare*, March 2016.

without any logic, even justified the administration of serious abuse[24]. European Union law is part of this tradition, even if the legislator seeks to soften its harshness, and in some respects its incongruity, by modifying its vocabulary.

The initial objective was to spare the animal pain, stress or any other form of unnecessary suffering. The idea that protective legislation would so openly assume that it is sometimes useful to cause the animal to suffer might seem odd. Yet, it was never intended to be otherwise, unlike a system that punishes mistreatment or abuse. Reserving the necessity makes it especially possible to anticipate the cases in which the animal can present a danger. However, in European legislation, useful suffering does not result from the need to repress the aggressiveness of animals. It is useful because it allows the continued exploitation of animals for the satisfaction of human interests. Removing the reference to utility does not change the system, but leads to presenting it differently and, above all, as a given rather than a construct. Humans are definitively omnivores; humans are definitively the lords and masters of the planet; humans will definitively exploit animals. This is why the suffering of animals is inevitable, and the only suffering they will be spared is that which is avoidable … in a system designed to maximize their utility to humans, like all things, in the legal sense of the term.

The directive concerning the protection of animals kept for farming purposes is revealing. Point 20 of the Annex prohibits natural or artificial breeding methods which cause, or are likely to cause, suffering or harm to the animals concerned. This prohibition is weak, however, because, provided that Member States allow such breeding methods, it does not prohibit those that are likely to cause "minimal" or "momentary" suffering or that require interventions that do not cause "lasting harm". These soft phrases reflect an acceptance of a certain amount of suffering, rather than a desire to contain it.

It is always the idea of necessity, but a necessity of another order: a necessity which is not conjunctural (to protect humans from animals), but structural (to dominate the animal), which derives neither from the circumstances, nor from the nature, but from a system stemming from history and culture.

Protecting animal welfare is a constraint on those who use animals: if animal welfare were irrelevant, experimental protocols would be simpler and knowledge would advance more quickly; breeding, transportation and, above all, slaughter would be more efficient; the costs would be lower and the benefits higher. However,

---

24. It was not until the Act No. 99-5 of January 6, 1999, relating to dangerous and stray animals and the protection of animals, that the reference to necessity disappeared from Article L521-1 of the Penal Code.

it seems that the common factor in all forms of exploitation is that they minimize or even deny the suffering they inflict. Slave owners would not admit to abusing their slaves: not being concerned about their health would have been economically irrational, as they would have provided inferior work. While no ethical charter for slavery was ever proclaimed (and yet this is what Colbert's Black Code embodied in some respects), an ethic of animal exploitation developed that established convergence rather than opposition between human and animal interests. In the same way as overcoming the resistance of the most skeptical or asserting that the exploitation of the animal is not in contradiction with its sensitivity and its ethological needs, so the rules enacted in favor of animal welfare are presented in a favorable way for the economic actors and the professionals in contact with animals. The protection of the animal is not the manifestation of a sentience, but the expression of an economically rational choice, including for operations and activities for which the welfare of the animals may easily appear superfluous. What, if not cynicism, could justify worrying about the suffering of the animal as it is being led to the slaughterhouse and even more so at the very moment of its killing? What does it mean to protect calves "confined for rearing and fattening"[25] or to improve the welfare of chickens destined for meat production in the context of "intensive farming"[26]? Regardless of the techniques or practices used, the tools used and the expertise of the professionals, the exploitation of animals causes pain, stress, fear and other forms of suffering. So long as this suffering does not result in economic loss, why should it necessitate investments in building design, limits on transportation times, training of animal handlers and processes that slow down the rate of slaughter? Protecting the animal at the time of its death is, however, essential and not only in the interest of the animal itself. First of all, of course, it reduces the pain, stress and suffering that will inevitably be inflicted on the animal. Beyond that, it also meets a social expectation: the attention given to the animal influences the consumer's attitude towards animal products[27]. In addition, it would contribute to improving the quality of the meat. Last but not least, by reducing the stress of the animals, it reinforces, if only indirectly, professional safety in the slaughterhouses.

The limitation of the enterprise of protecting animals by improving their welfare is the fact that it is part of a system that fatally compromises the welfare of animals because they are living in an environment that they do not control, an artificial environment, shaped by humans to satisfy specific needs, to which they will adapt with difficulty. This difficulty increases further, because humans do not only build

---

25. Art. 1, Dir. No. 2008/119/EC on the "Protection of calves".

26. Cons. 7, Dir. No. 2007/43/EC on the "Protection of chickens kept for meat production".

27. Cons. 4, Regulation No. 1099/2009/EC on the "Protection of animals at the time of killing".

the environment of the animals: progress in zootechnics allows them to shape them, once again to meet specific needs – scientific, agro-industrial, aesthetic – which are all new sources of suffering and discomfort for the animals. With regard to broilers, the high growth rate of the species does not allow a satisfactory level of welfare and health for the animals to be ensured[28], and yet, the directive that is intended to organize their protection does not contain a single provision on this point.

At best, as Sabine Brels points out (Brels 2014, p. 421), it is about reducing suffering. Welfare accompanies suffering. The relevant legislation organizes this suffering and sets thresholds of permissible suffering for different animals and contexts, taking into account specifically human economic and cultural interests. Aside from the programmed disappearance of the use of animals in biomedical research through support (declared at least) for the development of alternative methods[29], the protection of animals does not threaten any human activity. Thus, the stated objective of Council Directive 2008/120/EC of December 18, 2008, which lays down minimum standards for the protection of pigs, is to find the best farming system to ensure their welfare[30]. In any case, the threat is highly relative. The end of the use of animals in experimental protocols hangs on the development of alternative methods, which are progressing slowly, particularly since they must not compromise human health or the environment[31].

4.2.2. Justifiable suffering

The institutionalization of suffering is not only based on the recognition of the inevitability of this suffering, given the system of exploitation of animals put in place by humans. It also results from the tolerance of certain forms of suffering that could be avoided. The suffering associated with various practices is perfectly documented and recognized, and they are therefore naturally the object of a

---

28. Cons. 4, Dir. No. 2007/43/EC on the "Protection of chickens kept for meat production".

29. The replacement requirement is not always understood as implying the search for a substitute method for animal testing. It would also be satisfied by proposing an alternative or different method (comp. for the application of EC Regulation No. 1907/2006 (REACH), CJEU, January 21, 2021, C-471/18 P – Germany/Esso Refining: The Court of Justice considers that animal testing is only possible if there is no other solution; consequently, when the European Chemicals Agency asks a registrant to complete its registration dossier with a study involving animal testing, the registrant may respond by producing alternative information to such a study).

30. Cons. 13.

31. See Commission Communication of June 3, 2015 on the European Citizens' Initiative "Stop Vivisection", C(2015) 3773 final.

principle of prohibition. However, there is no shortage of justifications for reducing it to nothing by making exceptions.

Respect for religious rites, cultural traditions and regional heritage, mentioned in Article 13 TFEU and set out in several instruments of secondary legislation, is the most visible justification. Thus, the stunning of animals prior to being put to death, which, together with immobilization, constitutes the essential protection of the animal at the time of its killing, may be set aside for considerations linked to the exercise of religious freedom (ritual slaughter)[32]. Respect for tradition and cultural heritage plays a part in the continuation of the force-feeding of geese and ducks, even though the cruelty of the process is not in doubt (Broom and Rochlitz 2015), and EU law prohibits feeding techniques that cause unnecessary suffering. The distinction between the useful and the unnecessary is contingent. Since "foie gras is part of the cultural and gastronomic heritage protected in France", and because foie gras is, in this gastronomic perspective, indelibly linked to fattening by force-feeding[33], pain becomes useful. The vacuity and inconsistency of the criterion of uselessness must once again be underlined.

Tradition in all its forms is not the only justification for animal suffering. It is also of an institutional nature, taking into account the distribution of authority between the Union and the Member States and the conditions of its exercise. The principles of subsidiarity and proportionality also allow the Union to ignore certain animals, or to establish thresholds below which the protective standards it enacts are inapplicable. The European legislator is mainly concerned with intensive livestock farming[34].

The economic imperative is also a powerful argument for limiting the raising of welfare standards. The cost of combating suffering must not lead to jeopardizing the efficiency of the system and the competitiveness of European actors in the field of

---

32. There is no obligation on Member States which could just as well, without disregarding religious freedom, impose prior stunning in all circumstances (so long as it is reversible and does not have a lethal effect; see CJEU, Grand Chamber, December 17, 2020, C-336/19, *Centraal Israëlitisch Consistorie van België and others v. Vlaamse Regering, RDLF 2021 chron. 8, note M. Oguey*), as well as slaughter in approved slaughterhouses (CJEU, May 29, 2018, C-426/16, *Liga van Moskeeën en Islamitische Organisaties Provincie Antwerpen VZW and others v. Vlaams Gewest*).

33. Art. L654-27-1 of the Rural and Maritime Fishing Code.

34. For example, the broiler directive is mainly aimed at intensive farming and does not concern the keeping of small flocks of chickens (Cons. 8, Dir. No. 2007/43/EC on the "Protection of chickens kept for meat production"). Curiously, the threshold (Art. 1) is fixed in absolute numbers (500 chickens), rather than in population density.

animal breeding and biomedical research. Animal welfare is not an absolute and must be reconciled with other imperatives, particularly health, social and environmental[35]. Thus, the recommendations concerning the progressive abandonment of carbon dioxide for pigs and water baths for poultry stunning are not retained because they do not appear to be economically viable "at present"[36].

The most recent texts are enriched with new justifications that will undoubtedly appear more acceptable to consumers, by directly weighing the interests of human beings against those of animals. It is no longer a question of demonstrating the convergence of interests in order to justify measures intended to protect animals, but their divergence, in order to justify the neutralization of these same protective standards. The need to preserve the safety of workers is thus abundantly evoked. This presentation is clever: the suffering of animals is all the more useful, not because it might serve a disembodied objective such as profitability or competitiveness, but because it responds to the protection of a priori vulnerable people, the workers. This rhetoric becomes a convenient argument to justify violence in slaughterhouses and especially in farms. The mutilation or isolation of animals (tail docking in sheep, beak trimming, dehorning), which should normally be banned in farms applying for the "AB" (Agriculture Biologique/Organic Agriculture) label, since it is intended to guarantee a high level of animal welfare (at least higher than that required in conventional agriculture), is nevertheless tolerated so long as the safety of workers is compromised[37]. It is a priori more convincing than the idea that such practices improve animal health, welfare or hygiene.

4.3. Normalized suffering

Animal welfare has two aspects: one negative, the absence of suffering (physical and psychological); the other positive, the satisfaction of its needs (physiological and ethological) (Brels 2014, p. 402). European legislation has gradually incorporated both. To the general bans on unnecessary suffering have been added

---

35. See, in particular, Cons. 12 of the Council Directive No. 2008/120/EC of December 18, 2008, laying down minimum standards for the protection of pigs; Cons. 10 of Directive No. 2007/43/EC on the "Protection of chickens kept for meat production"; Cons. 9 of Directive No. 1999/74/EC on the "Protection of laying hens"; and Cons. 11 of Regulation No. 1099/2009 on the "Protection of animals at the time of killing", which states that changes to the rules on the slaughter and killing of fish will depend on scientific assessments, as well as on "the social, economic and administrative implications".

36. Cons. 6 of Regulation No. 1099/2009 on the "Protection of animals during killing".

37. See Annex II, pt. 1.7.5 and 1.7.8 of Reg. EU No. 2018/848 of the European Parliament and of the Council of May 30, 2018 on organic production and labeling of organic products.

rules tending, depending on the species considered, to offer animals under the care of human beings living conditions compatible with their needs. According to the World Organization for Animal Health (OIE), the level of well-being of an animal depends on its nutrition (absence of hunger, thirst and malnutrition), its state of stress, both psychological (absence of fear and distress) and physical (the animal must have a certain level of comfort), its health (absence of pain, lesions and disease) and the possibility of expressing normal behavior for its species[38].

The notion of well-being is misleading, however, because it does not describe a state that would be opposed to ill-being, but rather an instrument for measuring the physical and psychological state of a living being in its relationship with its environment. An individual's well-being is thus likely to vary on a scale from "very poor" to "very good" (Broom 2001, p. 148).

This notion is also a mask: it conceals what animal welfare legislation is all about. Since animal suffering is unavoidable, the notion of welfare serves as a guide to organize the violence inflicted on them according to a logic of normalization. It is at the heart of the legitimate exploitation of animals. It justifies confinement, discomfort and killing, rather than realizing and guaranteeing the effectiveness of the famous five freedoms that each animal should enjoy as an individual[39]. This is evidenced both by the living conditions reserved for animals (see section 5.3.1) and by the mutilations to which they may be subjected (see section 5.3.2).

4.3.1. Living conditions

The desire to ensure the welfare of animals does not prevent mutilation, crowding, restrictions on freedom of movement or restraint. These practices are certainly not encouraged, and most are even, in principle, prohibited. However, if certain procedures are followed, certain regulations are observed, the welfare of the animal itself or the safety of the workers is taken into account, or there is an economic imperative (profitability, competitiveness), they can be considered. Stating animal protection rules thus legitimizes the exercising of different forms of violence and contributes to the unbalancing or distortion of the balance between the principle and the exception.

Thus, the freedom of movement set out in Point 7 of the Annex to Council Directive 98/58/EC of July 20, 1998 on the protection of animals kept for farming purposes is, in reality, the possibility of continuously or habitually restraining the

---

38. Article 7.1.2 of the Terrestrial Animal Health Code.
39. Article 7.1.2 of the Terrestrial Animal Health Code.

animal. It can be tied, chained or kept, provided that it is given a "space appropriate to its physiological and ethological needs in accordance with established experience and scientific knowledge". Article 1.10 of Annex III to the Council Regulation No. 1099/2009 of September 24, 2009, on the protection of animals at the time of killing, reflects an identical movement. Its purpose is not so much to prohibit the tethering of animals as to detail the conditions that must be met if they are to be tethered, without, however, specifying the basis for this necessity and who assesses it.

The aim of animal welfare protection legislation should normally be to reduce population densities in farms, improve animal comfort and gradually put an end to intensive and industrial breeding, this sanitary, social and environmental aberration[40]. The project is quite different and simply aims to adapt the conditions of life and death that this type of breeding offers to the animals so that they are a little less unbearable. For farms with more than six calves, Directive 2008/119/EC determines the living space vital for each animal according to its weight (Art. 3.1.b) and sets a minimum of 1.8 square meters for an animal whose mass is greater than 220 kilograms. Council Directive 2007/43/EC of June 28, 2007, which lays down minimum rules for the protection of chickens kept for meat production, stresses, unsurprisingly, that high stocking densities produce negative effects, while at the same time specifying, revealingly, that these negative effects are less when the premises where the animals are housed benefit from good environmental conditions (Cons. 4). The limit, expressed in a purely reificatory logic in kilograms per square meter (Art. 3)[41], is not so rigid. The threshold of 33 kg/m^2 (which represents approximately 22 individuals per square meter, the average weight of a broiler chicken being 1.5 kg at 30 days after birth), which must not be exceeded "at any time", is only a valid subject to an exemption. Exceeding this threshold is subordinated to conditions that finally reveal the relative attention that is paid to the welfare of the animals. An increase of 6 kg/m^2 (around four additional animals) depends only on the owner's decision to increase the density of their farm being notified to the competent authority and on each poultry house being equipped with a ventilation system "and, if necessary, with heating and cooling systems" (Annex 2, Point. 3) that allows for the control of ammonia and carbon dioxide concentrations in the atmosphere, as well as temperature and humidity. No improvement in living conditions is required to allow the addition of 3 kg/m^2 (bringing

---

40. On this issue, see the thematic dossier "Élevage industriel", *Revue semestrielle de droit animalier* 2/2014, p. 209 and following.

41. Comp. Council Directive 1999/74/EC of July 19, 1999 laying down minimum standards for the protection of laying hens: the density is expressed in individuals per square meter, which does not guarantee greater comfort (Art. 4.4: maximum nine hens per square meter; above all, for hens kept in cages, the minimum space is 550 cm^2 for unenriched cages – Art. 5.1.1 – and 600 cm^2 for enriched cages – Art. 6.1.a – which represents more or less the area of an A4 sheet).

the total to approximately 28 individuals per square meter). It is sufficient that an inspection of the farm has never revealed any major defects and that the daily mortality rate is less than 1%[42]. Again, if the owner provides sufficient explanation for an exceptional mortality rate, the maximum density of 42 kg/m² can be attained. However, these animals will not have the opportunity to enjoy the well-being that such an environment is intended to provide for very long. Their natural longevity of a dozen years will be abruptly interrupted after 35 days, when they will have reached a weight of about 1.9 kg. The life expectancy of animals is not explicitly a determinant of well-being. On the contrary, its promotion seems tacitly based on an ephemeral existence devoted, until exhaustion, to production.

The issues are not limited to the living space of the animals. The Livestock Directive 98/58/EC does not require owners to provide natural light compatible with their needs. It does allow the use of artificial lighting, as long as its duration corresponds to the duration of natural lighting, but it only prevents animals from being subjected to permanent lighting or darkness (Annex, Point 10)[43]. As for the environment in the buildings (air circulation, dust levels, temperature, relative humidity and gas concentrations), it retains the low and vague threshold of no harm to animals (Annex, Point 11). The sectoral approaches are in line with this. With regard to pig farming, Directive 2008/120/EC prohibits the exposure of pigs to any constant noise in the buildings in which they are kept, while allowing continuous noise not exceeding 85 decibels, which is already high, with 80 decibels corresponding to the risk threshold for human hearing[44]. To the extent that continuous noise is constant and stable, this requirement is not very clear.

4.3.2. *Mutilation*

There are no general rules on the mutilation of farm animals. Directive 98/58/EC refers to the national legislation and the sectoral directives (pigs, calves, broilers, laying hens) offer protection of a rare indigence. As if to distance the violence of the law a little more, the vocabulary used is polite and the legislator does not hesitate to resort to euphemisms.

The mutilation of chickens is hidden in a section soberly entitled "surgical interventions". It is difficult to decipher that mutilating surgical interventions, other than for therapeutic or diagnostic purposes, are in fact authorized, as always under

---

42. For details, see Annex V.

43. Comp. Annex 1, Point 5 of the Directive 2008/119/EC of December 18, 2008 laying down minimum standards for the protection of calves.

44. Annex 1, Chapter 1.1 of Directive No. 2008/120/EC on the "Protection of pigs".

certain conditions. Beak trimming is reduced to a welfare purpose (avoiding feather pecking and cannibalism) and presented as a last resort, when "other measures to prevent" these phenomena "are exhausted" (Annex 1, Point 12 of Directive 2007/43)[45]. How is the extent of other measures and their failure assessed, and by whom? Above all, is reduction in density one of the relevant alternatives? The castration of male chickens is not supported by any particular justification and is not subject to any age limitation (in comparison, beak removal will take place before 10 days), nor is it subject to the administration of analgesic or painkiller. These mutilating surgeries seem very far from veterinary medicine. While they are performed on the advice (spaying) or under the control (castration) of a veterinarian, they are, however, being performed by qualified personnel[46].

This normalization of suffering is even more explicit when mutilations are performed on pigs. The immediate and long-term pain associated with partial tail docking, partial cutting and grinding of teeth, and castration is not denied. Since these activities are a source of suffering, should not a text intended to protect animals at least prohibit them? The legislator has, instead, chosen to refine the violation to physical integrity. These practices are therefore legal, so long as they are carried out according to a certain protocol[47]. Operations on the tail and teeth must be in the interest of the animals' welfare, when injuries are observed and no other measure has been able to prevent tail-biting or "other vices", the text specifies, as if a pig could manifest a habitual disposition to evil, and mutilation could teach virtue or remedy a serious imperfection! These practices then are not meant to be routine, but to be considered in a subsidiary manner, after the failure of a decrease in breeding density and the enrichment of the environment with appropriate materials to satisfy research and manipulation needs (Lerner and Algers 2013, p. 374). Yet, they persist[48]. Again, the

---

45. Comp. Council Directive 1999/74/EC of July 19, 1999 laying down minimum standards for the protection of laying hens. The protection is even looser. Point 8 of the Annex prohibits "all mutilation", except beak trimming. Member States have the option of allowing this in order to "prevent feather pecking and cannibalism". There is no need to establish the reality of the evil, or to implement other measures as a priority to ward it off. It is the animal's welfare that justifies this routine mutilation. Protection is limited to a question of age (chicks under 10 days old) and the intervention of qualified personnel, without any specification of the qualifications in question (which is not always the case; see Art. 4 and Annex 4 of Directive No. 2007/43 on the "Protection of chickens kept for meat production").

46. Being the persons who have received the training, the broad outlines of which are set out in the directive (Art. 4 and Annex 4).

47. Cons. 11 of Dir. 2008/120/EC of December 18, 2008 laying down minimum standards for the protection of pigs.

48. See also recently, concerning the French pig industry, European Commission, DG(SANTE) 2019-6603, *Final report of an audit carried out in France from June 17, 2019*

prohibition lacks force, as the text suggests that they can be performed on very young individuals, since, below seven days after birth, anesthesia and prolonged analgesia are not required.

Castration is even more liberal: it is not subject to any particular justification. Curiously, the rhetoric of animal welfare and breeder safety has not been used. Castration can therefore be widely practiced by farmers without them first measuring the degree of aggressiveness of the animals and trying to decrease it by other techniques, and especially without them worrying about the taste and smell of the meat offered to consumers (Parois et al. 2018, p. 23 ff.). Once again, protection is reduced to little. The veterinarian will be able to be replaced by someone with training.

Welfare, which is at the heart of animal protection legislation, is the most tangible sign of a willingness to consider animals no longer as simple things, agricultural products or laboratory equipment, but truly for what they are: living and sentient beings. It also masks the violence that is mercilessly employed on animals in farms, laboratories and slaughterhouses. This violence is based on the normalization of stunning and killing procedures, not all of which may meet the imperative of not causing the animal to suffer, and of confinement conditions and mutilation techniques; a violence which is deployed on a multiplicity of exceptions, largely devoid of content of generous principles, and on the paucity of welfare standards, which are poorly constraining[49] and poorly sanctioned[50].

---

to June 21, 2019 in order to evaluate Member State activities to prevent tail-biting and avoid routine tail-docking of pigs, Ares (2020)1188011 – February 25, 2020.

49. See, for example, the reference to guidelines, guides to good practice or to the experience acquired for the implementation of the standards, or the formulations providing farmers a very wide latitude (Annex to the "livestock" directive No. 98/58/EC) to treat injured or sick animals (isolated "where necessary", provision of dry and comfortable bedding "where appropriate", consultation of a veterinarian "as soon as possible") or to ensure the protection of animals in the open air (only "where necessary and possible").

50. In the event of non-compliance, sanctions must be "effective, proportionate and dissuasive" (Art. 23, Regulation No. 1099/2009/EU on the "Protection of animals at the time of killing"; Dir. No. 43/2007/EC on the "Protection of chickens kept for meat production"; Art. 60, Dir. 2010/63/EU on the "Protection of laboratory animals"). In addition to the fact that such precision lacks generality (according to Article 10 of the "livestock" directive No. 98/58/EC, accompanying the transposition of sanctions into national law is presented as a simple possibility; as for the directives on the protection of pigs (No. 2008/120/EC) and on the protection of calves (No. 2008/119/EC), they do not contain any precision), Member States have, here again, significant scope for interpretation. In France, violations of welfare standards are punishable by a 4th class fine (Code rural et de la pêche maritime, Art. R 215-8 (killing), Art. R215-4 (breeding) and Art. R215-10 (experimentation)), or €750 (Art. 131-13 of the Penal Code).

4.4. List of abbreviations

CETS	Council of Europe Treaty Series
Comp	Compare
Cons	Consultation
Dir	Directive
EC	European Communities
ETS	European Treaty Series
EU	European Union
OIE	World Organization for Animal Health (formerly Office International des Epizooties)
REACH	Registration, Evaluation, Authorization and Restriction of Chemicals
Reg	Regulation
TFEU	Treaty on the Functioning of the European Union

4.5. References

Brels, S. (2014). Le droit de la protection du bien-être animal : évolution mondiale. *Revue semestrielle de droit animalier*, 2, 399–423.

Broom, D.M. (2001). The use of the concept Animal Welfare in European conventions, regulations and directives. *Food Chain*, 148–151.

Broom, D.M. and Rochlitz, I. (2015). Le bien-être des canards pendant la production de foie gras. Report, Cambridge University Animal Welfare Information Service, Cambridge.

Dubos, O. (2017). L'Union européenne peut-elle écouter le "silence des bêtes". *R.A.E.*, 1.

Hervouët, F. (2015). Sensibilité animale et droit de l'Union européenne. In *Sensibilité animale. Perspectives juridiques*, Bismuth, R. and Marchadier, F. (eds). CNRS éditions, Paris.

Lerner, H. and Algers, B. (2013). Tail docking in the EU: A case of routine violation of an EU Directive. In *The Ethics of Consumption. The Citizen, the Market and the Law*, Röcklinsberg, H. and Sandin, P. (eds). Wageningen Academic Publishers, Wageningen.

Marchadier, F. (2018). La protection du bien-être de l'animal par l'Union européenne. *Revue trimestrielle de droit européen*, 251.

Marguénaud, J.-P. (2018). La promotion des animaux au rang d'êtres sensibles dans le Traité de Lisbonne. *Revue semestrielle de droit animalier*, 2, 13–18.

Parois, S., Bonneau, M., Chevillon, P., Larzul, C., Quiniou, N., Robic, A., Prunier, A. (2018). Odeurs indésirables de la viande de porcs mâles non castrés : problèmes et solutions potentielles. *INRAE Productions Animales*, 31(1), 23–36.

Sowery, K. (2018). Sentient beings and tradable products: The curious constitutional status of animals under Union Law. *Common Market Law Review*, 55(1) [Online]. Available at: https://ssrn.com/abstract=3090363.

5

How Do the Regulations and the Various Stakeholders Take the Pain of Animals Subjected to Experimental Procedures into Account?

Muriel OBRIET

Association Transcience, Paris, France

5.1. Animal experimentation: figures and regulatory approach to animal pain

5.1.1. *European Commission reports*

On February 5, 2020, the European Commission (2020a) published a report on statistical data on the use of animals for scientific purposes in the 28 Member States of the European Union during the years 2015–2017, as well as a report (European Commission 2020b) on the implementation of the Directive on the protection of animals used for scientific purposes, adopted on September 22, 2010 (Directive 2010/63/EU) (Official Journal of the European Union 2010)[1]. These reports were

---

1. This Directive has an ambitious objective, as evidenced, respectively, by Consideration 10, which states that "this Directive represents an important step towards achieving the final goal of full replacement of procedures on live animals for scientific and educational purposes as soon as it is scientifically possible to do so. To that end, it seeks to facilitate and promote the advancement of alternative approaches […]", as well as Consideration 12, which states,

Animal Suffering,
coordinated by Florence BURGAT and Emilie DARDENNE. © ISTE Ltd 2023.

prepared on the basis of data provided by the Member States. The annual statistical data sent by the Member States to the Commission only take into account live vertebrate animals and cephalopods and only if they were included in a "procedure", that is, used in an experimental project. The annual reports also include the number of animals used in the creation and maintenance of genetically modified animal lines.

The Directive also requires Member States to produce data every five years on animals killed without having been used in experimental procedures, such as: animals from the creation or maintenance of genetically altered lines that are in excess or that do not present the expected characteristics, animals killed for the removal of their organs and tissues and over-aged breeding animals. This five-year data, relating to the year 2017, has been published for the first time since the entry into force of the Directive on February 5, 2020 (European Commission 2020a).

5.1.2. Global data on animal experimentation

The figures tell us that the number of animals used for experimental purposes by the 28 Member States fell by 4.6% between 2015 and 2017 (the latest reference year): from 11,178,344 to 10,664,749 animals (European Commission 2020a). This decrease is unspectacular and is spread very unevenly across the different Member States. Moreover, this number does not reflect the reality, in that it only concerns animals that have been used in a procedure. Additionally, there are also animals that are bred and killed without having been used in a procedure, and for which there was no visibility until the publication of the five-yearly data in 2020. For 2017 (when the first five-year data is available), the number was 12,597,816 (European Commission 2020b, pp. 37–42). The total number of animals used for scientific purposes in 2017 in the 28 EU Member States was therefore 23,262,563, more than twice the number reported in 2013 by the European Commission and reported widely since then (European Commission 2013)[2].

"Animals have an intrinsic value which must be respected. There are also the ethical concerns of the general public as regards the use of animals in procedures. Therefore, animals should always be treated as sentient creatures, and their use in procedures should be restricted to areas which may ultimately benefit human or animal health, or the environment."

2. According to this report: "In the EU, the total number of animals used for experimental and other scientific purposes from the data collected in 2011 in accordance with the provision of the Directive for this report is just under 11.5 million (with data from France from 2010). This is a reduction of over half a million animals used in the EU from the number reported in 2008."

If we examine at the annual data for France, after an increase between 2015 and 2016 (+0.9%), the use of animals declined very slightly (-0.4%) between 2016 and 2018, and more significantly between 2018 and 2019 (-2.4%) settling at 1,865,403 (Ministère de l'Enseignement supérieur, de la Recherche et de l'Innovation 2021). These numbers only include animals used in a procedure.

5.1.3. *Data on the suffering of animals subjected to experimentation*

In addition to the overall number of animals, there is a need to consider the intensity of pain, suffering and stress experienced by the animals in the context of research projects in which they were included. To this end, two values should be considered: the number of animals involved in procedures of severe – the most painful and/or stressful – or moderate classification (we will discuss the classification provided for in the Directive later) and the number of animals reused in multiple procedures.

In the European Union, the percentage of animals subjected to procedures in the severe classification increased from 8% of total procedures in 2015 to 11% in 2016, a percentage maintained in 2017 (European Commission 2020a), representing 1,023,138 animals. In other words, there were 204,130 additional animals subjected to severe procedures in 2017, compared with 2015, even though the number of uses decreased slightly between these two years and Member States were supposed to implement the 3Rs principle[3].

The reuse of animals, a source of cumulative suffering and stress that is very difficult to assess, is nevertheless encouraged by public authorities as a way to reduce the overall number of animals used. However, this is not a reduction method in the sense of the 3Rs principle. The average reuse rate in the European Union is 2.2% and remained stable between 2015 and 2017. However, we note that for

---

3. Article 1 of Directive 2010/63/EU, on the protection of animals used for scientific purposes, sets out the purpose and scope of the Directive. The rules apply to breeders, suppliers and users of animals in all their tasks. All must apply the "3Rs" principle: replacement, reduction, refinement. Note, however, that replacement and reduction are irrelevant to breeders and suppliers. It is important to understand the scope that Russell and Burch intended for the 3Rs principle. Firstly, they set out a hierarchy of methods that is thus reflected in the Directive and that should be applied in the same order by researchers: firstly replacement, then reduction and – for animals that are still used in procedures – refinement. Secondly, this principle applies to all projects whenever the designer plans to use live animals. Therefore, it is not equivalent to apply the 3Rs principle and use alternative methods, which are non-animal methods.

"routine production" (vaccines and other biological products), reuse is as high as 12% and, in higher education and training, 8% (European Commission 2020a).

If we take the case of France, the rate of reuse is on the rise, from 0.74% in 2014 to 2.02% in 2019, a rate very close to the European average. Regarding the degrees of severity, between 2014 and 2019, the proportion of severe procedures in relation to the total number of procedures increased from 9% to 13.8% (with a peak at 18.7% in 2018). Similarly, the rate of procedures classified as moderate in severity has steadily increased from 31% in 2014 to 47.5% in 2019, while the rate of procedures classified as mild has steadily decreased; these represented 54% of procedures in 2014, whereas they represented only 32.4% in 2019. Non-recovery procedures have remained at fairly stable levels, around 6% (Ministère de l'Enseignement supérieur, de la Recherche et de l'Innovation 2021).

France is far ahead of all other EU Member States in the number of animals used in procedures classified as severe without the "competent authorities" being able to provide any scientific justification. The retrospective assessments of the projects concerned are not published on the French Ministry of Research website.

5.1.4. Assessment of pain in animals and practices that are ethically acceptable according to the Directive

If we compare the principles and declarations of intent set out in the consultations of the Directive with the articles themselves, we note a significant impoverishment in the content of the articles. This difference increases when we consider the content of some of the annexes, to the point that we might wonder how the parliamentarians who drafted the consultations could have agreed to vote on these annexes as they were written; in particular, Annexes 4 (killing methods) and 8 (determination of the severity classification of procedures).

Some examples of killing methods considered ethically acceptable are listed in Annex 4:

– use of a perforating rod for reptiles;

– use of carbon dioxide for birds and rodents (except fetuses or newborns);

– cervical dislocation for birds, rodents and rabbits (this "practice" is performed without prior sedation, except for animals weighing more than 1 kg);

– concussion or percussion of the cranium for fish, amphibians, reptiles and also for birds, rodents, rabbits and even newborn dogs and cats;

– decapitation for birds and rodents (if other methods cannot be used);

– electrical stunning (which is not a killing method) for fish, amphibians, birds, rabbits, dogs, cats and other small carnivores and large mammals.

Most of these methods are not permitted in the United States, for example, where a veterinarian is also required at the time of killing. In any other context, they would be considered to be acts of cruelty and subject to prosecution if disclosed.

Non-human primates benefit from what could be described as "preferential treatment", since the only authorized method of killing them is an overdose of anesthetic with prior sedation. This method, which is the only ethically acceptable one, should logically be applied to all species.

Annex 4 further specifies that other methods may even be used (without giving examples) "on unconscious animals, provided that the animal does not regain consciousness before death" and "on animals used in agricultural research when the aim of the project requires that the animals are kept under similar conditions to those under which commercial farm animals are kept […]". On the other hand, there is no specific mention in this annex of the need for specialized training for personnel responsible for killing, the quality of the equipment used to cause death, the presence of a veterinarian or of possible inspections at this very particular moment in the process. Their "mission" being over, no further attention is paid to these animals. They are reduced to the state of waste, to be disposed of as soon as possible.

Annex 8 is devoted to the evaluation of the severity category of procedures (the classification of severity should be included in the project presentation). Everyone will appreciate the objectivity of the evaluation grid by reviewing some examples of "moderate" procedures (the level between "mild" and "severe"):

– acute dose-range finding studies or chronic toxicity/carcinogenicity tests, with non-lethal end-points;

– surgery under general anesthesia and appropriate analgesia, associated with post-surgical pain, suffering or impairment of general condition (examples include thoracotomy, craniotomy, laparotomy and orthopedic surgery);

– models of tumor induction;

– irradiation or chemotherapy with a sub-lethal dose or an otherwise lethal dose but with reconstitution of the immune system;

– creation of genetically altered animals through surgical procedures;

– use of metabolic cages involving moderate restriction of movement over a prolonged period (up to five days);

– evoking escape and avoidance reactions when the animal is unable to escape or avoid the stimulus.

Would the legislator have classified the severity of these procedures as "moderate" had they been applied to humans? Animals – and at least all mammals – have the same pain perception system as we do.

This classification of procedures is particularly important when it comes to assigning a "moderate" or "severe" classification to a project (which may include multiple procedures). It should be noted that if animals are to be reused, they must have previously undergone only "mild" or "moderate" procedures. Reuse is normally not permitted following a "severe" procedure (and obviously not possible in the case of a "non-recovery" procedure). Retrospective assessment of the project (evaluation of the results obtained in relation to the expected results and verification of the conformity of the means implemented with the means initially planned) is only required for procedures classified as "severe" or projects using non-human primates. Projects classified as "moderate" are therefore, a priori, exempt (although Member States are able to introduce this obligation into their national regulations). It is understandable that the users of animals for scientific purposes have a strong interest in having the bar for the "severe" classification set as high as possible, so that as many projects as possible remain in the "moderate" classification and thus escape some of the requirements (or prohibitions) that apply to the "severe" classification.

If we refer to the Commission's implementing decision of November 14, 2012 (European Union Law 2012) and specifically to Part B (section 8), we see that it is possible for Member States to take some liberty with the regulation: "If the 'severe' classification is exceeded, whether pre-authorized or not, these animals and their use are to be reported under Severe." In this way, the Commission explicitly recognizes that some procedures exceed the "severe" classification (which is never envisaged in the Directive) and concomitantly that these procedures may not have been previously authorized (which is in total contradiction with the provisions of the Directive).

5.1.5. *Silenced pain and suffering*

At this point in the analysis, can we consider that we have produced an exhaustive list of gaps in the regulations? Clearly not, as we shall see.

5.1.5.1. *Invisible practices in published documents*

We will only discuss here two practices that reveal the absence of ethical rules at certain steps in the procedures, but there are undoubtedly many others of which we are unaware.

How are rodents identified in the laboratory? Most often by amputating a phalanx (known as toe- or digit-clipping), usually between 7 and 10 days after birth. While it would be possible to tattoo a leg or tail, the advantage of phalangectomy would – according to a recommendation published in February 2021 by the CNREEA (2021a) (Comité National de Réflexion Ethique sur l'Expérimentation Animale, the French National Committee for Ethical Reflection on Animal Experimentation) (CNREEA 2021b) – also be the genetic characterization (genotyping) of the animals and thus the limiting of manipulations. However, the CNREEA recognizes that this technique is "mutilating and painful" and that "due to the small size of newborn rodents at the time of the procedure, attempts to cut only the distal phalanx result in a large part of the finger, or even the whole finger, being amputated". We recall here that although newborn mice or pups do not yet have the motor skills to express a response to the painful stimulus, they nevertheless feel the full intensity of the pain (Sternberg et al. 2004, pp. 420–426).

Among the measures recommended by the CNREEA is the following: "The number of amputations will be limited to one phalanx per leg, will not concern the thumb and, as far as possible, the hind legs will be privileged [...]." How would these measures make this practice ethical? It should be totally condemned and the development of non-invasive methods should be promoted, such as genotyping by skin swabbing, eye discharge (tear) collection and stool or hair tuft analysis (the latter method being widely used in cattle breeding). Other EU Member States practice phalangectomy, as is the case in France, although ear biopsy (by punch) is more widely used for genotyping mice. On this point, the European Commission's report on the implementation of the Directive indicates that the use of sampling methods considered non-invasive – and not requiring project authorization – represents less than 2% of samples (European Commission 2020b, pp. 55–57). Although, a priori, the removal of a phalanx requires a project authorization, scientists remain very discreet about this type of practice, which never appears in published documents.

How do researchers elicit behaviors from animals that they would not spontaneously perform in certain projects? One method, commonly used with non-human primates in lesional, pharmacological, electrophysiological, brain imaging studies that include operant conditioning procedures, is the "positive reinforcement" method. In studies on learning in primatology, this method consists of giving the animal a drink or food that it appreciates as soon as a task has been correctly performed, in order to motivate it to continue the work. However, the positive reinforcement method has been misused in research laboratories to the extent that – in order to get the animal to quickly perform repetitive tasks as expected of it, or for it to accept being placed in a restraining chair for a blood test or other sampling – it may be deprived of food or drink. Rationing can be of varying duration depending on the "goodwill" of the animal. This method is contrary to the regulations since it undermines the satisfaction of the physiological needs of the animals (Article 33 of the Directive: care and housing), and yet it is widely used. The CNREEA refers in a February 1, 2021 paper on the practice of "water control" (a euphemism to avoid talking about deprivation) used in non-human primates in scientific projects (CNREEA 2021a). While the paper states that deprivation of food and/or water for a prolonged period of time – a method then assimilated with negative reinforcement ("punishment") – is unacceptable, it implicitly recognizes the existence of such practices. Indeed, among the manifestations that should attract the attention of the staff, and which would express the feeling of thirst, we read that the animal "drinks its own urine or compulsively licks every drop of water present in its environment". Behaviors such as "apathy, aggressiveness, self-directed behaviors or stereotypies" are also cited, behaviors that are clearly indicative of the harmful effects of long-term deprivation.

The persistence of such practices leads to the inference that they are not identified during veterinary inspections (which should be annual for facilities using non-human primates) as regulatory violations and are therefore not sanctioned. Nor do they appear in published documents, such as non-technical project summaries.

5.1.5.2. Psychological suffering: evoked but hidden

As noted above, the current regulatory framework is totally ineffective in accurately estimating the physical pain caused to animals used for scientific purposes, which could be accurately measured and effectively managed if the means were available.

However, the legislator wished to go further by referring in various sections of the Directive to the suffering, anguish and stress of animals. This acknowledges that they are affected emotionally and psychically by the experiments imposed on them, without, however, providing references that would have enabled those involved in animal experimentation to understand what psychological suffering in animals covers. While physically painful sensations generate psychological suffering (and in particular anguish and stress in the face of the possible repetition of intrusive or constraining acts), many other factors contribute to this suffering beyond the technical acts related to experimental procedures: deprivation of freedom (for non-domestic animals), deprivation of relationships with humans (for domestic animals, especially dogs and cats), deprivation of conspecifics and/or separation of the mother from her young, restricted environment without pleasant stimuli, multiple manipulations and restraints and, in particular, anxiety-provoking conditions preceding the killing.

However, suffering is a subjective experience that resists measurement. It is therefore illusory to think that we could use a chart to assess the severity of projects, as we might do to determine, albeit imperfectly, a level of physical pain. The inherent subjectivity of psychological suffering as experienced by an individual – human or animal – subjected to physical pain, deprivation or being placed in conditions incompatible with their emotional and social needs, prohibits any general approach.

Ultimately, as much by ease as by lack of empathy, the psychological suffering of animals is concealed during the conception of the projects as it is during their ethical evaluation. In concrete terms, they are denied the status of "suffering beings" that would give them access to our moral consideration. We can therefore affirm that the harm caused to animals used for scientific and educational purposes is far more considerable than statistical surveys and other reports would indicate.

5.2. How are the regulations regarding the assessment of pain in animals used for scientific or educational purposes applied?

5.2.1. *Upstream of the project*

Although Article 20 of Directive 2010/63/EU recommends that Member States ensure that all breeders, suppliers and users are approved by the "competent authority", there is nothing to prevent users from obtaining supplies from non-approved farms, whether within the European Union or elsewhere. The large pharmaceutical companies have breeding facilities wherever their subsidiaries are located and, if possible, in countries where legislation is less protective of animals, or even non-existent. In France, the percentage of animals from non-approved farms was 18.5% in 2019 (up 3% compared with 2018), including 12.3% from non-approved farms in the European Union (Ministère de l'Enseignement supérieur, de la Recherche et de l'Innovation 2021), proof that they are still not banned and that they continue to supply animals, without being subject to standards and inspections in accordance with the provisions of the Directive. Animals from non-approved farms are mainly fish, rodents (including transgenic mice from American or Chinese farms), primates, birds and dogs. Clearly, these animals are subject to the law of profitability, produced at the lowest cost (and sometimes even captured in their natural environment, in the case of primates and certain reptiles) and transported over thousands of kilometers in conditions that are very difficult to control.

Genetically modified animals – most often mice – are manufactured by the millions and considered as mere genetic material. Some of them are even genetically modified to develop a "harmful phenotype" (i.e. one that causes permanent discomfort and/or pain in the animal carrying it) that will begin to express itself as soon as they are born, therefore even before the research project begins.

5.2.2. At the time of project design

The designer must include the issue of the pain, suffering and stress of the animals that will be subjected to the different procedures in the presentation of their project. This is the prospective evaluation, and the classification of the project (severe, moderate, mild or non-recovery, based on the distinctions established by the Directive) will depend on this. The severity classification is included in the application for administrative authorization sent to the competent authority, but how will the project designer proceed to assign such a classification to their project? By referring to the specialist literature, by consulting colleagues, by asking veterinarians? Or simply by referring to Annex 8 of the Directive? The exercise may prove impossible in the case of the development of a new, and therefore unlisted, technique. Apart from the fact that Annex 8 grossly underestimates the suffering of animals subjected to procedures, it is also tautological, incomplete and confusing. It defines procedures of moderate severity in section I as follows: "Procedures on animals as a result of which the animals are likely to experience short-term moderate pain, suffering or distress, or long-lasting mild pain, suffering or distress as well as procedures that are likely to cause moderate impairment of the well-being or general condition of the animals shall be classified as 'moderate'." It is explained to the reader that a procedure can be classified as "moderate" if its effects are moderate. The same type of definition is used for the "mild" or "severe" classifications.

The designer will then refer to section II "Assignment Criteria" to hopefully understand how to determine the severity classification to assign to their project. They are told that the following should be taken into account: the type of manipulation (without defining what is meant by manipulation), the nature and intensity of the pain, suffering, distress or lasting harm caused by the procedure (without providing an evaluation grid), the cumulative suffering during the course of a procedure (without specifying how the effects of cumulative suffering are to be evaluated) and the prevention from expressing natural behaviors (without listing these according to the species considered). Suffice to say, the project designer is no better off than they were before, since this list is not a list of "classification criteria" for procedures, as the title implies, but a (non-exhaustive) list of factors that influence the level of pain and stress experienced by the animal, without any indication of how to quantify their isolated or cumulative effects.

No doubt to compensate for this lack of standards and scales that would ensure objectivity and homogeneity in the evaluation of the severity of procedures, to which scientists could refer, the drafters of the Directive decided to give examples in section III that would allow the designer to assign their project to a particular severity classification.

This section is in fact a "catch-all" in which we find, in no particular order:

– technical procedures (examples of surgical procedures, biopsies, electric shocks, irradiation);

– effects of certain manipulations (immobilization stress);

– activities related to the use of animals (breeding of genetically modified animals);

– restrictions or deprivations (diet modifications, fasting, use of metabolic cages);

– studies that necessarily include multiple procedures (acute toxicity dose-range finding studies, pharmacokinetic studies, congener deprivation studies).

What could the project designer do with this heterogeneous and incomplete assembly? The attribution of a severity classification is thus performed in a very approximate way, with a good dose of partiality, according to each designer's own idea of the sensitivity of animals.

While the issue of housing conditions must have been widely discussed during the drafting of the Directive, and while the drafting of the corresponding Annex 3 was able to draw on a wealth of technical data from breeders and veterinarians, the same could not be said of the issue of assessing the severity of projects, which is dealt with in Annex 8. While Annex 3 extends over 18 pages, in which there are even separate tables to define the dimensions of the enclosures granted to semi-aquatic or semi-terrestrial anurans according to the length of their bodies (see

p. 37 of the Directive), Annex 8 has to make do with four pages full of approximations, testifying to the lack of expertise that presided over its writing.

5.2.3. *Before the start of the project*

Before an administrative authorization is issued for a project using animals, it must have been favorably evaluated by a competent authority. In France, administrative authorizations are issued by a dedicated department of the Ministry of Research and the evaluation of the project is entrusted to "ethics committees for animal experimentation" considered as competent authorities by the administration. Their composition is defined by regulation (Art. R214-118; see Légifrance (n.d.a)).

If the committee has five members, it must include three members with an activity related to animal experimentation, one veterinarian, and a fifth member for whom the only requirement is that they be "not specialized in questions related to the use of animals for scientific purposes".

In order to give its opinion, the ethics committee for animal experimentation must first ensure that the designer has applied the 3Rs principle and, above all, verify that no method not using live animals would have been likely to provide results at least as satisfactory as the animal model (Replacement). However, how can ethics committees carry out this task properly, when no member has a priori expertise in the field of alternative methods, especially since there are many such methods and it would be necessary to be able to choose the most appropriate one in the context of the project to be evaluated? Due to lack of time and expertise, committee members (who are volunteers) refer to the rationale provided by the project developer, which is almost always the same in all projects: namely, that if the project requires a whole organism, the use of live animals is essential.

The committee must then rule on the "cost/benefit" ratio of the project; that is, the committee cannot give a favorable opinion if the ratio between these two elements is less than 1. However, how could it not give a favorable opinion knowing that "expected" benefits – in other words, expected benefits in the field of human or animal health that the designer has every interest in maximizing – are being compared with estimated costs that correspond to the "prospective" evaluation of the pain, suffering and distress suffered by the animals subjected to the procedures? The animals are not able to give their opinions. Whether in good or bad faith, the "costs" in terms of animal suffering will most often be minimized by the designer who finds themselves – and it must be recognized that this is an extenuating circumstance – rather unprepared to carry out this evaluation exercise correctly. The members of the local ethics committee are at just as much of a loss. As for the veterinarian member of the committee, who is often an employee of the structure to which this committee is attached, and who does not always have expert skills in animal algology for all the species used (from fish to primates, including cephalopods), their opinion does not present all the guarantees of impartiality or expertise that would be expected. Finally, the fifth member of the committee, who is usually a representative of an animal protection association, will only be able to put forward their empathetic perception of what the animals will suffer, and their voice will not carry much weight in the debate. These elements could explain why, in France, no project was rejected in 2017 (European Commission 2020a, table p. 7), that year being the reference year for this report.

5.2.4. During and after the project

5.2.4.1. Support for designers

However, it should be pointed out that the evaluation of the project does not stop at its prospective evaluation: researchers are also asked to verify throughout that it conforms with what was envisaged in the application presentation, in particular by collecting information on the pain, suffering, distress or lasting damage actually experienced by the animals subjected to the procedures. This request meets the expectations of the Directive (Art. 54, section 2): "Member States shall collect and make publicly available, on an annual basis, statistical information on the use of animals in procedures, including information on the *actual severity of* the procedures [...]" (emphasis added). To assist researchers in this assessment process for which they did not necessarily have appropriate methods and tools, the Commission established an expert working group that met in December 2011 and May 2012 and whose work resulted in the publication of a "Severity Assessment Framework" booklet (European Commission 2012).

This working document, published in July 2012 – which is not regulatory in nature and therefore could not be enforced in case of non-compliance with the recommendations contained therein – was to be widely distributed by each of the Member States in their respective national territories to users of animals for scientific purposes. The drafters of the document identified a number of factors that can contribute to a better assessment of the severity of procedures throughout a project, so that the necessary refinement measures (analgesia, post-operative care, cage design) can be applied. At the end of the project, the observations collected should enable improvements to be made in subsequent projects. According to the guide, the ability to assess true severity will require, among other things, teamwork, adequate ongoing training of all involved personnel, day-to-day assessment systems, and effective and well-documented protocols for assessing behavior and clinical signs. Actual severity should be assessed on an individual basis, based on daily observations. All of this seems perfectly relevant.

5.2.4.2. *Does the European Commission's guide really serve the interests of animals?*

One sentence in the paragraph dealing with severity indicators jumps out at us, however (see p. 6): "The aim should be to: achieve the best possible quality of life for the animal; ensure that any suffering due to scientific procedures is recognized and minimized, but to remain consistent with the scientific objectives."

Those last words are enough to call the two intentions that precede them into question and to put the impact of this "guide to best practice" into perspective. They refer us to Article 14 of the Directive: in paragraph 1, "Member States shall ensure that, *unless it is inappropriate*, procedures are carried out under general or local anesthesia [...]"; in paragraph 2, "When deciding on the appropriateness of anesthesia, the following shall be taken into account [...] *whether anesthesia is incompatible with the purpose of the procedure*"; and in paragraph 4, "An animal, which may suffer pain once anesthesia has worn off, shall be treated with pre-emptive and post-operative analgesics [...] provided that *it is compatible with the purpose of the procedure*" (emphasis added). Wherever we look, the scientific purpose of the procedure always takes precedence over the interests of the animal.

Who decides whether anesthesia or analgesia is compatible with the purpose of the procedure? The designer of the project ... who is both judge and jury in this situation. They may or may not decide to take the advice of the user establishment's designated veterinarian, and, if they do, whether or not to follow it. The same applies to the choice of the moment when the animal will be euthanized, that is, when the end-point, defined in the project presentation, will have been reached. Article 13 of the Directive states that "In choosing between procedures [...] death as the end-point of a procedure shall be avoided as far as possible and replaced by early and humane end-points." Here again, however, the designer may well judge that, in their opinion, in view of the clinical signs observed, this end-point has not yet been reached. If close to achieving the desired outcome, the designer may be tempted to prolong the life of the animal for a few hours or days, notwithstanding the signs of suffering and distress that indicate that the predefined end-point has been reached.

The booklet on procedure severity assessment (European Commission 2012) contains a number of examples that should enable project designers to determine in advance the severity classification of their projects. Project summaries are accompanied by an evaluation grid with six categories of criteria (each of which in turn includes up to five criteria): appearance, body functions, environment, behaviors, procedure-specific indicators and other observations. Take one example: on page 42, an abstract refers to a project to evaluate a potential therapy for multiple sclerosis. This project will use eight mice of a particular strain adapted to this type of research. The evaluation grid indicates among the undesirable effects: pain due to injections of the inflammatory adjuvant in the first instance (this pain and the distress induced may be sufficiently severe to consider euthanasia), then loss of tail tone, weakness of the hind limbs, hypo-mobility, paralysis of the limbs, urinary disorders and weight loss of up to 35%, with this condition evolving into chronic neurological deficits. The new therapeutic agent will then be administered, which may cause serious side effects (possibly requiring euthanasia).

What analysis have the experts gathered by the European Commission made of this project?

"A prospective classification of SEVERE is deemed appropriate as the procedure is expected to cause severe impairment of the animals' general well-being and condition." Leaving aside the fact that the use of the term "well-being" in this context is misplaced, to say the least, the classification seems to us to correspond to the reality of the suffering and distress that will be caused to this group of mice. However, the experts go on to state: "[...] the retrospective severity classification may be MODERATE depending on the duration of study and the implementation of early HEP [humane end-points] as indicated here [in the grid]".

So what are these sufficiently early end-points – according to the Commission's experts – that will trigger the euthanasia of the animals and allow the project to pass in the final evaluation to the "moderate" severity classification? They are listed in a column entitled "Humane end-point for any one of the following criteria", otherwise referred to as "HEP" in the rest of the text. The following is an exhaustive list: bilateral forelimb paralysis for more than 24 hours, bilateral hindlimb paralysis for up to five days; self-mutilation; persistent urinary retention (inability to empty bladder); paresis; 35% weight loss; ceasing to eat or drink for more than 24 hours; non-recovery from experimental autoimmune encephalomyelitis (EAE) three weeks after the onset of clinical disease; and clinical signs of intercurrent disease (such as hunching) (European Commission 2012, p. 43).

The same advice is given in the booklet for other projects that were assigned to the "severe" classification in the pre-evaluation, so that they can be moved to "moderate" severity in the final evaluation. The solution is quite simple: just indicate that end-points were applied early; in other words, more abruptly, that animals were euthanized before they died. This example shows how the primary purpose of the booklet (to help project designers determine the severity class of their projects) is misused.

As a reminder, the statistical data transmitted to the competent authority (usually the Ministry of Research of the Member State) by the animal user establishments will take into account the final evaluation and not the preliminary evaluation.

All texts (regulatory or simply informative) point to the fact that animal interests are secondary and that arrangements are possible to circumvent the regulations, so that unorthodox operations and practices are thus authorized, and even encouraged.

This very ambiguous position of the European Commission can only encourage users to take less account of animal suffering in their evaluations and, consequently, to underestimate it in the data collected and published by the Member States.

5.3. The obstacles to taking animal interests into account

Although associations have been actively campaigning for some 40 years in France and in Europe for the improvement of the fate of animals used in laboratories and for their replacement by non-animal methods, although regulations aimed at protecting animals used for scientific purposes were introduced in 1986 in the European Union, and although the majority of public opinion is opposed to animal experimentation, the results obtained in favor of animals used for scientific purposes are extremely disappointing. We offer some explanations.

5.3.1. *Market law and globalization*

The European regulation gives priority to "a proper functioning of the internal market" (others would say, the preservation of "free and undistorted" competition between the Member States), which is mentioned as a primary point of reference in Consideration 1, with animal welfare – as a value of the European Union – being mentioned only as secondary.

Article 2, paragraph 2 of the Directive perfectly illustrates the choice of the European legislator: "When acting pursuant to paragraph 1 [for a broader protection of animals falling within the scope of this Directive] a Member State shall not prohibit or impede the supply or use of animals bred or kept in another Member State in accordance with this Directive, nor shall it prohibit or impede the placing on the market of products developed with the use of such animals in accordance with this Directive." If a Member State refuses to allow animals bred in another Member

State to enter its territory for use in a research project, it may be subject to infringement proceedings.

In addition, multinational chemical and pharmaceutical companies relocate to countries that offer them the best economic conditions; they sometimes create their own breeding facilities on site, or buy from local breeders who are not subject to animal protection regulations. Globalization also allows them to undertake research that would be unauthorized, or tightly controlled, in the European Union, such as that involving certain genetic manipulations on non-human primates, or the use of protected species.

Transgenic animals – and especially mice, the animal of choice for researchers since they reproduce quickly, are inexpensive and easy to handle – are produced (since we are talking about production that can be described as industrial) in a few highly specialized laboratories around the world (mainly in China and the United States) and the majority of research centers globally are supplied by them. What independent authority checks how things are done in these farms and in the European research laboratories located around the world that use them? Obviously none.

5.3.2. The power of lobbyists

Even though we recognize the sincerity of certain researchers, who are genuinely convinced that there is no salvation for experimental science without the use of animals, the intentions of others are not always selfless and, although they are undoubtedly in the minority, these are the most "offensive" actors.

In this field, as in so many others, lobbying groups are at work. Behind the humanist discourse that affirms that only animal experimentation can eradicate deadly diseases and save our children, there is a "corporatist" mobilization of professional groups that aims to defend particular interests, often commercial, or to preserve certain dominant, mandarinate positions acquired over a long period of time.

In France, the most important lobbying group is undoubtedly GIRCOR (Groupe Interprofessionnel de Réflexion et de Communication sur la Recherche[4]). The neutrality of this name contrasts with the commitment of its website "Recherche animale"[5] (GIRCOR n.d.). GIRCOR was formed in 1991 and, from the beginning,

---

4. The French Interprofessional Group for Reflection and Communication on Research.
5. Animal research.

the CNRS (Centre National de la Recherche Scientifique, French National Center for Scientific Research) and INSERM (Institut National de la Santé et de la Recherche Médicale, French National Institute of Health and Medical Research) have played a prominent role. The stated objective of the association was to inform the public about the animal model and on the medical advances associated with animal experimentation, as well as the conditions under which research was being carried out. The association was to bring together public and private research organizations. However, over the years, it has opened up to other "partners/members", such as chemical and drug manufacturers and animal breeders (such as Charles River Laboratories or the Institut Clinique de la Souris).

GIRCOR is a member of the European Animal Research Association (EARA), which explains in its brochure (EARA 2022) that it is necessary, among other things, to "create a favorable climate for animal research by influencing European political decision makers", "lead pan-European initiatives to counter pressure on the laboratory animals supply chain and fight for the right to use laboratory animals in research" and, *ultimately,* "to influence public opinion". GIRCOR is listed in the European Union's directory of lobbyist organizations (GIRCOR 2022), and in France, it is the active relay to public authorities of the positions supported by EARA.

5.3.3. *Intentions but a lack of voluntarism*

We have noted that the Directive envisages multiple exceptions to the provisions it sets out: it also contains loopholes that allow Member States to apply these in a highly flexible manner. Its scope is therefore restricted. In addition, many concepts are imprecisely defined, which contributes to their heterogeneous application, depending on the Member States. Indeed, how is it possible to know what the legislator is talking about when they use the following terms:

– "Competent authorities", a notion used both to describe the bodies responsible for evaluating projects and those that issue administrative authorizations, without defining the qualities expected of them?

– "Alternative approaches", sometimes considered as alternatives to animal testing and sometimes as variations of the 3Rs rule?

– "Effective, proportionate and dissuasive sanctions", the last two adjectives leaving room for subjective interpretation when transposing them into national law?

– "Appropriate proportion of inspections", without any indication of how to determine this proportion?

– "Transparently evaluated project", without any explanation of how and to what this transparency will apply?

The Directive is so vague on certain points that the European Commission has perceived the need, in the years following its publication, to produce booklets intended to "assist the Member States and other bodies affected by this Directive to arrive at a common understanding of the provisions contained in the Directive". The Commission thus published five booklets (European Commission, Department of the Environment, Animals Used in Scientific Purposes), a sort of "practical guide" designed by working groups of experts. It is regrettable that nowhere in these documents is it specified who the experts are and how they were recruited.

However imperfect, these guides did have the merit of providing a more precise framework and some benchmarks. The "Severity Assessment Framework" guide, previously mentioned, was the first to be published in 2012. This was followed by the guide on "Project Evaluation" in 2013, and the guides on "The Education and Training Framework", "Animal Welfare Bodies and National Committees" and "Inspections and Enforcement" in 2014. The main shortcoming of these texts is that they have no binding power; they are not imposed on the Member States, which can therefore take them into account more or less rigorously, or even ignore them.

Indeed, on the first page of the booklets published in 2014 is a "disclaimer" that clearly states that the document "provides some suggestions on how the requirements of the Directive may be met. The content of the document does not impose additional obligations beyond those laid out in the Directive".

5.3.4. *A biased and uninformed evaluation of projects*

We should remember that the authorities responsible for evaluating projects are at the center of the evaluation system and that, as such, their members should obviously be untainted by any conflict of interest. In France, the composition of committees responsible for the ethical evaluation of projects, mentioned above, as well as their functioning, does not guarantee the expected impartiality. Mostly, they are attached to the research institution for which they carry out project evaluations. Their members, as employees of the institution, find themselves in the delicate position of having to evaluate the projects of their peers (who may themselves have to evaluate their own projects), the only constraint imposed by the regulations being that they are not themselves involved in the project they are going to evaluate. As they do not have expertise in non-animal approaches and rely only on the often limited expertise of the veterinarian in animal algology, they do not have sufficient objective elements of appreciation to verify that the project scrupulously applies the

3Rs principle and, in particular, that no alternative method could replace the use of animals.

As for the transparency of the evaluation, which is required by Article 38, paragraph 4 of the Directive, it is hard to know what this consists of. Indeed, meetings of the ethics committees are not public and no minutes are accessible, except to the individuals involved in the project or to representatives of the administrative authority.

Neither is transparency practiced at the level of national authorities. In France, CNREEA is positioned within CNEA (Commission Nationale de l'Expérimentation Animale, the National Commission on Animal Experimentation). This national committee must notably "establish the annual national report on the activity of ethics committees and formulate recommendations with a view to improving their practices" and also "establish an annual activity report addressed to the president of the National Commission on Animal Experimentation" (Art. R214-134; see Légifrance (n.d.b)). However, requests from associations for annual reports and activity reports from the CNEA, documents of an administrative nature that should be publicly accessible, were still unanswered in March 2021 (six months after the requests).

5.3.5. *Lack of qualifications of personnel using animals*

The fact that the suffering of animals used for scientific purposes is systematically underestimated by the texts, and by those involved, inevitably reflects, in one way or another, on the content of the regulatory training intended for personnel involved in animal experimentation; Articles 23 and 24 of the Directive provide only very general indications as to the skills that these personnel must acquire. The European Commission's 2014 guide on the education and training framework supplemented these far too imprecise articles (European Commission 2014).

In France, what does the Ministry of Agriculture provide for the training of personnel who are required to participate in a project using animals? A technical instruction from the General Directorate of Food issued on February 28, 2019 (Ministère de l'Agriculture et de la Souveraineté alimentaire 2019), to the departmental directorates in charge of population protection (Directions Départementales chargées de la Protection des Populations, (DDPP)) specifies the procedures for the instruction of applications for the approval of training in animal experimentation.

A detailed document written by the CNEA completes the ministerial instruction. It describes the specific training courses for project designers, applicators and handlers using animals: they include a basic module with content on the regulations[6] and a complementary module which specializes according to the animal species and experimental procedures[7]. There are no prerequisites for applicators and handlers. Following on from this training, which could legitimately be described as "express", designers or applicators may take an additional 22-hour module in surgical procedures: according to the Ministry of Agriculture's instruction, this is only an "initiation" to surgery, and individuals taking this module will not automatically be recognized as competent by the authorities. We are reassured. It is planned that acquisition will continue under an experienced tutor, without any indication of the duration of this tutorship. It should also be pointed out that no diploma or certificate of professional qualification is awarded as a result of this training.

How can we claim that applicators are properly trained on all aspects of their job in barely 54 hours of practical training (training on simulation tools is never mentioned)? As for maintaining these skills, in France, this only consists of a three-day course every six years, on general or technical topics. This training will be validated by the person in charge of follow-up on the competences of the establishment, on the sole basis of the program and confirmation of the trainee's attendance.

It seems incredible when we compare this training for personnel practicing animal experimentation with the training for those working in veterinary medicine. In France, to obtain the professional qualified veterinary assistant (*Assistant vétérinaire qualifié*, AVQ) certification, it is necessary to hold a baccalaureate or equivalent and to have successfully completed approximately 350 hours of training over the course of a year. Although they provide technical assistance to the practitioner, the holder of an AVQ certificate cannot perform any technical procedures on the animal. The holder of the professional specialized veterinary assistant (*Assistant vétérinaire spécialisé*, AVS) certification, a qualification

---

6. The first module is purely theoretical and lasts for 25 hours for designers, 13 hours for applicators and 7 hours for handlers.

7. The second module includes practical work that may be performed on live animals. It will cover minimally invasive experimental procedures by species group; basic knowledge of a species group; recognition of signs of distress, pain and suffering specific to the species; anesthesia and analgesia for the species group; euthanasia methods; management and monitoring of animal health and hygiene, animal facility equipment and materials; and the design of experimental procedures and projects All this in 32 hours for designers and applicators and 27 hours for animal handlers. The topics "pain", "analgesia and anesthesia", "end-points" and "euthanasia" will each be covered in 2 hours for designers and applicators!

recognized by the Ministry of Agriculture and by the French National Union of Private Practice Veterinarians (Syndicat National des Vétérinaires d'Exercice Libéral, SNVEL), will hold a baccalaureate or equivalent and will have successfully completed 24 months of training. They will be able to assist the veterinarian for the care and the complementary examinations and provide pre-, per- and post-operative surgical assistance. However, they will not be able to perform any technical act (such as sampling, blood sampling or suturing) in the absence of the practitioner, whereas a laboratory technician will be able to do so after a week and a half of training.

The laboratory rabbit does not benefit from the same technical skills of the individual who will perform a puncture or an abdominal surgery on it as the pet rabbit taken to the veterinary clinician. However, is the laboratory animal still an animal, a sentient living according to the French Civil Code? Clearly not. It does not seem to matter that a clumsy technical gesture causes pain or that a failed intervention causes death. The animal is only experimental material that no attentive proprietor cares about.

5.4. Conclusion

While the European directives of 1986 and then 2010 do indeed testify to the intention of European parliamentarians to improve the treatment of animals used for scientific and educational purposes and to reduce their numbers, and while their fate may appear less terrifying than that of animals subjected to vivisection in the 19th century, described by the historian Jean-Yves Bory (Bory 2013), we can, however, deplore the *minimal* application of the texts in most Member States of the European Union and the often biased interpretations of the different actors, which work against the interest of the animals.

We do not have enough space here to present what political action working towards transitioning to non-animal research should be. The Transcience association (Transcience n.d.) has set itself the priority objective of bringing these issues to the national and European political arena.

The stakes related to animal experimentation are high; the players are powerful, and the fields of application are many and evolving. There is no single, simple solution to support the transition to non-animal research. Complex strategies that take into account many parameters must be considered, which implies gaining skills and approaching the problem systematically: blocking factors must be considered within the framework of a system of interactions, rather than in isolation. However, it is also necessary to work on rebalancing the forces at work, in other words, those who seek to influence decision-makers, so that they commit to animals used in laboratories, must give themselves the financial, media and legal means to do so. It is up to the associations and other committees to be able to build solid and powerful collaborations in the years to come, to counterbalance the lobbyist groups that defend animal experimentation with the public authorities.

5.5. References

Bory, J.-Y. (2013). *La douleur des bêtes : la polémique sur la vivisection au XIXe siècle en France*. Presses Universitaires de Rennes, Rennes.

CNREEA (2021a). Avis et recommandation sur le contrôle hydrique utilisé chez les primates non humains dans les projets scientifiques. February 1st [Online]. Available at: https://www.opal-association.org/Controle%20hydrique_210201.pdf.

CNREEA (2021b). Recommandation sur la technique d'amputation de phalange comme méthode d'identification et de caractérisation génétique chez les rongeurs. February 3rd [Online]. Available at: https://www.sbea-c2ea.fr/wp-content/uploads/2022/05/recommandation-sur-la-technique-d-amputation-de-phalange-comme-m-thode-d-identification-et-de-caract-risation-g-n-tique-chez-les.pdf..

Commission européenne, Département de l'environnement. Animals used in scientific purposes: https://ec.europa.eu/environment/chemicals/lab_animals/pdf/guidance/severity/fr.pdf; https://ec.europa.eu/enrironment/chemicals/lab_animals/pdf/guidance/project_evaluation/fr.pdf; http://ec.europa.eu/environment/chemicals/lab_animals/pdf/guidance/education_training/fr.pdf; https://ec.europa.eu/environment/chemicals/lab_animals/pdf/guidance/animal_welfare_bodies/fr.pdf; http://ec.europa.eu/environment/chemicals/lab_animals/pdf/guidance/inspections/fr.pdf.

EARA (2022). About EARA Membership [Online]. Available at: https://www.eara.eu/about-us#:~:text=About%20EARA%20membership%20%7C%20EARA&text=Since%20its%20founding%20in%202014,other%20countries%20around%20the%20world.[8]

European Commission (2012). Guide sur le cadre d'évaluation de la gravité des procédures. 11 and 12 July [Online]. Available at: https://ec.europa.eu/environment/chemicals/lab_animals/pdf/guidance/severity/fr.pdf.

European Commission (2013). Rapport de la Commission au Parlement européen et au Conseil du 05/12/2013 : Septième rapport sur les statistiques concernant le nombre d'animaux utilisés à des fins expérimentales et à d'autres fins scientifiques dans les États membres de l'Union européenne, 05/12/2013: https://eur-lex.europa.eu/legal-content/FR/TXT/PDF/?uri=CELEX:52013DC0859&from=FR.

---

8. EARA's objectives and strategies are explained in the three documents found at the bottom of this page.

European Commission (2014). Direction de l'environnement. Guide sur le cadre d'enseignement et de formation [Online]. Available at: http://ec.europa.eu/environment/chemicals/lab_animals/pdf/guidance/education_training/fr.pdf.

European Commission (2020a). Commission staff working document accompanying the document. Report from the Commission to the European Parliament and the Council on the implementation of Directive 2010/63/EU on the protection of animals used for scientific purposes in the Member States of the European Union. 5th February [Online]. Available at: https://d144bb38-73b9-4d2e-bc69-5ed140189b94.filesusr.com/ugd/7f38fb_a65e06fae34c49fc868749c25a6e21c9.pdf.

European Commission (2020b). Commission staff working document [Online]. Available at: https://d144bb38-73b9-4d2e-bc69-5ed140189b94.filesusr.com/ugd/7f38fb_a65e06fae34c49fc868749c25a6e21c9.pdf.

European Commission (2020c). Rapport de la Commission au Parlement européen et au Conseil du 05/02/2020 : Rapport de 2019 relatif aux statistiques concernant l'utilisation d'animaux à des fins scientifiques dans les États membres de l'Union européenne en 2015-2017: https://d144bb38-73b9-4d2e-bc69-5ed140189b94.filesusr.com/ugd/7f38fb_d3f88251fb3c4f158ab26d9a549f0a25.pdf.

European Commission (2020d). Rapport de la Commission au Parlement européen et au Conseil du 05/02/2020 sur la mise en œuvre de la directive 2010/63/UE relative à la protection des animaux utilisés à des fins scientifiques dans les États membres de l'Union européenne [Online]. Available at: https://d144bb38-73b9-4d2e-bc69-5ed140189b94.filesusr.com/ugd/7f38fb_b0689e0cf80f4cfd8494491f5eb13cc9.pdf.

European Union Law (2012). Décision d'exécution de la Commission du 14 novembre 2012 : 2012/707/UE : Décision d'exécution de la Commission du 14 novembre 2012 établissant un format commun pour la transmission des informations conformément à la directive 2010/63/UE du Parlement européen et du Conseil relative à la protection des animaux utilisés à des fins scientifiques [notifiée sous l (europa.eu)].

GIRCOR (n.d.). GIRCOR [Online]. Available at: https://www.recherche-animale.org/.

GIRCOR (2022). Transparency register [Online]. Available at: https://ec.europa.eu/transparencyregister/public/consultation/displaylobbyist.do?id=058386922 152-70.

Légifrance (n.d.a). Article R214-118 – Code rural et de la pêche maritime - Légifrance (legifrance.gouv.fr).

Légifrance (n.d.b). Article R214-134 – Code rural et de la pêche maritime - Légifrance (legifrance.gouv.fr).

Ministère de l'Agriculture et de la Souveraineté alimentaire (2019). DGAL/SDSPA/2019-175 : Ministère de l'Agriculture et de l'Alimentation – Direction générale de l'alimentation – Service des actions sanitaires en production primaire – Sous-direction de la santé et de protection animales – Bureau de la protection animale [Online]. Available at: https://info.agriculture.gouv.fr/gedei/site/bo-agri/instruction-2019-175.

Ministère de l'Enseignement supérieur, de la Recherche et de l'Innovation (2021). Enquêtes statistiques sur l'utilisation des animaux à des fins scientifiques [Online]. Available at: https://www.enseignementsup-recherche.gouv.fr/cid70613/enquete-statistique-sur-l-utilisation-des-animaux-a-des-fins-scientifiques.html.

Official Journal of the European Union (2010). Directive 2010/63/UE du Parlement européen et du Conseil du 22 septembre 2010 relative à la protection des animaux utilisés à des fins scientifiques [Online]. Available at: https://eur-lex.europa.eu/LexUriServ/LexUriServ.do?uri=OJ:L:2010:276:0033:0079:fr:PDF.

Steinberg W.F., Smith, L., Scorr, L. (2004). Nociception and antinoception during the first week of life in mice. *The Journal of Pain*, 5(8), 420–426.

Transcience (n.d.). Transcience [Online]. Available at: https://www.transcience.fr/.

6

Altruism Towards Animals and the Economy

Romain ESPINOSA

Centre international de recherche sur l'environnement
et le développement (CIRED), CNRS, Paris, France

6.1. Introduction

Economics is a discipline that, like many social sciences, was mainly built around and for human beings. While public economics shares the foundations of utilitarian theory, à la Bentham or Stuart Mill, it has paid little attention until very recently to the question of animal welfare and, more generally, to altruism in human beings.

In line with utilitarian philosophy, the normative branch of economics has sought to discuss the appropriateness of public policy through a consequentialist lens: a society that increases the happiness of its citizens is preferable to a less happy society. To judge the level of happiness in society (called *social welfare*), economists have sought to aggregate individual levels of happiness (called *utilities*). In so doing, they have decided to consider only the selfish part of individuals' happiness and exclude altruistic preferences from social considerations, among them altruism towards animals (Espinosa 2019). In other words, economists have regarded society's happiness as the sum of its citizens' purely selfish happiness. However, a number of recent works have challenged this status quo and now argue for including animals (directly or indirectly) in discussions on societal choices[1].

---

1. One notable exception is Blackorby and Donaldson (1992). In their study, the authors focus on animal welfare for its own sake and not through the altruism of human beings. This work,

In his 2018 work, "Animal Welfare and Social Decisions: Is It Time to Take Bentham Seriously?" Johansson-Stenman puts forward an innovative discourse on how to consider animals in economics and, in particular, questions the legitimacy of their inclusion in social welfare calculations. The author explains that economics has almost unanimously excluded animals from its considerations, but that this approach is contrary to the very principles of the utilitarian philosophy from which economics claims to draw. He proposes five ways of viewing animals in economics. To the speciesist view of utilitarianism focused exclusively on humans, Johansson-Stenman (2018) proposes that animals should, at the very least, be considered through the altruistic preferences of certain humans in society. In other words, animals would have instrumental value: improving their welfare would also improve the welfare of altruistic humans.

This view of animal consideration through altruism is also the one adopted by Fleurbaey and Van der Linden (2021) in a work on egalitarianism and animals in economics. The authors, while asserting that "it is time to introduce animals into welfare economics", nevertheless only consider the happiness of animals through the existence of altruistic citizens in society. In their theoretical model, they conclude that, even while animals are indirectly valued, societal choices should favor animals. They argue that the most altruistic citizens in society are also those who are willing to pay the most for animals. Thus, at the same income level, an altruistic person will have lower happiness than a selfish individual if animals are mistreated. In a society that aspires to greater equality among human beings, greater consideration should be given to the most disadvantaged, namely the altruists, and thus, by transitivity, to the animals.

In a recent article, Nicolas Treich and I (Espinosa and Treich 2021) also propose a discussion on the relationship between humans and animals in societal choices. This work focuses on the degree of speciesism in a society and seeks to understand how society's overall preferences towards animals may influence policy and/or economic activity. The theoretical discussion shows, for example, that a society concerned with animal welfare will have an interest in limiting animal husbandry when it occurs under poor conditions. Paradoxically, if animals are treated well, a welfare-conscious society might want more animal husbandry, since well-treated animals would enhance social welfare. Nevertheless, the study also presents the result of an animal welfare perception survey in which we ask several social groups

---

very much ahead of its time, discusses animal exploitation in the broadest sense (animal husbandry and experimentation) and justifies considering the interests of animals through their sentience. The authors point out the risk of regarding animals solely through the lens of altruism, insofar as consideration for animals is not derived from their intrinsic experiences, but from the attachment of humans to them.

about how they see the value of a life for a farmed animal. Perceptions of what constitutes a life worth living are radically different across social groups: livestock professionals are much more likely to consider an animal's life worth living, even in a near-intensive livestock operation, while animal activists have very high demands for livestock conditions that can produce a positive benefit on an animal's entire life.

These different discussions show that the question of animal welfare can be integrated in different ways in economics. While the historical status quo tends not to consider animals in societal choices, a number of recent works call for a better consideration of them. Social choice debate argues, at a minimum, for an indirect consideration of animals, namely through the lens of human altruism. Fleurbaey and Van der Linden (2021) note that it is difficult to measure the well-being of animals, let alone compare it to that of humans, but economics has developed tools to measure altruistic considerations towards them.

6.2. Methods for assessing altruism towards animals

While theoretical work in economics has paved the way for the consideration of animal interests through human altruism, an important question is how this altruism should be measured and incorporated into social choices. We will see, firstly, how economists typically measure social gains in a non-altruistic framework (see section 6.2.1) and how we can extend this to altruistic considerations (see section 6.2.2).

6.2.1. *Utility, social welfare and willingness to pay*

In general, the aim of public economics is to measure the gains to society associated with an economic activity or public policy. In the context of economic trade, in order to determine whether an activity is beneficial to society, economists perform a cost–benefit analysis. If the costs of the activity exceed its benefits, then the action is said to reduce society's welfare. Since this society is composed of consumers and producers, economists aggregate the gains and losses of each member of society to determine the net gain of the economic activity as a whole. Economists thus seek to measure what they call the "total surplus", that is, the total gain in utility (welfare) for society.

The total surplus of an economic activity is defined as the difference between the costs of production and the consumer's "willingness to pay". Consider the following example: an individual is looking to buy a carton of soy milk and is willing to pay up to €5 to purchase this product, which corresponds to their willingness to pay, in other words, the maximum price they are ready to pay to obtain the product. This €5 can be seen as a monetary representation of the pleasure they will derive from the product. Beyond this, the product will cost too much, compared with the pleasure the individual will derive from it. Under €5, the consumer will buy the product because it will give them a greater pleasure than the price paid. We can therefore consider that the individual derives a pleasure equivalent to €5 for the carton of soy milk. In other words, willingness to pay is a monetary equivalent of the pleasure that the individual derives from the product.

Let us now consider the question from the perspective of the producer of the soy milk carton. They face production costs for creating and marketing the product, which are a net loss to society. Indeed, social well-being is greater when production costs are low (this is wealth saved). Thus, the producer incurs fixed costs in the production of the carton of soy milk and only agrees to sell their product for a price higher than the production costs: at a production cost of €1 per carton of soy milk, the producer will only agree to sell their product for prices over €1.

The social welfare generated by economic trade is then calculated as the difference between the benefit (the consumer's willingness to pay) and the cost (the production cost) associated with the activity concerned. In this example, the sale of a carton of soy milk creates the equivalent of €4 of well-being for society.

For market goods, as in the previous example, it is quite easy to calculate consumers' willingness to pay for a product. By observing market behavior, we can see the price range at which consumers are willing to buy a product. By increasing the price, we should observe a section of consumers switching products or leaving the market because their pleasure in consuming the product becomes lower than the price.

However, the issue is more complicated with respect to animal welfare, and there are four main reasons why considering the market situation at any given time is not sufficient to measure human altruistic considerations towards animals. Firstly, animal products can be considered as "credence goods", specific goods whose full characteristics we never fully observe, even after we have consumed them (Emons 2001). Thus, since we do not know some of the characteristics of a product, it is impossible for us to estimate with certainty the pleasure we derive from its consumption. Animal products fall into this category for consumers concerned with animal welfare. This is because it will always be impossible to know the full extent of the treatment of animals during the product's manufacturing process. An altruistic consumer will therefore always be uncertain about their enjoyment of a product.

The second limitation of the simple market analysis of animal welfare concerns is that it does not capture the full range of consumer demands. For example, consider two products: a box of six battery eggs for €1.50 and a box of six free-range eggs for €2. Consumers who are willing to pay 50 cents more for free-range hens eggs will buy the second product, but looking only at the proportion of consumers who actually buy this product ignores all the consumers who might be willing to pay between 1 cent and 49 cents for the hen welfare. Analyzing market shares as they are at a given moment thus underestimates consumer altruism for animal welfare.

The third limitation of market analyses is that they focus only on market goods. The question of altruism towards animals goes beyond the simple framework of trade and generally concerns all the relationships that humans may have with animals. Thus, a person who does not hunt may have altruistic consideration towards a hunted animal. This consideration is not captured by a market situation because there is no economic transaction for it to be expressed.

The fourth limitation is that some citizens do not participate in economic activities related to animal exploitation. For example, the willingness to pay of vegans or citizens who refuse to go to shows involving wild animals is not taken into account when analyzing sales because they are *outside* the market. Their altruistic considerations, which are surely the most important because they consider that no product currently on the market respects animal welfare enough to meet their altruistic motivations, are excluded from the analysis, which again leads to an underestimation of the altruism of citizens towards animals.

6.2.2. *Measuring willingness to pay for animal welfare*

In the discussion above, we saw that economists measure social gain as the difference between an individual's willingness to pay for a good and the cost of producing that good. This reasoning, while obviously applicable to physical goods, can also be extended to non-material goods such as a change in legislation. The social welfare gain of a new legislation would be the difference between the costs of that legislation and the willingness of all citizens to pay for its implementation. The main problem with these non-market goods is the absence of a market (and thus of a price mechanism) to enable the willingness to pay in a natural setting to be estimated.

In order to measure the willingness to pay for animal welfare, social scientists have developed two types of tools. On the one hand, for market goods, some studies use "choice" experiments, in which study participants are presented with several products and must choose, hypothetically or in reality, which to buy. The products presented vary according to their characteristics and price. For example, the participant has the choice between a box of free-range eggs at €2.20 and a box of battery eggs at €1.30. By varying the characteristics and prices of the products, economists are able to estimate how much an individual is willing to pay for the characteristics of interest.

On the other hand, in order to evaluate the willingness to pay for both market and non-market goods, economists have also developed "contingent" valuation methods. These techniques have been used extensively in environmental economics, where researchers aim to measure the satisfaction that a population derives from collective goods, such as environmental protection, which by definition have no market price. Contingent valuation methods use hypothetical questionnaires, in which individuals are asked to express the maximum amount they would be willing to pay to implement the legislation, or to acquire the good, in question. Since these studies are hypothetical in nature ("How much would you be willing to pay if it were possible?"), researchers try to minimize over-reporting bias (namely, the willingness to report being willing to pay more than we would if it actually cost money) by asking participants to respond in the most honest way possible ("cheap talk scripts"). The objective of contingent valuation methods is to estimate the *maximum* amount that citizen-consumers would be willing to pay for a good or a public policy. From a methodological point of view, there has been much debate in the field about the best way to estimate this maximum amount. Four main methods can be identified, all with their advantages and disadvantages (Fonta et al. 2010):

a) A first method consists of asking individuals what they would be willing to pay for a measure to be put in place or for a specific characteristic of a product (such as free-range farming). Researchers formulate the question as follows: would you be willing to pay €2 more per week to have all chickens in France raised in the open air? Participants can answer these questions in a binary way, which limits the information we can obtain from them (i.e. we only know if the individual is ready to pay more, or less, than €2) but which makes the situation closer to a market situation where a consumer decides whether or not to buy a product.

b) The second proposed method consists of sequentially asking several questions similar to the one presented above. If an individual declares that they are not willing to pay €2, then they are asked if they are willing to pay €1. If they are willing to pay €1, then we ask them if they are willing to pay €1.50, and so on. This iterative process thus allows us to circumscribe the individual's willingness to pay for animal welfare within a fairly narrow range, which provides more information than the previous technique. Nevertheless, participants in such surveys are often influenced by the starting point of the questions and, as this is chosen by the designers of the study, may induce a bias on the part of the researcher according to their preconceptions. Another risk is that participants may become bored with the same questions.

c) The third possibility proposed by researchers is to present consumers with a list of ranges of amounts (less than €1, between €1 and €4, between €4 and €7, and so on.) and to ask them the maximum amount they would be willing to pay for the good or measure concerned. This method, like the previous, allows for a good identification of the willingness to pay of participants within a possibly small range, but reduces the risk of fatigue. However, this method is subject to amplitude bias: the range of choices offered may affect the responses of participants. Here again, since the range of choices is chosen by the researcher before the study, there is a risk of creating bias in the responses. For example, it is likely that individuals will say they are willing to give more if the maximum range proposed is "€50 or more" rather than "€10 or more".

d) The fourth tool used to measure willingness to pay is to use open-ended questions. This method is perhaps the most intuitive and consists of asking individuals: "Up to how much are you willing to pay per week for free-range chickens in France?" The advantage of this technique is that it contains strong statistical information, because we know the exact maximum amount the respondent is willing to pay. However, these questions are the furthest from the reality of consumer choices. When we are at the supermarket, we do not ask ourselves how much we would be willing to pay at most, but simply whether we are willing to pay more or less than the price displayed. Participants may thus have difficulty estimating the true economic impact of their statement, or may even be unable to answer the question because of a lack of context.

6.3. Main results

Willingness-to-pay analyses have focused on welfare issues in the production of meat or, more broadly, animal products for food consumption. Here, we review several of these studies that seek to measure how much consumers would be willing to pay to improve the welfare of these animals.

In general, we can distinguish two types of situation. On the one hand, some researchers have tried to measure consumers' willingness to pay for spontaneous market changes (see section 6.3.1): if consumer altruism turns out to be high enough, then it will become profitable for companies to offer more animal-friendly products. On the other hand, some studies have focused on changes in legislation (see section 6.3.2). We have seen above that there are a number of limitations to market analysis, including the problem of consumer coordination. In this case, the state may want to legislate to set a minimum standard of respect for animal welfare. This second set of studies therefore aims to measure whether the level of altruism in society is high enough to compensate for the economic losses associated with stricter regulation and thus remains anthropocentric.

6.3.1. *Examples of spontaneous market developments and altruism for animals*

6.3.1.1. *Example of mobile slaughterhouses*

In a study of Swedish consumers, Carlsson et al. (2007) address the issue of slaughter methods, and in particular mobile slaughterhouses. The rise in trade in live animals in recent decades has led to an increase in the number of animals being transported over long distances before being slaughtered. This transportation induces very difficult living conditions for the animals concerned, thus reducing their well-being and increasing the risk of mortality. In addition, the long-distance transport of animals increases the risk of spreading infectious diseases and is also harmful to the environment. While there is a real interest in on-farm slaughtering, a key question is whether the altruistic considerations of consumers are strong enough for the industry to find these mobile slaughterhouses profitable enough to set up.

The study by Carlsson et al. (2007) seeks to measure the willingness to pay of Swedish consumers through a choice experiment. To do this, the authors sent a questionnaire by mail to 1,600 randomly selected Swedish citizens. They asked them to choose which of the two products they would prefer to buy. The two beef or chicken products vary according to several characteristics, including transportation to the slaughterhouse. The researchers used statistical methods to infer what respondents would be willing to pay for the use of a mobile slaughterhouse, rather than transportation to a slaughterhouse away from the farm.

The results of the study show a significant willingness to pay for cattle to be killed on site. Consumers are willing to pay an average of 10% more for products from mobile slaughter. Given the additional cost associated with implementing this alternative slaughter method, the authors estimate that 18–45% of consumers would be willing to actually purchase these products if they were available on the market. Altruistic motivations would thus spontaneously improve cattle welfare through market mechanisms (i.e. without government intervention). However, researchers observe a negative willingness to pay for chickens (consumers would be willing to pay less for mobile slaughter), which they do not explain.

6.3.1.2. *Example of labels*

Many studies on animal welfare, such as Carlsson et al. (2007), have been conducted, and a key question is why market mechanisms do not improve animal welfare if so many consumers are willing to pay for these changes. In a recent work, Mulder and Zomer (2017) suggest several answers, among them a lack of information on the market. Consumers may not understand or trust what is behind the labels. In addition, consumers may prefer collective action (see the next section for legislative developments).

In their study, Mulder and Zomer (2017) used a dual mechanism (a choice experiment and the contingent valuation method) to measure the willingness to pay for improved living and killing conditions (life span, access to the outdoors, stunning technique for slaughter, density) for broilers. From their representative sample of 1,603 Dutch citizens, the authors report a high willingness to pay for chicken welfare: €3 more per chicken for better stunning methods and €2 more for outdoor access.

This study is an interesting example because it illustrates the possibility that the willingness to pay of respondents to take collective rather than individual action for animal welfare can be calculated. The authors analyze three types of collective procedures: the fact that a large number of citizens also adopt a responsible purchasing attitude, a collective agreement or a change in legislation. In all three cases, consumers are willing to pay more for chicken. For the authors, this is proof that the market is failing when it comes to animal welfare and that spontaneous altruism on the part of consumers can only be revealed through collective action.

6.3.2. *Examples of legislative developments and altruism for animals*

The studies presented above illustrate that market mechanisms can help improve animal welfare in cases where altruistic consumer preferences are sufficiently strong. However, the problem of coordination may prevent improvements in animal welfare, even though a significant proportion of the population would like to see such changes. In this case, economists have been interested in the willingness to pay for legislation, rather than for products.

6.3.2.1. *The example of the European directive on chickens*

The first example of a study we can cite is that of Bennett et al. (2019), regarding the implementation of the EU Broiler Directive. The aim of this European directive, which came into force in June 2010, was to improve the conditions under which chickens are kept, by providing a common European framework on feed, access to water, bedding, ventilation, heating, noise, light, cleaning and even veterinary inspections. The authors of the study sought to assess how much a representative British citizen would be willing to pay to implement this measure. Through a survey of respondents residing in the United Kingdom, the researchers asked 655 participants how much they would be willing to pay per week, in addition to their food bill, for this measure to be implemented. The survey used payment cards (see above) ranging from £0.05 to £4 or more.

The survey results show that only a small proportion of respondents say they are not willing to pay anything at all for the implementation of the legislation. Indeed, 82.2% of respondents indicate a willingness to pay for the measure. The statistical work shows that 50% of Britons are willing to pay £21.50 or more per year to implement the Directive. Taken against the population as a whole (23.4 million households), the authors estimate that UK citizens would be willing to pay a total of £504 million for this Directive. This amount could be seen as representing the national level of altruism of UK citizens to improve the welfare of broilers. At the same time, an independent report on the study calculated the costs of implementation of this Directive for the UK and concluded that the new legislation would cost £21.7 million. This example illustrates a situation where human altruism towards animals can be satisfied by state intervention: the "altruistic" benefits of helping animals are 23 times greater than the associated costs.

6.3.2.2. The example of the Twenty Measures for Animals

In a recent project, students at Sciences Po Paris worked on developing a program of measures aimed at improving animal welfare in France (2020). After one year of work, they analyzed the cost to the public authorities of implementing 20 selected measures (Vingt Mesures pour les Animaux). This program was backed by a dozen national parliamentarians and received the support of over 18,000 citizens. This study also sought to measure the willingness of the French to pay for each of these 20 measures through a survey of a representative sample of the population (1,500 respondents). In order to measure willingness to pay, the questionnaire used contingent valuation methods with two types of responses (open-ended responses and responses with payment cards). The unique nature of this work is in its analysis of the willingness to pay for 20 measures affecting very different animals (farm, as well as domestic and wild animals and animals used in animal experimentation).

In the context of this survey, the first results (see Table 1.1) presented show a high willingness to pay for the welfare of many animals (the results presented are averages per person). We present below Espinosa's estimates (corrected for the warm-glow effect). The highest willingness to pay is observed for the issue of slaughter: the French are willing to pay an average of €22.64 per year to ban slaughter without stunning. The lowest willingness to pay concerns the introduction of vegetarian menus in canteens (€9.14) or the prohibition of forced feeding in the production of foie gras (€7.85).

Respondents are willing to pay more for domestic animals (sterilization of cats and identification of dogs and cats), as well as for wild animals (bans on dolphinariums and shows involving animals). The French also say they are concerned about the cruelest practices in animal husbandry, such as the method of stunning pigs (end of carbon dioxide gassing) and raising chickens in cages.

Measure	French citizens' willingness to pay
Making the first visit to the veterinarian to identify pets, free and mandatory	€17.30
Conducting sterilization campaigns for stray cats	€14.79
Improving calf bedding by introducing edible elements	€10.38
Improving the fiber diet of calves to combat deficiencies	€9.90
Banning badger and fox digging	€13.04
Banning all forms of hunting of animals kept in captivity	€12.50
Establishing mandatory labeling of processed egg products, following the system already in place for single eggs	€9.89
Banning the production and sale of fur in France	€15.62
Introducing a daily plant-based menu in all school canteens	€9.14
Implementing an animal ethics course in school curricula	€8.90
Banning industrial "factory farm" breeding	€13.46
Banning slaughter without stunning	€22.64
Banning animal dissection in primary and secondary schools	€9.61
Including animal-free experimentation experts on all animal testing ethics committees	€12.15
Banning the cutting of teeth in piglets in favor of grinding	€11.73
Banning the use of carbon dioxide to stun and kill pigs in favor of other alternatives	€13.07
Subsidizing circuses to convert to animal-free shows	€14.40
Banning the breeding and acquisition of dolphins and orcas in dolphinariums	€13.47
Banning forced force-feeding in foie gras production	€7.85
Banning the keeping of egg-laying hens in cages	€14.39

Table 6.1. *Results of the "Vingt Mesures pour les Animaux" project (Espinosa 2022)*

6.3.3. *Meta-analyses of the willingness to pay for animals*

While previous studies have highlighted the diversity of scopes for assessing human altruism towards animals, two meta-analyses have sought to explain the common trends underlying this work. Lagerkvist and Hess offered the first meta-analysis on the willingness to pay towards farm animals in 2011. The authors provided an initial overview of this field of research based on 24 studies. This first meta-analysis was then completed by Clark and his co-authors (2017), who took new studies into account and analyzed a total of 54 works on the willingness to pay towards animals.

In their meta-analysis, Clark and his co-authors focused on farm animals. Most of the studies considered were from European countries (56%) and primarily analyzed issues associated with eggs and pork. As the sample sizes of these analyses varied, the authors of the meta-analysis provided a weighting to each study according to the number of respondents involved in each survey: studies with a larger sample size received a higher statistical weighting.

This meta-analysis provides several insights into human altruism towards animals. The first result is that a positive willingness to pay to improve the living conditions of animals is observed in the vast majority of the studies considered[2]. Secondly, the authors note that statistical methods have improved over time, making such analyses increasingly accurate. Thirdly, the researchers note a strong heterogeneity in altruism towards animals. Cattle (meat or milk), then poultry are the animals towards which altruism is the highest. Altruism appears to be lower towards fish and pigs. It is therefore likely that altruism would increase with our level of proximity to animals. However, we can note three alternative hypotheses to this, as I mention in a recent work (Espinosa 2021).

Firstly, it is possible that the measures proposed in the surveys to improve the condition of animals vary significantly for different animals. Respondents may be willing to pay more for measures with the greatest impact, yet such measures are specifically proposed for cattle. Secondly, survey participants may have different levels of knowledge about the living conditions or vital needs of animals. If we are unaware, for example, that the vast majority of chickens in France are intensively reared, it is difficult to understand why we would need measures to help them.

---

2. Indeed, much work concludes that there is a positive willingness to pay towards farm animals: Bennett and Larson (1996), Bennett (1998), Bennett and Blaney (2003), Bateman and co-authors (2008), Seibert and Norwood (2011) and Tonsor and Wolf (2011).

This second explanation is considered by a previous meta-analysis by Carl Johan Lagerkvist and Sebastian Hess (2011). In this work, the authors show that the studies that explain the most about animal husbandry conditions to participants are those that induce the highest willingness to pay. The authors conclude that the population remains under-informed on the subject of animal welfare. They characterize animal welfare as a credence good, in other words, a product for which we cannot really know its utility because we do not have all the information about it. The authors believe that the willingness to pay towards animal welfare may be greater than estimated, because people are optimistic about the living conditions of animals.

The final important finding of the Clark and co-authors study concerns the relationship between altruism levels and socio-demographic characteristics. The researchers show that women and individuals with higher levels of education report being willing to pay more for animal welfare. The most affluent households also declare, quite naturally given the financial constraints of the most modest households, to be ready to spend more on animals. Finally, these studies generally highlight a lower level of concern for animals among older people, without any conclusion on an age effect (people care less about animals over time) or a generational effect (modern generations are more sensitive to the animal condition). These findings are aligned with the results of many studies on the topic that show greater concern for animals among women and people from educated, urban backgrounds (Herzog et al. 1991; Discroll 1992; Eldrige and Gluck 1996; Vrij et al. 2003; Kendall et al. 2006; Erian and Phillips 2017).

6.3.4. Is willingness to pay the result of altruism?

An important question raised by these willingness-to-pay studies is whether the price that consumers are willing to pay reflects altruistic motivations. Willingness to pay to improve living conditions in farms does indeed seem to stem from altruistic motivations, but other phenomena could be at work, such as social pressure, or self-image issues. In a recent work, Frey and Pirscher (2018) propose some response elements. The authors set up an analysis to determine the willingness to pay of German consumers while measuring the respondents' level of altruism through a scale established in the psychology literature. In this study, consumers were asked to indicate how much they would be willing to pay for four animal-friendly measures: an end to the slaughter of male chicks, an extension/increase in farm space for pigs, the systematic use of painkillers for the castration of piglets and an extension/increase in farm space for laying hens.

The study, conducted with participants at the University of Halle, provides evidence to support the hypothesis of a strong link between willingness to pay and altruism. Indeed, for three of the four measures studied, individuals with higher altruism scores also indicate a stronger willingness to pay. However, these correlations lose their explanatory power when other explanatory variables are added to the statistical model. The authors explain this loss of explanatory power by the fact that the altruism scale chosen is not necessarily adapted to altruism towards animals, which could differ from altruism towards humans or an altruistic propensity in environmental matters. However, in recent work with Nicolas Treich (Espinosa and Treich 2021), we show that individuals who are most committed to humans also pay more for animal welfare, which also reinforces the idea of a strong correlation between a general altruism factor and willingness to pay towards animals.

6.3.5. *Does social pressure affect our altruism towards animals?*

Among the reasons that may affect this willingness to pay, Bennett and Blaney (2002) were interested in the relationship between the moral weight of animal welfare and social consensus. The authors sought to understand whether our moral considerations for the animal condition, and thus our altruism towards them, depend on the collective perception of the subject. In an experiment with a sample of students from the University of Reading, the authors measured participants' willingness to pay for more protective legislation for pigs being killed in two scenarios. In the first case, students were presented with the measure as highly consensual (supported by associations such as CIWF and by the majority of the population). In the second case, the measure was presented as not very consensual, with differing scientific opinions on the effectiveness of the method provided by law.

The study authors showed that a majority of students (61%) support this legislation. The average willingness to pay to implement this legislation is estimated at £1.37 per week across the sample (out of an average weekly food budget of £21.73). However, the results show that this support is strongly influenced by the level of social consensus presented. The average willingness to pay was £2.75 per week when high social consensus was presented, as opposed to £1.09 per week for low social consensus. The authors conclude that the presence of a strong social consensus towards animal welfare reinforces the moral weight in individuals, who therefore become more altruistic towards animals.

6.4. Limitations and perspectives

Contingent valuation methods and choice experiments provide a good approximation of the degree of altruism of human beings towards animals. Through the examples given, we can see that these methods make it possible to discuss a wide range of situations, from animal husbandry to hunting and domestic animals. Different altruistic considerations are observed for different species. This willingness to pay varies according to the moral weight that an individual gives to their activity towards animals, which seems to capture the idea of altruism. The amounts calculated turn out to be relatively high and sometimes enable the emergence of spontaneous mechanisms on the market (such as labels). In some cases, however, the state must play a coordinating role and change legislation to bring altruisms together.

An important limitation is that these methods quantify animal welfare in monetary terms. Other methods have recently been proposed to see the extent to which humans value the lives of animals in the same way that researchers have valued human life. In a recent study, Weathers and co-authors (2020) explain that the lives of humans are often analyzed by the DALY (disability-adjusted life year) indicator. One less unit of DALY can be conceptualized as losing one year of healthy life. This indicator has proven to be very useful for comparing the impact of very different diseases or accidents in humans.

The objective of Weathers and his co-authors was to propose a similar indicator, allowing the comparison of animal abuse situations for different species (cattle, pigs, chickens) and for different farming situations (cage or free-range farming). The authors constructed the SAMY (species-adjusted measure of suffering-years) scale, from an online questionnaire given to US respondents. In order to define equivalences between different situations of suffering, the authors asked questions including two scenarios, such as the following:

> The first program prevented 1,000 perfectly healthy pigs from contracting a disease that would have quickly killed them. The second program prevented X pigs from being unnaturally and disproportionately fattened, which would have led to bone fractures, respiratory problems and frequent heart attacks. What is the lowest value of X that would make you say that the second program reduced suffering more overall than Program 1 [1, 500, 1,001, 2,000, 5,000, 10,000, 100,000, 1,000,000]?

Such methods hold promise for discussing the social choice between human and animal interests. Indeed, one-third of the study's respondents indicated that they thought animal suffering should be considered at least in the same way as human suffering. These methods could include human–animal comparisons in the questions, allowing for the establishment of a common cross-species scale[3]. Such a scale would still be anthropocentric and would consider animals only through the lens of human altruism, but could represent a first major step towards considering the interests of animals. The shift to the direct consideration of animals is surely one of the greatest challenges facing the economics of the animal condition in the coming years.

6.5. References

Bateman, I.J., Burgess, D., Hutchinson, W.G., Matthews, D.I. (2008). Learning design contingent valuation (LDCV): NOAA guidelines, preference learning and coherent arbitrariness. *Journal of Environmental Economics and Management*, 55(2), 127–141.

Bennett, R.M. (1998). Measuring public support for animal welfare legislation: A case study of cage egg production. *Animal Welfare*, 7(1), 1–10.

Bennett, R.M. and Blaney, R.J. (2002). Social consensus, moral intensity and willingness to pay to address a farm animal welfare issue. *Journal of Economic Psychology*, 23(4), 501–520.

Bennett, R.M. and Blaney, R.J. (2003). Estimating the benefits of farm animal welfare legislation using the contingent valuation method. *Agricultural Economics*, 29(1), 85–98.

Bennett, R.M. and Larson, D. (1996). Contingent valuation of the perceived benefits of farm animal welfare legislation: An exploratory survey. *Journal of Agricultural Economics*, 47(1–4), 224–235.

Blackorby, C. and Donaldson, D. (1992). Pigs and guinea pigs: A note on the ethics of animal exploitation. *The Economic Journal*, 102(415), 1345–1369.

Carlsson, F., Frykblom, P., Lagerkvist, C.J. (2007). Consumer willingness to pay for farm animal welfare: Mobile abattoirs versus transportation to slaughter. *European Review of Agricultural Economics*, 34(3), 321–344.

Clark, B., Stewart, G.B., Panzone, L.A., Kyriazakis, I., Frewer, L.J. (2017). Citizens, consumers and farm animal welfare: A meta-analysis of willingness-to-pay studies. *Food Policy*, 68, 112–127.

Driscoll, J.W. (1995). Attitudes toward animals: Species ratings. *Society & Animals*, 3(2), 139–150.

---

3. For example, Wilks et al. (2020) ask participants whether they would prefer to save one human or 100 humans.

Eldridge, J.J. and Gluck, J.P. (1996). Gender differences in attitudes toward animal research. *Ethics & Behavior*, 6(3), 239–256.

Emons, W. (2001). Credence goods monopolists. *International Journal of Industrial Organization*, 19(3–4), 375–389.

Erian, I. and Phillips, C.J. (2017). Public understanding and attitudes towards meat chicken production and relations to consumption. *Animals*, 7(3), 20.

Espinosa, R. (2019). L'éléphant dans la pièce. Pour une approche économique de l'alimentation végétale et de la condition animale. *Revue d'économie politique*, 129(3), 287–324.

Espinosa, R. (2022). Animals and social welfare. *Mimeo*.

Espinosa, R. and Treich, N. (2020). Animal welfare: Antispeciesism, veganism and a "life worth living". *Social Choice and Welfare*, 56, 531–548.

Espinosa, R. and Treich, N. (2021) Moderate versus radical NGOs. *American Journal of Agricultural Economics*, 103, 1478–1501.

Fleurbaey, M. and Van der Linden, M. (2021). Fair social ordering, egalitarianism, and animal welfare. Egalitarianism, and animal welfare. *American Economic Journal: Microeconomics*, forthcoming.

Fonta, W.M., Ichoku, H.E., Kabubo-Mariara, J. (2010). The effect of protest zeros on estimates of willingness to pay in healthcare contingent valuation analysis. *Applied Health Economics and Health Policy*, 8(4), 225–237.

Frey, U.J. and Pirscher, F. (2018). Willingness to pay and moral stance: The case of farm animal welfare in Germany. *PloS One*, 13(8), e0202193.

Herzog Jr., H.A., Betchart, N.S., Pittman, R.B. (1991). Gender, sex role orientation, and attitudes toward animals. *Anthrozoös*, 4(3), 184–191.

Johansson-Stenman, O. (2018). Animal welfare and social decisions: Is it time to take Bentham seriously? *Ecological Economics*, 145, 90–103.

Lagerkvist, C.J. and Hess, S. (2011). A meta-analysis of consumer willingness to pay for farm animal welfare. *European Review of Agricultural Economics*, 38(1), 55–78.

Mulder, M. and Zomer, S. (2017). Dutch consumers' willingness to pay for broiler welfare. *Journal of Applied Animal Welfare Science*, 20(2), 137–154.

Seibert, L. and Norwood, F.B. (2011). Production costs and animal welfare for four stylized hog production systems. *Journal of Applied Animal Welfare Science*, 14(1), 1–17.

Tonsor, G.T. and Wolf, C.A. (2011). On mandatory labeling of animal welfare attributes. *Food Policy*, 36(3), 430–437.

Vrij, A., Nunkoosing, K., Knight, S., Cherryman, J. (2003). Using grounded theory to examine people's attitudes toward how animals are used. *Society & Animals*, 11(4), 307–327.

Weathers, S.T., Caviola, L., Scherer, L., Pfister, S., Fischer, B., Bump, J.B., Jaacks, L.M. (2020). Quantifying the valuation of animal welfare among Americans. *Journal of Agricultural and Environmental Ethics*, 33(2), 261–282.

Wilks, M., Caviola, L., Kahane, G., Bloom, P. (2020). Children prioritize humans over animals less than adults do. *Psychological Science*, 32, 28–38.

7

Causing Pain versus Killing

Tatjana Višak

Department of Philosophy and Business Ethics,
University of Mannheim, Germany

7.1. Introduction

In animal ethics, there is a broad consensus that causing animal pain matters morally and ought *ceteris paribus* to be avoided. That pain, or suffering more generally, ought to be avoided *ceteris paribus* means that it should be avoided unless there is some special fact that justifies it in a particular situation. For example, I may undergo some painful treatment at the dentist in order to prevent greater suffering that I would otherwise have experienced later on. In that case, the fact that the treatment benefits me overall may justify the dentist's painful actions. I may also decide to sacrifice some of my welfare for a greater benefit to others, or even to harm someone else in order to prevent greater harm to others. Whether and, if so, under what circumstances such things are justified is controversial in ethics. But in any case, causing someone to suffer is considered morally problematic in the sense that it is in need of a justification. This holds for the suffering of humans as well as for the suffering of non-humans. After all, in spite of many differences, humans and sentient non-humans have one important commonality: they are both subjects of well-being, and what happens to them can make them better or worse off. Their well-being matters to them, in the sense that it makes a difference for them how they feel: a difference they care about. Sentient beings have an interest in not suffering, and it is broadly agreed that this interest ought to be considered.

Some ethicists disagree. These ethicists hold that the moral community, that is, the scope of those who deserve moral consideration, should not include all sentient

Animal Suffering,
coordinated by Florence BURGAT and Emilie DARDENNE. © ISTE Ltd 2023.

beings. For example, contractarians conceive of ethics in general as an imaginary contract between moral agents. In pursuit of their rational self-interest, moral agents agree to accept some restrictions on their liberty under the condition that others do so as well. So, for example, they agree not to injure others provided that others will not injure them. In this view, morality is based on an imaginary agreement among rational moral agents in pursuit of their self-interest. Those sentient beings that are not rational moral agents are not parties in that imaginary contract and the contractors have no moral duties towards them, according to contractarianism. Kantianism also traditionally restricts the moral community to moral agents, that is, to those who can act on the basis of moral principles. According to Kant, the moral community consists only of those who can act on moral principles. As with contractarians, this excludes many sentient beings, both human and non-human. Nowadays, however, there are authors both in the Kantian and in the contractarian tradition who argue in favor of granting all sentient individuals' moral status (Rowlands 2009; Korsgaard 2016).

Utilitarianism is a moral theory that takes animal welfare seriously from the very beginning. For example, Jeremy Bentham (1963), one of the founding fathers of utilitarianism, already argued with regard to non-human animals that the question is not whether they can reason or talk, but whether they can suffer. Peter Singer (1995), one of the most influential contemporary utilitarians and animal ethicists, builds on Bentham's dictum in his groundbreaking work *Animal Liberation*. Singer argues that counting the welfare of non-humans for less than that of humans amounts to a form of discrimination similar to racism or sexism. Singer uses the label "speciesism" to denote wrongful discrimination on the basis of species. Like many other animal ethicists, Singer argues in favor of equal consideration of interests, that is, of well-being. According to this principle, same amounts of suffering matter equally, no matter whether the suffering individual is a dog, a cow or a human. Equal consideration of interests does not entail equal treatment, since differences in interests can justify different treatments.

Humans do a lot of harm to non-humans for minor self-interested preferences, such as certain gustatory pleasures or economic interests. For example, billions of animals suffer in intensive animal farming at any point in time, even though humans could survive and be healthy without consuming these animals' products. In fact, not consuming these products would have major benefits when it comes to human health and survival. Animal ethicists broadly condemn intensive animal farming as speciesist and morally unacceptable. The same holds for many other practices in which humans exploit non-humans.

Yet, even those who accept the principle of equal consideration of interests and take non-human welfare as seriously as human welfare do not necessarily condemn the routine killing of non-humans in animal husbandry and in similar practices. For example, some authors in animal ethics would accept practices of so-called "animal-friendly" animal husbandry or "humane carnivorism". These labels refer to all practices in which animals are granted pleasant lives and are killed painlessly for human consumption. The remainder of this chapter considers (and tentatively rejects) three different justifications for this position that can be found in the animal ethics literature.

7.2. Animals and the harm of death

The first justification of humane carnivorism rests on the assumption that death, in contrast to pain, does not harm an animal. In order to understand and evaluate this line of argumentation, we need to turn to theories about the harm of death. When we talk about the harm of death for an individual, we do not consider effects on others. Furthermore, in discussions about the harm of death, we talk about cases in which a life ends sooner rather than later. We contemplate a life that ends at a particular time, say t1, rather than at some later time, say t2. Thus, we do not compare mortality to immortality. We also do not talk about the process of dying, but simply about the fact that a life ends at some point in time rather than at a later point in time. The suffering that may be involved in the process of dying does not belong to the harm of death, thus understood. Lastly, we assume that the state of being dead is not as such good, bad or neutral for an individual. Rather, the welfare subject has ceased to exist, so there ⟍ nobody for whom it can be good, bad or neutral to be dead.

If death wer   at for some individuals than for others, this could justify killing some of   or purposes that would not justify the killing of the others. For example, if death were a lesser harm for some non-human animals, this might justify killing them for our gustatory pleasure, while it is not justified to kill humans for this purpose. Differences with regard to the harm of death would also justify killing some rather than others in cases in which someone had to be killed in order to prevent greater harm. For example, if we had to throw one individual out of an overcrowded lifeboat that would otherwise sink, we could base our choice on differences regarding the harm of death. If death was a lesser harm for a dog than it is for a human, we could sacrifice a dog instead of a human, for example. Lastly, if death were not harmful for cows, pigs and chickens, this could justify the practice of humane carnivorism and explain, as it were, why we are not allowed to kick these animals, while we are allowed to kill them. It is therefore important to consider what determines how harmful having a shorter rather than a longer life is for an individual.

7.2.1. *Frustration of wants*

One influential position, which we can call the "frustration view" on the harm of death, holds that death harms a being to the extent that it frustrates the fulfillment of their desires. Imagine that I have the desire to go to Paris tomorrow and I die tonight. In that case, the harm of death according to the frustration view consists of preventing me from fulfilling my desire to go to Paris and of preventing me from fulfilling all other desires that I had before I died and that remained unfulfilled due to my death. Dying later rather than earlier is not necessarily less harmful for an individual in that view. But it typically is less harmful, since people tend to have fewer and weaker desires for the future towards the end of their natural lifespans. Peter Singer accepted this frustration view on the harm of death throughout much of his career (Singer 2011). "Frustration" here is a technical term for an unfulfilled desire. What matters is that a desire remains unfulfilled. It does not matter whether an individual actually feels frustrated in the sense of being sad and angry about it. In fact, having died precludes the possibility of being sad or angry about anything. Yet, death may prevent individuals from fulfilling their desires, which thus remain unfulfilled.

Beings that have a conception of their own existence across time usually have plans and projects for the nearer and further away future, along with the general desire to go on living. In contrast, beings that lack a conception of their own existence across time lack a desire for continued life. They only have immediate and short-term desires, such as the desire to escape frightening or painful situations, the desire to eat and the desire to rest. Thus, according to the frustration view, death is typically a greater harm for normal adult humans than for sentient non-humans, since the former typically wish to continue living and have all kinds of plans for the future. Most non-human animals, in contrast, do not have a conception of their own existence across time. They live in the moment. So, death counts as a significantly lesser harm for them in this view. Unborn and newly born babies, as well as some mentally severely impaired humans, are comparable to non-human animals in this regard. Singer (2011) argued that death is, for this reason, not particularly harmful for these individuals. In this view, death at some particular point in time is good for an individual just in case continued life would frustrate more of their current desires than death. Most proponents of the frustration view hold that the relevant desires are idealized desires rather than actual desires. For example, the relevant desires must be well informed and rational.

On the basis of this account of the harm of death, Singer argued that death is not a great harm for most non-human animals. He also argued that abortion and infanticide do not harm the baby in question, since it has no future-directed desires that death frustrates. What desires particular individuals actually have is, of course, an empirical question. It is very relevant when it comes to the practical implications of the frustration view on the harm of death. It does seem true, though, that most sentient non-humans, as well as human babies and some severely mentally impaired humans, live solely in the present. If so, death does not harm them, or not very much, according to the frustration view.

7.2.2. Deprivation of value/life comparative view

An alternative account of the harm of death does not focus on the frustration of what the individual wants. Instead, it focuses on the loss of what would have been valuable for the individual in question. It conceives of the harm of death as the deprivation of the well-being that the individual would otherwise have experienced in the future. This so-called deprivation view on the harm of death does not consider how much a being wants their future, but rather how much value the future would have had for the individual in question (Bradley 2009). So, for example, if a zebra dies, the animal is thereby deprived of the good and bad experiences that it would otherwise have had, had it lived longer. Depending on whether its future would have been good, bad or neutral for the zebra, dying at a particular time rather than at a particular later time is harmful, beneficial or neutral for it.

Of course, we do often not know when an individual would otherwise have died and what would have happened until then. The deprivation view only tells us that depending on the counterfactual scenario, death at a particular time harms or benefits the individual to some degree. In practice, we may only be able to make informed guesses about what would have been the case.

In this view, death is harmful for all and only individuals who would otherwise have had future life with a positive welfare level. This includes individuals that do not have future-directed desires, such as young babies and certain non-human animals. Death is good in this view for individuals that would otherwise have had a bad future. Killing such an individual would be beneficial for it and would thus be a case of euthanasia. Since this view compares the actual life of an individual to the life that it would otherwise have had (in the counterfactual situation in which it lived longer), it is also called the life comparative view. (Note that claims about the goodness or badness of death do not automatically imply any particular view about the ethics of killing.)

7.3. Population ethics

The second possible justification of humane carnivorism rests on a particular view in population ethics. Population ethics deals with the question of how to promote welfare if what I do has an impact on who will live and how many will live. The impersonal total view in population ethics holds that our concern about the promotion of welfare should be focused on the overall amount of welfare in the universe, rather than on making it the case that better instead of worse lives are lived. If what matters is the amount of welfare in the universe, then killing an animal need not be a problem, even if it harms this animal. After all, bringing another animal into existence that would not otherwise have existed and whose life contains at least as much welfare as the future of the killed animal would have contained can replace the welfare loss that the killing brought about. In this section, I point out some implications of the impersonal total view and introduce some alternative views in population ethics. I tentatively reject the impersonal total view in favor of an alternative view.

In as far as we are to promote well-being, we need to compare outcomes in terms of well-being. But well-being can be understood as either a personal or an impersonal good. "Personal good" refers to the goodness of lives, while "impersonal good" refers to the goodness of the universe. What kind of goodness is the goodness that determines the goodness score of an outcome? In other words: what kind of goodness determines what we have reason to do? What kind of goodness is morally significant? According to impersonal views, this is impersonal goodness. Personal good is only considered to be ethically relevant (but not significant) and it is connected to impersonal good via a conversion function, as will be explained below. In contrast, according to person-affecting views, personal goodness is morally significant (Bader forthcoming).

Proponents of impersonal views tend to accept both kinds of good but consider only impersonal good to be ethically significant. Personal good then has to be converted into impersonal good via a conversion function. This is analogous to converting one kind of currency into another. Even if the conversion rate were 1:1, we still had two different currencies. For example, the conversion function from personal good to impersonal good that the impersonal total utilitarian accepts is linear: one unit of personal good counts for one unit of impersonal good. This means that, according to impersonal total utilitarianism, an outcome is better (in terms of impersonal good) the more personal good it contains. Each additional unit of personal good makes the outcome better from the point of view of the universe, as it were, by exactly one unit.

It may be helpful to contrast the impersonal total view with prioritarianism. They are both impersonal views, and therefore they both need to convert personal good into impersonal good. As we saw, the impersonal total view has a conversion function of 1:1, since every unit of personal good counts for one unit of impersonal good. Prioritarianism, in contrast, counts one additional unit of personal good that comes to a well-off individual for less than one unit of personal good that a bad-off individual gains. While one additional unit of personal good is (by definition) exactly the same amount of *personal* benefit, prioritarians discount the value of additional units of personal good, depending on how well off the recipient already is. So, in the case of *bad-off* individuals, one unit of personal good is converted into one unit of impersonal good, but in the case of *well-off* individuals, one unit of personal good is converted into *less* than one unit of impersonal good. The better-off an individual already is, the less one additional unit of personal value counts towards the impersonal value of the outcome: the conversion function is not linear but concave. This is what "giving priority to the worst-off individuals" means. What ultimately matters for both of these impersonal theories is not personal but impersonal value. The goodness of the outcome for both views is determined by adding up the amount of *impersonal value* that it contains.

Except for the impersonal total view and prioritarianism, there are a variety of further impersonal views. For example, there is the impersonal average view, variable value views and critical level views. For all impersonal views, personal and impersonal good can come apart. I already explained how they may come apart in the case of prioritarianism. On the impersonal average view, if only miserable people exist, it can make an outcome better to add a group of somewhat less miserable people, since this raises the average level of welfare, for example from -10 to -5. Yet, adding additional miserable lives rather than no lives at all does not make it the case that better rather than worse lives are lived. So, adding additional bad-off people is not something that a person-affecting view would recommend.

Different impersonal and person-affecting views on promoting welfare have different implications for the ethics of killing. For example, a counterintuitive implication of an impersonal average view would be that we could make the outcome better by killing all but the best-off individuals. After all, that would (at least *ceteris paribus*) raise the average level of welfare. I am not aware of anyone who defends this position, though.

The impersonal total view implies the replaceability argument. Classical utilitarians were proponents of the impersonal total view, which is still the most commonly accepted view among utilitarians today. Peter Singer (2011) famously discussed this argument in relation to the ethics of killing non-human animals. If we kill a cow that would otherwise have had a pleasant future, the killing diminishes the overall amount of welfare in the universe. Thus, it makes the outcome impersonally worse. But if we bring another cow into existence that would not otherwise have existed and whose life is at least as good as the future life of the killed cow would have been, the overall amount of welfare remains the same. The replaceability argument has been used to justify the routine killing of animals in practices such as meat and dairy production, aquaculture and animal experimentation. Peter Singer (2011) also mentions it in relation to a possible practice of breeding human babies as sources of spare organs.

A precondition of the replaceability argument is that the involved animals' lives are good. If they were bad, the killing would not present a welfare loss after all and nothing needed to be replaced. Simply killing the miserable individuals would improve the situation. In practice, it is questionable whether the animals in the above-mentioned practices have pleasant lives. But at least in principle, there could be practices in which individuals would routinely be killed that would meet the conditions. In these practices, the impersonal total view would allow routinely killing and replacing animals, at least if we bracket other negative effects on overall welfare. (The effects of the practices on the environment, climate, health and resource use would of course need to be considered in a full utilitarian evaluation. Singer (2011) takes these effects to count heavily against the practices in any realistic scenario.)

According to a person-affecting view, killing an animal that would otherwise have had a pleasant future reduces welfare, understood as a personal good. In other words: it makes a life worse. Bringing an animal into existence that has a pleasant life and would not otherwise have existed does not benefit this animal, assuming non-comparativism. According to non-comparativism, existing cannot be better, worse or equally good for a welfare subject than never existing. This is because existence and non-existence are non-comparable in terms of personal goodness. Thus, bringing an animal into existence rather than never bringing it into existence does not improve this animal's life. So, according to the person-affecting view, the practice of killing and replacing an animal makes a life worse while it makes no life better, *ceteris paribus*. Therefore, proponents of person-affecting views reject the replaceability argument. (We can distinguish between wide and narrow person-affecting views, but I will now do so here. Even though these views are importantly different, they agree in their rejection of the replaceability argument, which is our main concern here.)

I consider (wide) person-affecting views more plausible than impersonal views, since I think it matters that individuals lead better rather than worse lives. But the total amount of welfare in the universe as such does not matter. I think that lives are the units that can be better or worse (for the one who lives them) in a meaningful way. I therefore take it to make a morally significant difference that better rather than worse lives are lived. But the total amount of welfare in the world is not something in itself that matters. If we could bring about more total welfare in the universe by a mere addition of a well-off individual, I would think that this is morally neutral.

7.4. Metaethics

The third justification of the claim that killing sentient non-humans, in contrast to causing them pain, is not a problem that rests on a particular position in metaethics. It rests on the view that our normative reasons for action (or what is morally right or wrong) cannot be based on any objective value, because there are no objective values. Therefore, welfare cannot be an objective value either and the fact that killing diminishes an individual's welfare cannot as such make it wrong. According to this subjectivist view about value, valuing subjects confer value on things. So, welfare, just like anything else, is valuable if and only if and because some subjects value it, perhaps under some idealized conditions. The badness of death, in this view, cannot consist of depriving an individual of what would have been objectively good for them. Instead, the badness of death consists of preventing the subject from getting what they actually want, such as, perhaps, going to Paris tomorrow or simply continuing to live.

This subjectivist view in metaethics goes together with the frustration view about the harm of death. In fact, subjectivism is incompatible with the deprivation view on the harm of death, since the latter presupposes that welfare is good for the subject and the more of it, the better, independently of the subject's valuing attitudes and desires. Peter Singer, for example, was a metaethical subjectivist throughout most of his career. He also accepted the frustration view on the harm of death, as mentioned above. When he became an objectivist, he abandoned the frustration view and accepted the deprivation view on the harm of death (Višak 2014).

If value and (thus) normative reasons for action are based on these preferences in one way or the other, then it is relevant what preferences animals actually have. If animals have a preference not to be in pain but lack a preference for continued existence, then this can explain why killing them as such is not a problem, assuming subjectivism in metaethics.

7.5. Conclusion

This chapter is not supposed to settle the issue as to whether killing animals as such is morally problematic, but it indicates what it takes to defend one view or the other in this debate. More specifically, this chapter explored the three major lines of argumentation that are used in the ethical literature to defend the view that even though animal welfare matters, killing animals, even on a massive scale, may be morally unproblematic.

Those who accept that some things are good independently of whether or not they are valued, and that welfare is among these things, are likely to accept the deprivation view about the harm of death and hold that death can be harmful for sentient non-humans. Those who accept the frustration view about the harm of death, perhaps because they are metaethical subjectivists, are likely to argue that death as such does not harm those individuals that do not have any future-directed desires. Independently of whether or not death is harmful for a particular animal, it depends on one's view in population ethics whether one holds that bringing an animal into existence that would not otherwise have existed and whose life contains at least as much welfare as the future life of the killed animal would have contained can outweigh the welfare loss that the killing brings about. This so-called replaceability argument is based on the impersonal total view in population ethics, which evaluates outcomes on the basis of the total amount of welfare that they contain. The person-affecting view, in contrast, evaluates outcomes on the basis of whether they bring it about that better rather than worse lives are lived.

For what it is worth, I am personally drawn towards non-speciesism and the principle of equal consideration of interests, a (wide) person-affecting view in population ethics in conjunction with non-comparativism, as well as objectivism about value and the deprivation view on the harm of death. This combination of views entails that killing harms animals just in case they would otherwise have had a pleasant future and that bringing other animals into existence cannot in any way compensate for this harm. Of course, many animals that are currently killed in intensive agriculture and similar practices would not otherwise have had a pleasant future. But if death does not harm them for this reason, this is only because we treat them in a way that seriously harms them in the first place. Of course, this way of treating sentient beings is problematic according to a non-speciesist position.

In any case, we should not forget that practices in which we routinely kill animals – such as fishing and animal husbandry – are nearly always easily avoidable and they cause a lot of pain and suffering for animals. Therefore, even if killing these animals as such were morally unproblematic, the pain and suffering that these practices involve would already count heavily against them.

7.6. References

Bader, R.M. (forthcoming). Person-affecting utilitarianism. In *Oxford Handbook of Population Ethics*, Bykvist, K. and Campbell, T. (eds). Oxford University Press, Oxford.

Bentham, J. (1963). *An Introduction to the Principles of Morals and Legislation*. Hafner, New York.

Bradley, B. (2009). *Well-Being and Death*. Oxford University Press, Oxford.

Korsgaard, C.M. (2016). A Kantian case for animal rights. In *The Ethics of Killing Animals*, Tatjana, V. and Robert, G. (eds). Oxford University Press. Oxford.

Rowlands, M. (2009). *Animal Rights: Moral Theory and Practice*. Palgrave MacMillan, New York.

Singer, P. (1995). *Animal Liberation*, 2nd edition. Pimlico, London.

Singer, P. (2011). *Practical Ethics*, 3rd edition. Cambridge University Press, New York.

Višak, T. (2014). Review of *The Point of View of the Universe: Sidgwick and Contemporary Ethics*, de Lazari-Radek, K. and Singer, P. (eds). Oxford University Press, New York, 2014, *Ethical Perspectives*, 21(3), 469–471.

8

Wild Animal Suffering

Oscar HORTA

University of Santiago de Compostela, Spain

There is a tendency to imagine the life of animals when they are not the victims of harms by human hands as being very positive, as an ideal of how things should be. This, among several other factors, such as the popularity of environmentalist views, is one of the reasons why many people still have what we can refer to as an idyllic view of the life of animals in the wild[1]. According to this view, animals live happy lives as long as we do not harm them in any way. This is a very nice thought, one we should all deeply wish were true.

Unfortunately, however, there are reasons to question this idyllic view. First, all around the world, people are helping wild animals in different ways. Rescue centers for orphaned, sick or injured wild animals, as well as cases of wild animal rescues from ponds, frozen lakes, or natural disasters are examples of this that appear in the media every now and then. Animals can also be aided indirectly on a very large scale by measures aiming at the promotion of human interests. The best example of this is that of wild animal vaccination programs, which have targeted different diseases to avoid zoonotic outbreaks, saving in the process vast numbers of animals from great amounts of suffering and slow deaths (Animal Ethics 2020a).

These initiatives, and their positive effects in relieving the animals of some serious harms, are at odds with the idea that animals have great lives in the wild. If

---

1. For exceptions, see Mill (1969 [1874], pp. 373–402), Gould (1994) and Dawkins (1995), Darwin (2004 [1901]). Current attitudes toward wild animals among animal advocates and the general public have been studied, respectively, in Morris and Thornhill (2006) and in Waldhorn (2019).

Animal Suffering,
coordinated by Florence BURGAT and Emilie DARDENNE. © ISTE Ltd 2023.

the idyllic view of nature were right, there would be no need for these actions and measures, since animals could not possibly benefit from them. Still, they have made a substantial difference for the animals they have helped. Had these animals not been aided, many of them would have suffered painful deaths. We may think that the animals in these situations are an exception, and that, in general, animals in the wild live happily. However, this does not seem to be an adequate representation of how things work in ecosystems. There are different factors that can be harmful for wild animals, and can cause them to suffer and die prematurely. Hence, our efforts to save them from some of the harms they would otherwise undergo can be very important, and deserve much more attention than the one they have received to date.

This chapter will consider this question, by explaining what wild animal suffering consists of, what the main factors that cause it are and what can be done to prevent it or reduce it now and, especially, in the future. To do this, section 8.1 starts by providing an explanation of the meaning with which the term "wild animal suffering", and other related ones, have been used in the debate about this question. Section 8.2 then explains the reasons why wild animal suffering may be much more significant than most people think, and might actually prevail over positive well-being. Next, section 8.3 presents several feasible ways of helping wild animals, some of which have been implemented already for a long time. Section 8.4 summarizes the case for helping wild animals, which can be seen as a cumulative argument encompassing increasingly strong considerations. Subsequently, section 8.5 introduces the epistemic objection that we cannot have the kind of knowledge necessary to help wild animals. It then presents a series of responses that can be given against this objection. Section 8.6 indicates what kind of work is now needed in order to learn more about how to successfully help wild animals and to increase the attention that is given to this question. Finally, section 8.7 concludes, indicating some of the key ideas that need to be taken into account when thinking about wild animal suffering.

8.1. What does the term "wild animal suffering" mean?

8.1.1. *The harms we are talking about when we speak of wild animal suffering*

When some people first get across the term "wild animal suffering", they imagine that it has something to do with their conservation status. This is understandable, given the current prevalence of both conservationist thinking and disregard for animals as individuals. However, it is a serious misconception. Groups of animals like populations or species do not suffer; only their individual members do. Accordingly, wild animal suffering does not have to do with animal populations or species as such, but with the experiential well-being of their individual members. It therefore has no relation with the number of animals or their conservation status, their biological fitness, their diversity, the kind of influence they have in their ecosystems, or the extent of the areas where they live. It just has to do with how individual sentient animals feel.

There are different circumstances that can negatively affect the animals' well-being. As a result, two different meanings have ended up being given to the expression "wild animal suffering". First, the term has a broad meaning that can cover all the different ways in which wild animals can be harmed, including both anthropogenic (i.e. caused either directly or indirectly by humans) and natural harms. Examples of the former include harms caused by hunting, fishing, poisoning; injuries suffered in collisions with human vehicles; etc. Examples of the latter include starvation, thirst, cold, disease, parasitism, etc. Second, "wild animal suffering" has a more restricted meaning that is used to cover harms that are totally or partially natural. The latter would occur when animals are hurt as a result of a combination of anthropogenic and natural factors. At first sight, it seems that the first meaning should be the one that makes more sense, as the expression "wild animal suffering" does not point at any circumstances in particular under which wild animals may be harmed. However, while anthropogenic harms have traditionally received a great deal of attention, natural harms have been often overlooked. This has happened in the literature in animal ethics, in animal welfare science and in animal advocacy. As a result of this, the second meaning of the term has become prevalent in the literature, to single out and vindicate concern for animal suffering caused by factors that are partly or totally natural, and to name work in helping animals undergoing such harms in both academic work and advocacy (Tomasik 2015a; Faria 2022; Horta 2022; Animal Ethics 2020a; Johannsen 2020). Note that due to humans' constant intervention in the wild, including anthropogenic effects on climate, it might be argued that in fact many of the harms we would think to be natural actually result from a combination of both natural and indirectly anthropogenic factors.

Finally, it is worth noting that the word "suffering" is typically used in the expression "wild animal suffering" in a very loose way. That is, it is not just used to name mental states with negative valence, which is what it means, strictly speaking. Rather, it has been commonly used as a loose shortcut to name any kind of harms suffered by individual animals. These can include suffering, as well as other harms, such as death, which have a negative effect on any aspect of their experiential well-being.

8.1.2. *The animals we are talking about when we speak of wild animal suffering*

In order to understand adequately wild animal suffering, it is also important to clarify what animals we are referring to. The term "wild animal" has different meanings. It is often used to name animals belonging to species that have been domesticated. Alternatively, it is sometimes used to name those living in wild areas where human impact is not very significant. But none of these terms adequately describes what is relevant of the situation of some animals that makes the use of the term "wild animal suffering" adequate to refer to the harms they suffer. Rather, the animals to which this term better applies are those that do not live under direct human control. In other words, those that are not in captivity (as those living in factory farms, for instance) or semi-captivity (as grazing goats living outdoors). An elephant living in a circus and a fox living in a fur farm are subjected to human control, and the (very significant) harms they suffer are fully anthropogenic. Instead, a feral cat or a pigeon living in an urban environment, not being held in captivity, may face some anthropogenic harms, as well as face many natural ones that may not differ from those that animals in the wilderness suffer. The term "wild animal suffering" in its standard usage thus applies in the case of animals not living in captivity. Note also that the word "wild" has absolutely no implication concerning any "ferocious" traits these animals might exhibit.

8.1.3. *Other related terms*

Another term that is sometimes used in order to name how good or bad the lives of these animals are, as well as the study of this topic, is "wild animal welfare". Still, this term has also been used to name the study of the situation of captive wild animals or of animals living in the wild affected by human action (Kirkwood 1992; Kirkwood et al. 1994; Sainsbury et al. 1995; Jordan 2005; Feber et al. 2016; JWD Wildlife Welfare Supplement Editorial Board 2016). In addition, efforts to reduce the harms suffered by wild animals are sometimes referred to as "helping wild animals". This, again, is a loose expression that can include both cases where animals in need receive actual assistance and cases where other types of measures prevent beforehand the harms that animals would otherwise suffer (Tomasik 2015a; Palmer 2019; Animal Ethics 2020a).

8.2. What the lives of wild animals are like

8.2.1. *Factors causing wild animals to suffer*

Now that we have seen how wild animal suffering can be defined, let us look at what it consists of. Assessing accurately the experiential lives of nonhuman animals and how different circumstances may affect them is not easy. Still, there are some reasonable inferences we can make about how their lives can be like under certain conditions. Natural factors threatening animals are very diverse, and include, among others, disease, parasites, lack of food and water, extreme weather conditions, harmful variations in their environments (such as increases and decreases in, for instance, salinity or humidity), conflicts and accidental injuries (Cooper 1999; White 2008; McCue 2010; Wobeser 2013; Faria 2022; Ray 2017). Our own experience when undergoing such harms shows us that they can be very hard to stand, especially when they cause intense pain. The same is true for nonhuman animals. However, unlike what can often happen in our case, there is often no relief whatsoever for them. They cannot enjoy the access we may have to medical treatment, housing, security, food, etc. As a result, we can expect them to suffer very significantly. In fact, we can also, in some cases, assess this by noting how such situations boost their stress (McLaren et al. 2007; Boonstra 2013).

In addition, we can consider certain factors that can be indirect indicators of the presence of negative experiences and of their proportion with respect to positive ones, and yet are observable and measurable. One such indicator which can be used as a proxy for suffering is death (Ng 1995; Horta 2017; Hecht 2021). This is because the factors that typically kill animals in the wild include most of the factors that also cause them to suffer. Animals who die due to lack of water, or starve to death, or are killed by parasites, disease or infected wounds, or freeze to death, etc. are very likely to suffer very significantly in the process. Some wild animals may die quickly, but many undergo protracted deaths that may be very painful. If their lives are long enough, and if they are sufficiently free from substantial sources of harm, animals can also have positive experiences that make their lives better. They die very young, though. This means that they may have to undergo the significant suffering present in the processes that lead to their death without having enough time to enjoy any pleasurable experience. This means that suffering is very likely to prevail in the lives of these animals, thus outweighing pleasure. That is, they live lives which can be concluded to be net negative for them; lives which, from the point of view of the animals themselves, would have been better not to be lived.

8.2.2. *The extent of the harms wild animals suffer*

Unfortunately, many wild animals are likely to be in this situation, as they die shortly after coming into existence. This is related to the fact that the vast majority of animals have reproductive strategies that consist of bringing large numbers of offspring into existence. To be sure, some animals reproduce by just having one offspring at a time and invest a great deal of energy in trying to ensure the survival of their progeny. This happens, for instance, in the case of large mammals like ourselves. But these are a tiny minority. Many animals reproduce by laying hundreds, thousands or sometimes millions of eggs – sunfishes, for instance, reproduce by laying up to 300 million eggs (Fraser-Bruner 1951). It is very difficult for these animals to survive and make it to maturity. In fact, the study of age-specific mortality among many animals indicates that many of them die when they are very young. Others may survive for a bit longer. But, on average, in relatively stable populations, only one offspring per parent will be able to reach maturity and reproduce. This happens especially among fishes, amphibians and reptiles, as well as among many birds and mammals. This is also true for most invertebrates that represent, by several orders of magnitude, the vast majority of animals (Tomasik 2015b).

Because most animals reproduce by having large numbers of offspring, and because the majority of these die when they are very young, it is possible, for the reasons explained above, that the majority of the animals that come into existence may have lives where suffering prevails. Furthermore, it is also possible that aggregate suffering is larger in size than aggregate positive well-being among wild animals in general. This would be so because those who survive their juvenile stages, and do not suffer the fate described above, still often face severe situations of suffering caused by factors such as the ones mentioned above. So we might be too optimistic if we thought that the lives of adult animals are great and typically contained very large amounts of pleasure that could outweigh the suffering of those dying in their youth. There are animals who are likely to have happy lives, but for many others the opposite is probably the case (Ng 1995; Faria and Paez 2015; Faria 2022; Horta 2017, 2022; Johannsen 2020). This is even more relevant as the number of sentient animals living in the wild is very significant – according to some estimations (Tomasik 2015b), it could be of up to between 10^{18} and 10^{22}.

Moreover, the fact that premature death is the norm among many animals can also be harmful in itself, in addition to being negative by occurring in painful ways. According to the prevalent view in philosophy today about the reason why dying can be harmful, this is so because death deprives us of all opportunity to enjoy future goods in our lives (Nagel 1970; McMahan 2002; Scarre 2007). If this is so, then that means all sentient animals may be harmed by death when they cease to exist. According to this, short-lived wild animals would be harmed not only by the suffering they undergo while dying but also by their premature deaths.

We might think that in the case of many animals this would not be the case since they are not sentient, at least not when they are very young. We cannot rule out that this is the case among some animals. The behavior and physiology of many different animals has now been documented, though, and there is a significant amount of evidence that show vertebrates and a very large number of invertebrates are sentient (Allen and Bekoff 1997; Gregory 2004; Sneddon 2004; Low et al. 2012; Broom 2014; Carere and Mather 2019). So, while this argument, if successful, would bring us good news in the case of certain animals, it is unfortunately unlikely that it can be successful in the case of most of the others. Moreover, if indeed some animals are not sentient once they hatch and only become conscious at a later stage, this would mean that those dying before that time would not have suffered, but all those dying afterwards would. Therefore, if the number of animals dying not long after the time when they become conscious is high, suffering may still prevail in these animals' populations. Note that this sets aside the fact that it is difficult to believe animals that have just hatched (for instance, sea turtles trying to reach the sea or small fishes trying to find food) are not sentient.

8.2.3. *Some promising ways of helping animals in the wild*

We may at first think that, as wild animal suffering is so massive, reducing it is a hopeless cause. But it is not. We have also seen that there are different ways in which people all around the world are already helping wild animals in need. In some cases, they do so on their own, when they encounter an animal they can rescue. In other cases, initiatives promoted by private organizations or public institutions can make a difference for a much larger number of animals. These efforts could be expanded. A good strategy may consist of investing more resources in initiatives set up to help wild animals that are likely to be supported both by the general public and scientists[2]. In this way, the knowledge gained in studying these questions can inform actual projects and policies helping many wild animals, as well as foster further research on the topic. Let us now turn to some examples of interventions that appear to be especially promising.

---

2. A study by Animal Ethics (2020b) indicated that scholars and students in life sciences consider research on vaccination, helping animals that are victims of weather events, and helping animals in urban environments as topics of work that are both interesting and likely to be supported in academia.

8.2.4. *Vaccination*

Wild animal vaccination programs have been implemented for decades already[3], targeting diseases as diverse as rabies, tuberculosis, brucellosis and anthrax, among others. These diseases have been successfully eradicated in large areas in the wild thanks to animal vaccination (Rupprecht et al. 2003; Turnbull, et al. 2004; Koenig et al. 2007; Garrido et al. 2011; Gormley et al. 2017). There are several ways in which animals are vaccinated, a common method consisting of the distribution of oral baits containing the vaccine by helicopters.

What is especially relevant here is that vaccination programs all around the world have been well researched and monitored once implemented. This means we have both the knowledge and the technology that are needed to make much more progress in this area. One advantage of these measures is that, in addition to being desirable for the sake of helping animals themselves, they can get significant support and funding due to their benefits for human beings. Actually, they can benefit from the rise of the One Health paradigm in life sciences, according to which humans' and nonhuman animals' health should be safeguarded together (Monath 2013).

8.2.5. *Rescuing animals affected by weather events*

Another way of helping animals that looks promising today has to do with measures helping animals affected by extreme weather events or other natural disasters. We are all familiar with efforts aiming at rescuing human beings when such events occur, as well as with precautionary measures introduced to minimize the harm these events can cause to humans. There have already been efforts to design and implement measures and protocols aiming at rescuing and preventing the harms to nonhuman animals who are the victims of these events (Anderson and Anderson 2006). Nevertheless, they are still very limited, and have often focused on domesticated animals, leaving wild ones behind. Wild animals can benefit from such initiatives in obvious ways, though, and we would think that this is something public opinion can be quite sympathetic about. These measures present another advantage: they should not be opposed by people who object to helping animals when the harms they suffer are not anthropogenic. This is because weather events have been affected by human activities affecting the climate, so the harms that they cause to nonhuman animals can no longer be considered to be purely natural (Palmer 2010, 2019; McCumber and King 2020).

---

3. See, for instance, Baer et al. (1971) for early work on this topic, on which there has been more than half a century of work.

8.2.6. *Helping animals living in urban, suburban, industrial and agricultural areas*

Many wild animals, especially small ones, live in agricultural or suburban areas, and others in the middle of towns and industrial areas. Human activity can be positive or negative for these animals in a variety of ways (Hadidian and Baird 2001; Hadidian and Smith 2001; Burger and Lunney 2004; Adams 2016). It could be perfectly feasible to start working now in designing and implementing programs that could help to harmonize human interests with those of the animals that live in those areas in ways that reduce their suffering, promoting the presence of those who tend to have better lives, rather than those who suffer more. Programs in these areas have the advantage that they would be easier to monitor and control than in other places, so they can be excellent starting points to test different ways of reducing wild animal suffering.

8.2.7. *Contraception*

Another area of work that has many potential benefits for animals in the wild is contraception, especially because it can facilitate other ways of helping animals (Cohn and Kirkpatrick 2015; Vinding 2016; Ansari et al. 2017). Suppose, for instance, that we eradicate a certain disease in an animal population, or that we are able to provide food to another whose members are starving. Suppose further, as it is very plausible, that these measures may cause these populations to increase significantly in the near future, giving rise to worse situations of suffering in them. In such cases, combining those ways of helping animals with contraception programs could avoid this undesirable effect while at the same time eliminate the targeted form of suffering.

Moreover, contraception and vaccination programs can reduce both anthropogenic and natural harms. There are different cases today of animals being killed to prevent them from passing certain diseases either to humans or to domesticated animals. When, in these cases, vaccination programs are introduced, they not only free the wild animals from the diseases causing them to suffer and sometimes to die, but also stop them being killed by humans. Examples of this include the choice between hunting down and vaccinating badgers against tuberculosis in the United Kingdom (Cassidy 2019), or between killing and vaccinating bisons against brucellosis in the Yellowstone area (United States Animal Health Association 2006). In other cases, animals are killed because their populations are no longer able to feed in certain areas and move on to other places inhabited by humans who then consider them to be a nuisance, and may kill them.

Contraception here can help them to have a better quality of life, by having more resources available, and also, again, can free them from being killed by humans.

8.2.8. *Reducing overall wild animal suffering in different ecosystems*

Finally, the study of the situation of wild animals with respect to their well-being can provide guidance for other, more important decisions that can affect a significantly larger number of animals. Conservationist policies and the reforestation of certain areas are cases in point. If the elements we have gathered can lead us to conclude that certain animals tend to have better lives than others, and that certain types of ecosystems are likely to contain less wild animal suffering than others, promoting them would be a way of having a tremendously positive impact for animals.

Examples of this include the protection of large herbivores. These animals reproduce by having just a few offspring to which they give much parental care, and on average tend to have longer life spans where they meet less important hardships than most other animals. Their lives tend therefore to be much better from the point of view of their well-being than those of most wild animals. These animals eat large amounts of biomass, which would otherwise be eaten by much smaller animals who reproduce in very high numbers, and who, for reasons already mentioned, would have significantly worse lives. Accordingly, if no other ripple effects occur, measures protecting these large herbivores may end up promoting scenarios with better overall aggregate and average lives for animals in the ecosystem where they are carried out (Pearce 2015; Faria and Horta 2019).

In conclusion, while wild animal suffering is widespread and extremely large in extent, there are already different ways of addressing it that are very beneficial for animals, that can be implemented in the short term or are being implemented already and that are likely to be supported by many people, including life scientists and policymakers.

8.3. The ethical case for helping wild animals, summarized

In light of what we have explored in previous sections, there seems to be a strong cumulative argument in favor of helping wild animals. There are a number of situations where wild animals are in need of aid due to the action of different factors that are harmful to them. In some of these cases, they are being helped, and it would be possible to provide them even more extensive help with further research and resources. The reason for doing this is very simple: if we can reduce animal suffering without causing more harm, it seems we should do it. This is something we can support even before taking into account other considerations concerning the amount of wild animal suffering there is in the wild (Gompertz 1997 [1824]; Bovenkerk et al. 2003; Hadley 2006; Nussbaum 2006, ch. 5). This is especially important as there are many animals that are not just undergoing some mild pain or discomfort but actually extreme forms of suffering, as it happens when they undergo a slow death. Moreover, many animals have very short lives ending in painful deaths that are likely to have more suffering than pleasure in their lives. Putting an end to their suffering when feasible seems to be even more important. It is even possible that the majority of animals are in this situation. And if this is so, it is actually also a possibility that suffering prevails in the wild. This is much more controversial, but it is not necessary to think that it is correct to support helping animals in the wild. If it is true, though, it gives us further reasons to try to improve the situation of wild animals. The importance this has is increased because of the huge number of sentient wild animals that exist, which is by many orders of magnitude higher than that of humans and also than animals harmed by humans through their use as resources (Tomasik 2015b).

8.4. Epistemic objections

We may conclude that we do not have any sound ethical reasons to oppose helping wild animals. However, there are other types of objections that do not challenge the ethics of helping wild animals but the idea that we can do so successfully. Among these objections, the most important ones are that we have very serious epistemic shortcomings limiting our capacity to make sound assessments of how to help wild animals. According to this, we would not be able to adequately assess how to have a positive impact for them that is not harmful in other much worse ways (Delon and Purves 2018). This is a valid point, but there are several reasons why it should not lead us to inaction, including the following:

First, we must bear in mind that, as this paper has stressed, our focus should now be in doing more research, rather than in taking action right now. Given this, if on the basis of the research already carried out we had reasons to believe that aiding some animals would cause more harm to others than good to these animals, then the recommendation that would follow would not be to do it. Rather, it would be to go on with our research until we get better knowledge about how to best act.

Second, while this objection is pessimistic about our chances to improve things, it seems to assume a very optimistic stance concerning the way things actually are now, given the vast amount of animal suffering in nature. This should lead us to be less reluctant towards our efforts to help animals. In addition, we should bear in mind that such unexpected consequences need not be necessarily negative ones. They could also be positive ones. This should be noted even though we should try to prevent unforeseen consequences in case they are bad.

Third, there is a way to minimize the possible unexpected negative effects of the implemented measures by carrying them out first in areas already significantly transformed by humans, and which humans continue to shape today, such as urban, suburban and industrial areas. Areas where agriculture has very significantly changed the previously existing ecosystems might also make sound candidates. Small-scale programs could be implemented in these areas first. The lessons learned from these pilot programs could be then used to act in safer ways in other places as well.

Fourth, humans are constantly intervening in all kinds of ecosystems to attain different aims, mostly anthropocentric ones, though also sometimes preservationist ones. This happens, for instance, when certain ecosystems are changed through agriculture or through the implementation of different forest or landscape management policies. Note also that disciplines that are regularly applied to guide interventions like these in different ecosystems, such as applied ecology and also conservation biology, are well-established scientific fields today. If this is so, and if we thus accept that there are sound ways to study the results of interventions promoting anthropocentric or preservationist goals, there is no reason to have a radically different view when our aim is to reduce the harms suffered by nonhuman animals.

Fifth, finally, we should not forget that, as we have seen above, different efforts aiding wild animals have been implemented and monitored for a long time already, sometimes on a very large scale, as in the case of vaccination programs.

In light of this, we can conclude that epistemic objections should not stop us from learning more about how to best reduce the harms that wild animals suffer. In the next section, we will see some ways in which this could be done.

8.5. Promoting scientific work in welfare biology

8.5.1. *How previous work can be very useful*

In recent years, a growing number of publications have started to address the question of wild animal suffering. Only a few of these have been authored by life scientists, however, as many have been approached from the viewpoint of practical philosophy, political theory or the philosophy of science (Dorado 2015). This means that while the defense of the normative case for working on reducing wild animal suffering is well underway, there is still a lot to be done when it comes to actual scientific work on the field.

This does not mean that such work is currently starting from zero, though. On the contrary, there is an abundant scientific literature concerning how the lives of animals in nature are. The amount of research already carried out in animal ecology is huge. These studies are not focused on the well-being of animals, which has not been a concern in academic research. However, it is not difficult to see how such a vast knowledge can provide us with the tools to make reasonable inferences about how different factors affect the well-being of animals. For instance, we saw above that death can be used as a proxy for suffering, although it is not always accurate. Studies about the limiting factors and the different causes of mortality that animal populations face can therefore tell us a great deal about the ways in which the animals in such populations suffer. So if we know, for example, that in some situations a certain number of animals starve to death, or die because of parasites, we can easily infer that they are suffering. We have also seen that the study of age-specific mortality in a certain population can give us some clues concerning the proportion of suffering against happiness that there is in that population. Work on age-specific mortality can be illuminating concerning the well-being of different populations of animals. Work on animal behavior can similarly provide some important clues about how animals may be doing from the point of view of their well-being. Other knowledge concerning the way different animals live and interact with their environment can finally provide us with indicators about their well-being, be it positive or negative.

This being so, it is interesting to note that, while field research would be enormously useful, a significant amount of knowledge can be gathered now by carrying out literature reviews focused on factors affecting wild animals negatively from the point of view of their well-being. Meta-analyses of such factors could indeed set the ground for future research.

8.5.2. *Why cross-disciplinary work is needed*

To some extent, we might think that the new work needed here would be an expansion of traditional animal welfare science. After all, it might be argued that what we need here is to move from assessing the factors that affect animals in captivity negatively and positively to assessing these factors for animals living outside direct human control. However, things are more complex than this. The lives of animals living in captivity are almost fully under human control. Humans can determine and change the different factors affecting these animals, including what their surroundings are like, what they eat, whether they get health care, whether they interact with other animals, etc. This does not happen, however, in the case of animals. Hence, in order to understand correctly what factors affect the positive and negative well-being of wild animals, it is not enough to develop ways of assessing such well-being. We also need to learn about how they relate with other organisms and their physical environment, and how the circumstances present in such environment can affect their well-being. In addition, as we have seen above, to successfully implement measures that can help animals without causing harm elsewhere, we need to be able to make sound predictions of the effects that such measures will have. This is part of the work carried out by the science of ecology. Other related disciplines, such as zoology or wildlife management, could also make relevant contributions. Therefore, it appears that the kind of work that is needed here is a cross-disciplinary one that integrates the knowledge of different fields with a focus on their relevance to the positive and negative well-being of animals[4].

This type of work has been referred to with the name "welfare biology", and described as the study of sentient living beings and their environment with respect to their suffering and happiness (Ng 1995; Faria and Horta 2019; Soryl et al. 2021). Such integration of knowledge from different fields would not be new, among other reasons because the sciences of animal welfare and ecology are interdisciplinary themselves as well.

8.5.3. *Benefits for the consideration of the problem and for policymaking*

The promotion of work in this new cross-disciplinary field would be useful not only because it would provide us with the necessary knowledge to inform adequate policies and projects that may make a difference for wild animals, but also because it would provide prestige to the study of this question and to consider wild animal suffering a serious matter that deserves our concern. Finally, academic work in this field would also be necessary to influence decision-makers to include the promotion

---

4. There is already cross-disciplinary work in life sciences combining the approaches of the sciences of animal welfare and ecology (see, for instance, Linklater and Gedir 2011; Cattet 2013; Beausoleil et al. 2018; Hampton and Hyndman 2018). Their aims are usually different from the reduction of wild animal suffering. They have been often motivated by a concern for the anthropogenic harms animals may suffer and for how such harms affect the results conservation scientists may obtain. At any rate, they are examples of how cross-disciplinary work combining these disciplines can be put into practice and of how more training in animal welfare science could be beneficial for ecologists and other life scientists as well.

of interests of animals in the aims to consider when designing new policies potentially affecting wild animals. In this way, it is more likely that we can succeed in making a positive difference for nonhuman animals in the future.

This is especially important because, large as the numbers of currently existing wild animals are, these figures pale in comparison to the number of animals that will live in the future. Accordingly, it makes sense to have a longtermist approach that maximizes our impact not only in the present but also for future animals too. Hence, it might be preferable today to promote courses of action that can maximize our success in fostering and consolidating the interest in the question, rather than our immediate impact reducing some of the harms suffered by animals.

8.6. Conclusion

To date, policies affecting wild animals have been appraised and introduced depending on their impact on human interests, or in some cases on the basis of conservationist and environmentalist considerations. Concern for wild animals requires that the promotion of the interests of animals should be incorporated among the aims that such policies should have.

This is not the case today, as most people are still unaware of the reality of wild animal suffering. Moreover, many identify the moral consideration of wild animals with conservationist views that have to do with animal biodiversity or with their habitats. Yet, the conditions that favor better lives and less suffering for animals are the ones that protect them from the sources of harm that they face, as sentient individual animals, in their lives, not as members of certain species, populations or ecosystems.

Despite this, we have seen that humans are already aiding wild animals in several ways and that there is a huge potential for such efforts to be increased much more significantly. In this chapter, we have seen some examples of particularly promising initiatives in that respect that have been implemented or could be implemented. In the future, it is very likely that helping them in more significant ways might be possible. We need to be more knowledgeable about this issue and raise awareness about the need to help animals. At the moment of writing this chapter, only two animal advocacy organizations are working in this field, which are Animal Ethics and Wild Animal Initiative. More outreach and research is necessary to expand concern about this topic among people sympathetic to the moral consideration of animals and the general public.

Wild animal suffering is huge in scale and has been largely neglected to date, but it is also a tractable area where a significant difference for animals can be made now and, especially, in the future.

8.7. References

Adams, C.E. (2016). *Urban Wildlife Management*. CRC Press, Boca Raton.

Allen, C. and Bekoff, M. (1997). *Species of Mind: The Philosophy and Biology of Cognitive Ethology*. MIT Press, Cambridge.

Anderson, A. and Anderson, L. (2006). *Rescued: Saving Animals from Disaster*. New World Library, Novato.

Animal Ethics (2020a). Introduction to wild animal suffering: A guide to the issues. *Animal Ethics*, Oakland [Online]. Available at: https://www.animal-ethics.org/introduction-wild-animal-suffering [Accessed 26 January 2021].

Animal Ethics (2020b). Surveying attitudes toward helping wild animals among scientists and students. *Animal Ethics*, Oakland [Online]. Available at: https://www.animal-ethics.org/survey-helping-wild-animals-scientists-students [Accessed 26 January 2021].

Ansari, A.S., Ayesha, B., Lohiya, N.K. (2017). Fertility control modalities in animals: An overview. *BAOJ Veterinary Science*, 1, a004.

Baer, G.M., Abelseth, M.K., Debbie, J.G. (1971). Oral vaccination of foxes against rabies. *American Journal of Epidemiology*, 93, 487–490.

Beausoleil, N.J., Mellor, D.J., Baker, L., Baker, S.E., Bellio, M., Clarke, A.S., Dale, A., Garlick, S., Jones, B., Harvey, A. et al. (2018). "Feelings and Fitness" not "Feelings or Fitness"– The raison d'être of Conservation Welfare, which aligns conservation and animal welfare objectives. *Frontiers in Veterinary Science*, 5, a296.

Boonstra, R. (2013). Reality as the leading cause of stress: Rethinking the impact of chronic stress in nature. *Functional Ecology*, 27, 11–23.

Bovenkerk, B., Stafleu, F., Tramper, R., Vorstenbosch, J., Brom, F.W.A. (2003). To act or not to act? Sheltering animals from the wild: A pluralistic account of a conflict between animal and environmental ethics. *Ethics, Place and Environment*, 6, 13–26.

Broom, D.M. (2014). *Sentience and Animal Welfare*. CABI, Wallingford.

Burger, S.K. and Lunney, D. (eds) (2004). *Urban Wildlife: More than Meets the Eye*. Royal Zoological Society of New South Wales, Sydney.

Carere, C. and Mather, J. (eds) (2019). *The Welfare of Invertebrate Animals*. Springer, Dordrecht.

Cassidy, A. (2019). *Vermin, Victims and Disease: British Debates over Bovine Tuberculosis and Badgers*. Palgrave Macmillan, Basingstoke.

Cattet, M.R. (2013). Falling through the cracks: Shortcomings in the collaboration between biologists and veterinarians and their consequences for wildlife. *ILAR Journal*, 54, 33–40.

Cohn, P. and Kirkpatrick, J.F. (2015). History of the science of wildlife fertility control: Reflections of a 25-year international conference series. *Applied Ecology and Environmental Sciences*, 3, 22–29.

Cooper J.E. (1999 [1982]). Physical injury. In *Noninfectious Disease of Wildlife*, Fairbrother, A., Locke, L.N., Hoff, G.L. (eds). Iowa State University Press, Ames.

Darwin, C. (2004 [1901]). Charles Darwin to Asa Gray, May 22nd, 1860. In *The Life and Letters of Charles Darwin*, vol. 2, Kessinger Publishing, Whitefish.

Dawkins, R. (1995). God's utility function. *Scientific American*, 274(6), 80–85.

Delon, N. and Purves, D. (2018). Wild animal suffering is intractable. *Journal of Agricultural and Environmental Ethics*, 31, 239–260.

Dorado, D. (2015). Ethical interventions in the wild: An annotated bibliography. *Relations: Beyond Anthropocentrism*, 3, 219–238.

Faria, C. (2022). *Animal Ethics in the Wild: Wild Animal Suffering and Intervention in Nature*. Cambridge University Press, Cambridge.

Faria, C. and Horta, O. (2019). Welfare biology. In *Routledge Handbook of Animal Ethics*, Fischer, B. (ed.). Routledge, New York.

Faria, C. and Paez, E. (2015). Animals in need: The problem of wild animal suffering and intervention in nature. *Relations: Beyond Anthropocentrism*, 3, 7–13.

Feber, R.E., Raebel, E.M., D'Cruze, N., Macdonald, D.W., Baker, S.E. (2016). Some animals are more equal than others: Wild animal welfare in the media. *BioScience*, 67, 62–72.

Fraser-Bruner, A. (1951). The ocean sunfishes (Family Molidae). *Bulletin of the British Museum (Natural History)*, 1, 89–121.

Garrido, J.M., Sevilla, I.A., Beltrán-Beck, B., Minguijón, E., Ballesteros, C., Galindo, R.C., Boadella, M., Lyashchenko, K.P., Romero, B., Geijo, M.V. et al. (2011). Protection against tuberculosis in Eurasian wild boar vaccinated with heat-inactivated *Mycobacterium bovis*. *PLoS ONE*, 6, e24905.

Gompertz, L. (1997 [1824]). *Moral Inquiries on the Situation of Man and of Brutes*. Edwin Mellen, Lewiston.

Gormley, E., Ní Bhuachalla, D., O'Keeffe, J., Murphy, D., Aldwell, F.E., Fitzsimons, T., Stanley, P., Tratalos, J.A., McGrath, G., Fogarty, N. et al. (2017). Oral vaccination of free-living badgers (*Meles meles*) with Bacille Calmette Guérin (BCG) vaccine confers protection against tuberculosis. *PLoS One*, 12, e0168851.

Gould, S.J. (ed.) (1994). Nonmoral nature. In *Hen's Teeth and Horse's Toes: Further Reflections in Natural History*. W.W. Norton, New York.

Gregory, N.G. (2004). *Physiology and Behaviour of Animal Suffering*. Blackwell, Ames.

Hadidian, J. and Baird, M. (2001). Animal welfare concerns and the restoration of urban lands. *Ecological Restoration*, 19, 271–272.

Hadidian, J. and Smith, S. (2001). Urban wildlife. In *The State of the Animals 2001*, Salem, D.J. and Rowan, A.N. (eds), Humane Society Press, Washington, DC.

Hadley, J. (2006). The duty to aid nonhuman animals in dire need. *Journal of Applied Philosophy*, 23, 445–451.

Hampton, J.O. and Hyndman, T.H. (2018). Underaddressed animal-welfare issues in conservation. *Conservation Biology*, 33, 803–811.

Hecht, L.B.B. (2021). The importance of considering age when quantifying wild animals' welfare. *Biological Reviews*, 96, 2602–2616.

Horta, O. (2017). Animal suffering in nature: The case for intervention. *Environmental Ethics*, 39, 261–279.

Horta, O. (2022). *Making a Stand for Animals*. Routledge, Oxford.

Johannsen, K. (2020). *Wild Animal Ethics: The Moral and Political Problem of Wild Animal Suffering*. Routledge, London.

Jordan, B. (2005). Science-based assessment of animal welfare: Wild and captive animals. *Revue Scientifique et Technique-Office International des Epizooties*, 24, 515–528.

JWD Wildlife Welfare Supplement Editorial Board (2016). Advances in animal welfare for free-living animals. *Journal of Wildlife Diseases*, 52, (supp. 2), S4–S13.

Kirkwood, J.K. (2013). Wild animal welfare. *Animal Welfare*, 22, 147–148.

Koenig, P., Lange, E., Reimann, I., Beer, M. (2007). CP7_E2alf: A safe and efficient marker vaccine strain for oral immunisation of wild boar against classical swine fever virus (CSFV). *Vaccine*, 25, 3391–3399.

Linklater, W.L. and Gedir, J.V. (2011). Distress unites animal conservation and welfare towards synthesis and collaboration. *Animal Conservation*, 14, 25–27.

Low, P., Panksepp, J., Reiss, D., Edelman, D., Van Swinderen, B., Koch, C. (2012). The Cambridge Declaration on Consciousness [Online]. Available at: http://fcmconference. org/img/CambridgeDeclarationOnConsciousness.pdf [Accessed 12 January 2021].

McCue, M.D. (2010). Starvation physiology: Reviewing the different strategies animals use to survive a common challenge. *Comparative Biochemistry and Physiology A: Molecular and Integrative Physiology*, 156, 1–18.

McCumber, A. and King, Z. (2020). The wild in fire: Human aid to wildlife in the disasters of the anthropocene. *Environmental Values*, 29, 47–66.

McLaren, G., Bonacic, C., Rowan, A. (2007). Animal welfare and conservation: Measuring stress in the wild. In *Key Topics in Conservation Biology*, Macdonald, D.W. and Service, K. (eds). Blackwell, Malden.

McMahan, J. (2002). *The Ethics of Killing: Problems at the Margins of Life*. Oxford University Press, Oxford.

Mill, J.S. (1969 [1874]). *Nature. Collected Works*, vol. 10, Routledge, London.

Monath, T.P. (2013). Vaccines against diseases transmitted from animals to humans: A one health paradigm. *Vaccine*, 31, 5321–5338.

Morris, M.C., and Thornhill, R.H. (2006). Animal liberationist responses to non-anthropogenic animal suffering. *Worldviews*, 10, 355–379.

Nagel, T. (1970). Death. *Noûs*, 4, 73–80.

Ng, Y.-K. (1995). Towards welfare biology: Evolutionary economics of animal consciousness and suffering. *Biology and Philosophy*, 10, 255–285.

Nussbaum, M.C. (2006). *Frontiers of Justice: Disability, Nationality, Species Membership*. Harvard University Press, Cambridge.

Palmer, C.A. (2010). *Animal Ethics in Context*. Columbia University Press, New York.

Palmer, C.A. (2019). Assisting wild animals vulnerable to climate change: Why ethical strategies diverge. *Journal of Applied Philosophy*, March 3rd.

Pearce, D. (2015). A welfare state for elephants? A case study of compassionate stewardship. *Relations: Beyond Anthropocentrism*, 3, 133–152.

Ray, G. (2017). Parasite load and disease in wild animals. *Wild Animal Suffering Research* [Online]. Available at: https://was-research.org/paper/parasite-load-disease-wild-animals [Accessed 5 October 2020].

Rupprecht, C.E., Hanlon, C.A., Slate, D. (2003). Oral vaccination of wildlife against rabies: Opportunities and challenges in prevention and control. *Developments in Biologicals*, 119, 173–184.

Sainsbury, A.W., Bennett, P.M., Kirkwood, J.K. (1995). Welfare of free-living wild animals in Europe: Harm caused by human activities, *Animal Welfare*, 4, 183–206.

Scarre, G. (2007). *Death*. Acumen, Stocksfield.

Sneddon, L.U. (2004). Evolution of nociception in vertebrates: Comparative analysis of lower vertebrates. *Brain Research Reviews*, 46, 123–130.

Soryl, A.A., Moore, A.J., Seddon, P.J., King, M.R. (2021). The case for welfare biology. *Journal of Agricultural and Environmental Ethics*, 34, 1–25.

Tomasik, B. (2015a). The importance of wild animal suffering. *Relations: Beyond Anthropocentrism*, 3, 133–152.

Tomasik, B. (2015b). How many wild animals are there? *Essays on Reducing Suffering* [Online]. Available at: http://reducing-suffering.org/how-many-wild-animals-are-there [Accessed 11 January 2021].

Turnbull, P.C.B., Tindall, B.W., Coetzee, J.D., Conradie, C.M., Bull, R.L., Lindeque, P.M., Huebschle, O.J.B. (2004). Vaccine-induced protection against anthrax in cheetah (*Acinonyx jubatus*) and black rhinoceros (*Diceros bicornis*). *Vaccine*, 22, 3340–3347.

United States Animal Health Association (2006). *Enhancing Brucellosis Vaccines, Vaccine Delivery, and Surveillance Diagnostics for Elk and Bison in the Greater Yellowstone Area: A Technical Report from a Working Symposium Held August 16–18, 2005 at the University of Wyoming*. The University of Wyoming Haub School and Ruckelshaus Institute of Environment and Natural Resources, Laramie.

Vinding, M. (2016). The speciesism of leaving nature alone, and the theoretical case for wildlife anti-natalism. *Apeiron*, 8, 169–183.

Waldhorn, D.R. (2019). Toward a new framework for understanding human–wild animal relations. *American Behavioral Scientist*, 63, 1080–1100.

White, T.C.R. (2008). The role of food, weather and climate in limiting the abundance of animals. *Biological Reviews*, 83, 227–248.

Wobeser, G.A. (2013). *Investigation and Management of Disease in Wild Animals*. Springer, Dordrecht.

9

Reflections on the Ethics of Veterinary Medicine

Philippe DEVIENNE

Practicing Veterinarian and Doctor of Philosophy, Vincennes, France

> *"My task which I am trying to achieve is, by the power of the written word, to make you hear, to make you feel – it is, before all, to make you see."*
>
> Joseph Conrad, *The Nigger of the "Narcissus"*, Preface, 1897.

9.1. Introduction

The ubiquitous position of the veterinary profession is reflected in the many ethical questions it comes across. It is, for example, the justification in helping sports animals to perform in horse betting, or major endurance races for horses, the euthanasia of litters of kittens, or the improvement of animal well-being techniques limited by the profitability constraint of breeding. Veterinarians encounter animals in great distress and owners who, for example, refuse euthanasia for emotional or religious reasons, or out of ignorance. They have to take a stand, even beyond issues of sanitation, on the use of animal meal in cattle feed. They must intervene when the economics of animal husbandry are contrary to the health of the animal. They encounter tensions between the economy of their own business (with its many charges and material costs) and the realization of expensive care for an animal presented by insolvent owners. Should they accept training offered on live animals (mostly pigs) in order to learn new surgical techniques? Do they have the right to remove an organ from a healthy animal, effectively excluding its consent, in order to

Animal Suffering,
coordinated by Florence BURGAT and Emilie DARDENNE. © ISTE Ltd 2023.

graft it onto another animal? Is it legitimate to ask whether a veterinarian can also be a carnist, hunter or aficionado, among others? Do all these ethical dilemmas not place the veterinarian in contradiction with their civil society, while they are a priori expected to be the first defender of the animal condition?

In response to the intense developments in research on experimental animals and the industrialization of animal husbandry, which led to appalling living conditions for livestock from the 1970s onwards, the landscape of animal ethics has seen the development of anti-speciesist theories. In veterinary medicine, research on animal pain and animal behavior, as well as the development of pet medicines, has partially, at least, changed the profession's view of animals. This approach followed the renewal of ethical questions which, in the 1970s and 1980s, no longer sought a foundation for ethics on what is right or wrong, but rather ethics applied to specific fields, particularly medicine. Indeed, the development of technosciences has opened up a field of questioning that was previously unheard of, imposing the search for new ethical pathways. Research in veterinary ethics has therefore been oriented towards ethics applied to conflicting situations in the practice of care and in the use of animals in our society. The task of veterinary ethics is thus to evaluate morally good or bad actions within a given situation, to arbitrate and to decide with the help of reasoning from normative ethics[1].

Can an ethical stance that is limited to the medical principles of the practitioner suffice? Is veterinary medicine ethical? Do the great universal principles not lose sight of specific animals? Can we summon emotions in veterinary ethical thinking? Is there a contradiction between veterinary ethics and animal husbandry? What is the role of justifications in veterinary ethics? Can veterinary ethics be taught? This survey of veterinary ethical thinking will uncover many aspects and aporias of a profession with multiple faces.

9.2. Is medical practice ethical?

9.2.1. *Veterinary medicine is the result of a scientific practice...*

The emergence of anatomical-clinical-medical science and the discovery of the infectious agents responsible for plagues in livestock laid the legitimate foundations for a veterinary profession built on the bedrock of a science superior to that of bonesetters and healers (Hubscher 1999). However, veterinary medicine until the 1980s was extremely reductionist: it considered the animal to simply be a body

---

1. Normative ethics is made up of different theories, such as deontological ethics, contractualism or utilitarianism, for example.

made up of organs and, in animal production, a thermodynamic machine producing, for example, meat, milk and eggs. This positivist attitude was decisive, not in denying, but in ignoring the existence of pain, suffering or consciousness in animals. It could be said that, certainly, things have changed since those days when professors, students and practitioners castrated horses and bull calves with *bruticaine*[2] and cats sterilized without anesthesia in sadly infamous *neutering boxes*, while fighting against what they called the anthropomorphism of the population. Different times, different ways…

However, we must recognize that we still *perceive* animals through this positivist lens. The practice of veterinary medicine does not escape this gap with the patient, which consists of seeing only the symptoms of the disease and not the sick animal, which is then only an object of care limited to a set of genetically based physicochemical dysfunctions. Words such as "misery", "isolation", "vulnerability", "distress", "boredom" and "fear" have been reduced in a neurophysiological ideology to terms such as stress and nociception.

The medical activities established on the basis of scientific investigation are constitutive of a practice qualified as irreproachable in the veterinary community, nowadays driven by approaches such as that of EBM[3], which guides the teaching and ordinal authorities in regulating professional practice. Therapeutics that have not been scientifically tested by proven methods, statistically evaluable and supported by evidence, are therefore a real Pandora's box that can cause significant harm to the animal. Society has relied, until now, on the competence of the veterinary profession to select and train its students, to sanction deviations and illegal practices of medicine and surgery by non-veterinarians and to establish sanitary regulations for the protection of animal and human populations. In return, such a professional attitude towards society marks a requirement of probity towards the animal. It is achieved technically by the application of established guidelines.

Veterinary technoscience has advanced vaccinations, surgery, imaging, medical biology and more. Hospitals and clinics have enabled the development of a very elaborate technology of care. Does this technological deployment echo a consumerist and economic perspective of care, or of the profitability of veterinary structures as professional service companies? This professional evolution has become even more significant with the advent of the financialization of the profession, which certainly enables the quality of the technical facilities of

2. Rollin's pun on the use of local anesthetics that are not analgesic enough when castrating horses (Rollin 2006).
3. Evidence-Based Medicine.

veterinary clinics and hospitals to be developed, but risks limiting the individual freedoms of practitioners who are subject to the profitability of the capital invested.

9.2.2. ... which establishes deontic actions qualified as irreproachable...

Veterinary medicine follows a set of deontic rules[4] (Sadegh-Zadeh 2012) that allow for successful diagnosis and medical or surgical treatment. Prescriptions, not truth values, determine *human action.* This enables an *approach qualified as irreproachable* when the veterinarian follows this deontic logic. Any action outside this set of prescriptions is unfit for the medical act, whether it is preventive, diagnostic or curative. These actions that allow for treatment are reported in journals on veterinary medicine and manuals in the form of nosological entities that describe the treatment (*cure*). This form of narrative recounts, for instance, clinical examinations, tables of biological and hematological data, and radiographic and ultrasound images, and is expressed in terms of arid *clinical case* reports written in an imposed style. This approach distances itself from the singular animal.

However, veterinary medicine does not guarantee ethical practices simply because it obeys deontic logic in its medical practice. Ethics also follow a deontic logic with its imperatives. As a matter of fact, there are no *specific criteria* for identifying the linguistic characteristics of ethical statements, nor, for that matter, any meta-ethical analyses (Laugier 2006). Ethical judgments cannot be reduced to statements containing deontics such as "must" or "be obliged to" in both universal and very specific contexts (Putnam 2013). It should simply be emphasized that the transition between the practice of the medical deontic imperative and the ethical position of *blamelessness* – where no blame could be attached in our ethical approach – is dubious at best.

---

4. Scientific veterinary medicine elaborates *speech acts* structured by *deontic logic* (*deon* = obligation) imposing established conducts for the prevention, diagnosis and treatment of animal diseases. It functions by using *deontic operators* that can be broken down into several subclasses: 1) obligation (mandatory; must; requires); 2) prohibition (forbid; prohibition; not allowed; wrong; unacceptable; immoral); 3) permission (permissible, allowed, admissible); 4) optionality (optional, voluntary); and 5) freedom (free, not obligatory). These operators are found in the legal sphere ("it is forbidden to steal"), in ethics ("we have a duty to respect our elders"), but also in veterinary medicine. For example, *obligation* ("The monitoring of biting dogs *is mandatory*"; "Reporting tuberculosis *is mandatory*"); *propriety* (if animal X presents clinical sign A, then it is *appropriate to* perform complementary examination B); *prohibition* (it *is forbidden* to issue antibiotics without a prescription), and so on (Sadegh-Zadeh 2012, Modal extensions of classical logic, p. 928).

9.2.3. ... while science cannot be the guardian of morality

The analysis of the semantic field also reveals to us that the conceptual categories contained in the discourses on biology do not totally *overlap* with the categories of ordinary discourse. In other words, the scope of the biological concepts of the animal, the biological concept of pain or the biological concept of death cannot be identical to the scope of the ordinary concepts of the animal, pain or death (Diamond 2011b, p. 151). The category of the biological discourse on death, including the cessation of vital functions, etc., cannot be superimposed with the category of the ordinary discourse on death, with its experiences including anguish, grief, sorrow and funeral rituals. Similarly, the biological notion of pain does not overlap with the ordinary notion of pain. In other words, there is a biological dimension of the animal (as there could be a biological dimension of the human), but neither the animal nor the human can be contained only within this biological dimension, and ethics will have to accommodate this difference.

While the profession can, almost, act with one voice, from a medical point of view, to coordinate national or international activities in case of epizootics, concerning the positions and actions to be taken in order to limit sanitary risks, for example, in the restriction of the use of antibiotics in animals within the framework of antibiotic resistance, it is not the same when it comes to ethical considerations.

Professional bodies establishing codes of ethics dwelt at length, between the 1970s and 2000s, on the internal rules of the profession, long before considering the question of duties towards animals, animal welfare or (belated) stances on, for example, bullfighting. Professional tensions are also present on other issues such as those concerning circus animals, ritual slaughter and veganism. In each case, these reflections are aiming to modify the practice.

Thus, we cannot know what is right or good to do in the many ethical questions we encounter, since we are steeped in our cultural, philosophical and religious contexts, for instance, which are often aporetic about them. Also, ethical resolutions are largely controversial (Putnam 2013). Within what framework can we consider the validity of such ethical reflections? There can be no objective foundation in ethics: only the framework of an intersubjective assembly can be envisaged in questionings that are, by nature, pluralistic.

This intersubjective assembly that constitutes the *ethics committee* cannot be limited to the veterinary profession alone. Such an attitude would then take on characteristics of corporatism, where the profession itself would become closed in. Indeed:

Professional goodwill does not allow for any new decision to be taken in a crisis situation if it is not enlightened and guided by a reflection of an order other than simple professional competence or simple technical coherence. [...] Ethics is precisely this reflection on the grounds of action and, consequently, on its content, meaning and responsibility (Misrahi 2006, p. 81).

A reflection on ethics needs contributors from outside the veterinary profession, to enable exchanges on all the professional aspects and difficulties that it encounters. Veterinary ethics must pass beyond the values of science and market logic. Dealing with issues such as the use of animal meal and cannibalism, for example, or the genetic modification of species, requires highly technical debates and therefore a particular competence among those involved (Doucet 2006). However, that *experts* specialized in these technicalities wind up being the guardians of a moral authority is not appropriate: ethics in the hands of scientific experts alone causes the very notion of ethics to disappear (Diamond 1995a). The intersubjective ethics committee takes on its meaning within a dimension analogous to that of a democratic debate, comprised of veterinarians, of course, but also of lawyers, philosophers, sociologists, ethologists, or even political scientists, economists, or *the man on the street*. Such a heterogeneous community makes it possible to obtain a synoptic vision of the scope of application of ethics.

9.3. What kind of ethics?

Health professionals in human medicine, aware that their training does not help them to solve ethical dilemmas, have wished for developments in medical ethics. The same was true in the 1970s and 1980s in French veterinary schools. It was at the request of students, in reaction to this technical veterinary care training, that a discreet breakthrough was made, outside the imposed programs. Veterinary medicine journals were also slow to present sporadic articles on ethics, despite the publication of books on veterinary ethics in the United States.

Principles established on the basis of consequentialism and deontologism, for example, have emerged, in order to establish the foundations of a medical ethical theory. Masterful ethical theories such as John Rawls' (1971) *Theory of Justice* suggested a similar development in medical ethics. It would be misleading and tedious to provide a catalog of the various ethical theories that would act as a recipe book for the ethical dilemmas encountered in veterinary medicine. Instead, we will consider a spatial approach outlining a field of reflection whose outline will be constituted, on the one hand, by a theoretical approach, *the Principles approach*, and, on the other, by an anti-theoretical approach, *casuistry* (Arras 2016).

9.3.1. *From Principles to casuistry*

9.3.1.1. *The Principles approach*

The Principles approach can form the basis for veterinary medical reflection.

In 1979, Beauchamp and Childress (2020) identified four principles of medical ethics:

1) beneficence, which is action to improve health status;

2) non-maleficence, the Hippocratic assumption of *primum non nocere* – meaning that we must act without harming;

3) respect for autonomy. The goal of medical action is to seek the patient's *autonomy*, to maintain or restore a *livable* existence;

4) justice, where the duty of fairness requires that patients be treated in a similar manner.

These principles are *starting points* for providing a reflective framework in human medicine. This framework can be extended to the practice of veterinary care.

This principled approach can be understood as a mix between deontological principles (autonomy and justice), according to Kant and Rawls, and consequentialist principles (non-maleficence and beneficence), according to Mills (Childress and Beauchamp 2020).

9.3.1.1.1. The consequentialist dimension of the Principles approach

Our medical decisions can be made according to consequentialism. The act will be better as long as the consequences are good, or better relative to other possible actions for the animal. However, the deciding on an act is a promise made on an "if all goes well" assumption. In fact, consequentialist theory may have some difficulty in assessing the consequences of a given act with any certainty. To question the validity of an expensive treatment, with significant side effects for an old animal, where at all costs, *we must do everything* for three or six months of (mere) survival, constitutes an ethical question. Under what conditions, and with what quality of life? Of course, EBM data, training and experience help with taking risks, for example, in an intervention where the veterinarian weighs the risks and benefits for the animal. Nevertheless, consequentialism remains grounded in uncertainty.

One form of consequentialism, utilitarianism, has been strongly criticized by Beauchamp and Childress: utilitarianism would favor immoral acts to maximize the value of utility, by *justifying rational choices*. Thus, the famous 3Rs rule (*reduce, replace, refine*), used in animal experimentation, is the application of a utilitarian theory which tends to maximize research in biology or medicine, and minimize the suffering of animals. However, the theory may lead to the sacrifice of a (small) number of animals for the sake of many human beings. This utilitarian position is also found in animal husbandry: the *welfare* slider can be positioned just above a minimal threshold, which is sufficient to *justify* the conditions of existence of many food animal species (Nussbaum 2012). More generally, utilitarianism obscures the actual needs of individuals in the name of a general value: utility.

9.3.1.1.2. The ethical dimension of the Principles approach

The Principles approach embraces obligations that are related to deontological ethics: autonomy and justice. Deontology in medical ethics values actions based on intention. Actions have value if they conform to the moral law. But here as well setbacks are not far away. Thus, for example, *free and informed consent* is a medical application of a deontological principle with respect to autonomy. It consists of a duty to inform the animal's representative before any act of cure. While this assumes that animal owners are totally autonomous, free from any constraints, it is necessary to recognize that the signed acceptance of the document is but a "hollow ritual": the owners are either in an emergency situation, or in panic, or ignorant, without any other possibility than to accept. Moreover, such a measure can be misused by the practitioner who acts *in accordance with the moral law* for fear of legal recourse if something goes wrong, which changes the meaning of *moral law* since "consent cancels out the wrong" (Ogien 2009, p. 58). This is a form of bypassing of a moral principle that consists of accepting the unacceptable.

9.3.1.1.3. General criticism of the Principles approach

We may question the relevance of theoretical philosophical models such as the consequentialist or deontological models for veterinary medicine ethics. It is as if there were a fascination for an ideal of universality in animal ethical rationality that would allow for the logical *derivation* of moral principles and their applications. These theoretical models emphasize a feature, such as autonomy or utility, that allow for the *justification* of moral action. However, they overlook other principles that will not be morally relevant. The very notion of principle in medical ethics has been sharply criticized under the term *principlism*, in which each principle may conflict with others. Ethical approaches through either Rawls' *Theory of Justice* or that of the utilitarians, despite the profound differences between them, have one thing in common, and that is the *universality of an ability* such as reason, or happiness and pleasure, or the absence of suffering (Plot 2011). This universality arises in an environment where consequentialist or deontological universalist ethics dominate in philosophy, based on impartial determinate *principles*, analogous to those used in the justice model.

We cannot limit moral concern to mere biological or naturalistic forms of animal and human life. Nor can we limit our responsibility to animals to legal criteria, where *justification* would be the key word, either from a scientific- or justice-based model (Diamond 2011d; Gilligan 2019). This raises questions about the propensity to follow models that are based on a universal dimension, setting aside particular positions:

> The universal rule is too vast to be precise, it is too general, too lofty, too far removed from the concrete richness of situations to be able to validly enlighten a worried conscience, anxious to act "as well as possible", who would question its duty (Misrahi 2006, p. 58).

Therefore, medical ethics cannot be limited to the search for an ideal that would opt for a neutral stance between reality and moral judgment, as if there were (or were not) a moral reality independent of particular situations. For example, the *principle of no-harm* can, far from the reality of situations, be in contradiction with the act of euthanasia – the *well-dying*.

The difficulty inherent in *principlism* lies in its ignorance of the particularities of the animal life context and its representative, owner or guardian, which are passed over in silence (Doucet and Dion-Labriea 2011). These principles do not provide "mechanical solutions or definitive decision-making procedures for moral problems posed in medicine" (Beauchamp 2019). Moreover, Beauchamp sees his set of four principles as neither general rules nor absolute relationships, but rather as *prima facie* principles[5] that function as obligations, rarely subject to *particular* conflicts.

9.3.1.2. The casuistic approach

A key moment in medical ethics was the renewal during the 1980s of casuistry as applied to bioethics and medicine by Toulmin and Jonsen (1988). Casuistry enables moral problems to be posed and solved by focusing less on principles or moral theories than on attention to circumstances and analogies with particular cases that have preceded them. The case is the atomic form of our moral judgments. In casuistry, a collection of paradigmatic cases is assembled. We will then make our ethical decisions in a particular situation by reference to these paradigmatic cases resolved in varying degrees. This is analogous to the jurisprudential approach in the

---

5. This approach postulates that problems in ethics are approached by using a priori principles.

justice model. The clinician must be able to resolve the particular case of each ethical situation if it presents a clear family resemblance with paradigmatic cases referenced by ethics committees (Loue 2002). These cases of casuistry may have the merit of *sticking* very closely to the ethical situation, where ethical theories would not be able to resolve the disagreements between the different protagonists.

However, this way of approaching ethics poses a major problem: can we, in ethics, rely on analogous situations that would claim to have sufficient concordance with the case to be dealt with in order to be able to resolve it? We are faced here with a question of identity in an inductive approach. Can the resolution of an ethical problem be generalized and applied to other similar cases? This would imply an *infallibility* in ethics that is not admissible (Putnam 2013).

9.3.2. *Intermediate versions between the great principles and casuistry*

9.3.2.1. *Towards a practical ethics that directs actions*

9.3.2.1.1. An attention to contexts…

There are alternatives to the great principles theory and the non-theory of casuistry. Several veterinary ethics textbooks (Rollin 2006; Mullan and Fawcett 2017) use the form of *narrative ethics* that outlines a fictional narrative close to real-life cases in order to provide ethical guidance on a case-by-case basis, such as, for example, futile medical care despite the veterinarian's disagreement, requesting euthanasia for cats that urinate or claw around the home, euthanizing a healthy pet following their owner's death, the question of the veterinarian's committed responsibility for an animal exhibiting hyperaggressiveness and so on. A given situation can be approached from a number of different directions using, for example, the deontic *justification* of respect for life, the consequentialist *justification* of suffering, and the experience of common sense, etc. Principlism itself has been reworked to be more practical. What can we expect from such ethics in veterinary medicine? This is ethics in which practitioners and caregivers would free themselves from a dogmatic approach, making choices that direct their actions, as Aristotle had proposed in his ethics of virtue (Aristotle 2004, II, 1103b26). An act would be judged valid as long as someone virtuous were performing it.

But how can we envisage such ethics? Martha Nussbaum (2006) proposes to start from the moral reflection on the Aristotelian *good life*, in order to discover how moral concepts such as kindness, generosity, compassion and care for the other make sense in "this teeming whole", against a background "which determines our judgment, our concepts and our reactions" (Wittgenstein 1994, section 629).

9.3.2.1.2. … in which emotions are rehabilitated…

Emotion is at the heart of our reactions concerning animals. Our lives are filled with emotions, such as those of attachment to our surroundings, of love or sorrow, but also, conversely, those of envy, jealousy and hate, and so on. We also know that emotions can be deceiving. Whatever the case, can they claim to institute acceptable value judgments? The aim here is not to reject emotions, which contribute to the general appreciation of a situation; on the contrary, emotions require us to take into account our own vulnerability in this world (Golstein 2011). Thus, according to Tronto (2009), the ethics of care brings to light virtues such as generosity or concern for the other, taking into account sensitivity, experience and imagination. In these ethics, emotions do not have to be eliminated: they even play an essential role in moral life, putting compassion back at the heart of the link between individuals, while denouncing the illusion of a human devoid of feelings or sympathy.

9.3.2.1.3. … to take into account animal vulnerability

What kind of compassion? It is the compassion that takes into account situations such as water or food deprivation, attacks on physical integrity, the absence of shelter and also of vital risks; in other words, compassion of the *vulnerability* of other animals or humans. However, this compassionate emotion can only be taken into account in the ethical framework if it is attached to reason; Nussbaum thus links reason and emotion in a continuous dialectic: *reason holds to compassionate emotion, compassionate emotion holds to reason* (Golstein 2011). She even speaks of "rational compassion" (Nussbaum 2012, p. 425). We will focus on two ethics of interest to us that extend *beyond compassion*: these are the *ethics of care* and the *ethics of capabilities*.

9.3.2.2. *Between the ethics of capabilities and the ethics of care*

9.3.2.2.1. Capabilities take into account the extent of our duties…

It seems crucial that a veterinary ethical decision must be concerned with the quality of life of the individual animal or group of animals. How should we act when an animal is suffering? How do we establish its needs? What is the impact of living conditions on the quality of a chicken farm? What living conditions are acceptable? According to Nussbaum, what matters is the individual creature and its dependence. She considers that care and its associated dependence are the necessary conditions to bring to the Rawlsian theory in order to attain a just society, where the animal can be taken into account. In fact, Nussbaum, in developing her position *beyond compassion*, proposes to use her concept of capability to develop a political and legal approach to the animal condition. The capability approach is a substantive approach to a theory of justice for both humans and animals:

> There is a considerable moral difference between a policy that promotes health and one that promotes health capabilities: it is the latter, not the former, that respects individuals' life choices (Nussbaum 2012).

What does "caring" mean? It means taking into account the necessary conditions of physical integrity, absence of suffering and so on, that is, helping others to develop their capabilities. Nussbaum proposes considering the particular animal – and its species – from a list of 10 capabilities:

Life: whether or not animals have a conscious interest in continuing their lives. Nussbaum states, however, that "moderate and respectful paternalism may justify the practice of euthanasia in the case of elderly animals in pain" (Nussbaum 2010, p. 258).

Physical health: it is under this heading that Nussbaum denounces the fact that animals raised for food purposes do not enjoy the same protection as others. For example, the food industry, like sports fishing and sports hunting, are sources of considerable injustice to animals and must be stopped.

Physical integrity: practices concerning mutilations, even if not very painful, but necessarily modifying the lives of the animals, must be prohibited. Nussbaum cites as an example the declawing of cats (surgery already prohibited in France), or the cutting of tails or ears in dogs.

Senses, imagination and thought; feelings: animals present emotions, conscious states. They can be, for example, jealous, loving, fearful or conscious (Devienne 2020).

Practical reason; affiliation; *other species; play; control of own environment.*

Nussbaum, through capabilities, adjusts our actions to give animals the opportunity to thrive. She refers to the ethological sciences, which rely on a descriptive theory of each species and its life form (Nussbaum 2012). The list of capabilities considers the extent of our duties to an individual of a given species. Capabilities are to be understood as a threshold effect to act, in practice approaching the concept of *animal dignity*. It is only in a second step that capabilities can be applied to groups or to numbers:

> The capability approach attaches no importance to large numbers as such; it is interested in the welfare of existing creatures and the harm done to them when their powers are wasted. [...] The harms that are

done to species thus occur through the harms that are done to individuals, and this individual harm should be the focus of moral attention in the capability approach (Nussbaum 2010, p. 244).

Contrary to the concept of capacity, the concept of capability makes it possible to take into account the necessary and sufficient conditions to be implemented so that a living being, human or animal, can flourish. The good would correspond to the lessening of situations of adversity and of what hinders this flourishing. The capability approach is close to deontological theory, in that it attaches importance, as Kant does (2019), to the respect of principles and to the person, considering them not as a means but as an end.

9.3.2.2.2. … and provide the substance of the care action…

Like the ethics of capabilities, the ethics of care are ethics that respond to the needs of the other, taking our emotions into account. In this way, it distances itself from an abstract morality aiming at universality. According to Tronto, moral philosophy, by its universal character, is based on a theory of justice that forgets proximity to the other, attention to the particular, concern for the other. The ethics of care is not strictly speaking a theory: its aim is not to build a morality. It does not question the issue of the cognitive capacities, notably conscience, of species to justify the use of animals. This is above all a *practice*, a way of doing things, of handling them. It shifts from values such as freedom, equality or autonomy, which were previously the pillars of ethical reflection, to reflective fields such as vulnerability and dependence on others. Veterinary care can borrow from Joan Tronto's extended definition of care as:

> A generic activity that includes everything we do to maintain, perpetuate, and repair our "world" so that we can live in it as well as possible. This world includes our bodies, ourselves, and our environment, all of which we seek to connect into a complex, life-supporting network (Tronto 2009, p. 143).

This activity, which is a priori much more extensive than that of veterinary practice, is nevertheless to be taken with interest: it is directed towards the vulnerable, encountered in the animals that surround us, but also in those environments that include wild animal species living in natural environments that we have weakened by our activities. In an agentive perspective, *Care* is a disposition to take care of the other and to pay attention to, care about, worry about and care for the vulnerable other.

It should be noted that the French language does not differentiate between types of care, whereas the English language offers two terms: *care*, meaning "to take care of", and *cure*, meaning "to care for" (Sadegh-Zadeh 2012). The concept of *care* contains not only solicitude and care, but also a set of tasks performed by care givers in farms or veterinary clinics. Thus, a veterinarian can *cure* without *caring* for the animal, as in the case of a surgical operation in which the duty of *care* is devolved to the nurse. It should also be emphasized that we speak of a relationship of *care* between the animal and the health professional, where vulnerability can be shared[6].

9.3.2.2.3. ... that targets the animal's vulnerability

This model of vulnerability is based on the relationship between two living beings, one in need, adrift, and one who practices care, who takes into account the concern of the former. While both are in a dissymmetrical position as regards care, no one can deny that they have found themselves vulnerable in their own histories, whether in their health, their professional lives or their emotions, where *someone else* may have been there to help them, reassure them, comfort them:

> Throughout our lives, all of us go through varying degrees of dependence and independence, autonomy and vulnerability. A political order that presumes only independence and autonomy as the nature of human life misses a great deal of human experience, and must somehow hide this point elsewhere (Tronto 2009, p. 181).

The question of care, of concern for the other, highlights the vulnerability of the other who is there, beside us, or close by. This relationship takes on an extreme meaning in these one-way, absolute dependencies. It is not, a priori, a matter of reciprocity, of interdependence, but rather of concern and care for the other, whether human, animal or environmental, in situations that threaten their development and integrity of life.

Care, and the manner in which it is narrated, defines a texture, "an unstable reality that cannot be fixed by concepts or by particular determined objects, but through the recognition of gestures, manners and styles" (Laugier 2006, p. 322). This approach to care is not a search for generality from an animal individual, but resides in the relational character of the particular itself, in contrast with the drive for generality. This attitude is recognition of the other in *my* own sensitivity, in *my* own vulnerability. It is a response, a self-transformation, in the practice of caring for *this* dependent animal. Indeed, care for the animal shows us how we are transformed

---

6. For many reasons, veterinarians and nursing staff are vulnerable socio-professional categories: suicide rates among veterinarians are well above the national average.

by what is lived, how we allow ourselves to be transformed – and this is indeed in a passive form – by what is lived (Emerson 1992), in the care, in this *exposure* (Cavell's own words) to death and life. The notion of value emerges from the way in which we understand what is told in our stories of care, in terms of success or failure, skill or clumsiness, or in the absence or presence of suffering. It is found in the uncertain destiny and worry, experienced at close quarters, that unites the caregiver and the animal in the stories told in surgery, in the difficult births, but also in the many euthanasia that we perform. These life stories that occur in the care of the individual are in fact the background to the shaping of the caregiver who carries out the care. Therefore, a care structure must be endowed with a certain degree of organization and social construction, of learning and skills, which allow for discernment, for help *on a case-by-case basis*, or for forming a necessary coherent response dictated by the imperatives of the practice. This medical learning is technical and theoretical, but also practical, in terms of experiencing encounters with other animals.

Care does not necessarily have a positive dimension: it can be neglected, poorly executed, absent, disrespectful, poorly paid or not take the animal into consideration. Care jobs are those involving pee-poo, vomit, diarrhea, bleeding and the like, where hygiene directly participates in the maintenance of life functions of the vulnerable animal. Care is dirty work (Molinier 2013). An animal left in its droppings and excretions suggests an absence of care. In fact, care work is something that is invisible, unnoticed, transparent and only noticed when it is deficient. Caring requires hygiene and attention to what needs to be done to preserve the life of the animal, keeping it from escaping from the place where it is confined; caring requires cleaning it, feeding it, watering it, administering medical care, re-dressing it, and then taking care, checking and checking again. The ethics of care emphasize the vulnerability and dependence of sick animals on their caregivers, putting care back at the heart of medicine, which is not reduced to pathology.

9.3.2.2.4. But the veterinary world is not reduced to pathology or care...

It could be said that veterinary care ethics have a clear family resemblance with *care* ethics. Tronto, however, excludes certain activities from care: (1) creative activity, (2) production, (3) destruction and (4) pleasure seeking.

9.3.3. *A profession subject to the economics of its business*

9.3.3.1. *The curses of the veterinarian...*

When we decide to take on a pet, whether it is purchased or adopted from a shelter, for instance, we care for it by providing for its basic needs. We help it to flourish and realize its capabilities. The aims of the ethics of care and of capability are not to empower these animals by giving them freedom (which they would be unable to enjoy), but to provide them with a measure of well-being. While we are making animals dependent on us, we, in turn, have a duty to care for them (Engster 2006). However, caring for an animal also has a cost.

While bartering may have been an effective measure in its time to treat animals, it cannot meet today's ever-increasing costs associated with the inherent burdens of any company and with developments in technoscience, both in diagnosis and in prevention and therapy, and this applies to both livestock and pet animals. Veterinarians are faced with a *double curse* in their practice: on the one hand, a curse linked to the verdictive in the diagnosis and prognosis of the sick or traumatized animal; on the other hand, a curse linked to the verdictive that condemns the animal to palliative care or euthanasia by announcing the cost of care that may exceed the financial means of the animal's owner or the veterinary enterprise. How do we reconcile this ethics of care with the unaffordable cost? Such measures require financial flexibility on the part of veterinarians, such as: deferred payments, insurance or association funds, to help pay for the care of indigent animal owners (Rollin 2006). Society does not currently provide for financial measures to help impecunious people care for their animals.

Veterinary medicine is not confined to animal care: it is not limited today to restoring health, but manages the reproductive capacities of animals. In pets, sterilization enables the regulation of proliferation and its associated diseases. It is possible to speak of care insofar as these sterilizations require technical qualities and skills, with the aim of limiting the proliferation of domestic species or liminal animals (Kymlicka and Donaldson 2016).

Veterinarians are subject to societal pressure that is ignorant of the genetic diseases generated by breeders who seek, for example, bovine, feline and canine hypertypes – of which the *English bulldog* undoubtedly constitutes the paradigm – for which the reckless consequences must be corrected medically or surgically. The profession takes into account these deviations by approaching the producers, but the recourse to a legislative authority is inevitable to frame such deviations.

9.3.3.2. ... *whose aporia is animal welfare on farms*

Veterinary medicine also works to improve and increase animal production, fertilization and genetic selection, and more. The veterinarian is a major actor in the development of breeding and experimentation through the control of pathologies, prophylaxis, epidemiological surveillance networks, medical assistance to production, insemination and the yield of animal production, whose end is not the animal itself but the producer-breeder. The treatment carried out by humans on livestock and experimental animals is mostly deplorable. Intensive confined so-called "industrial" breeding has led to a reduction in, and even made it impossible for professionals to detect animal pathologies to limit or even eliminate the work of veterinarians on individuals to concentrate on the herd as a whole (yet suffering is also individual). Intensive breeding produces diseases directly linked to high production levels, to a stressful environment due to the lack of space and to confinement, which prevents the manifestation of natural behaviors.

Moreover, it is difficult to speak of care in the strict sense of the word: unfulfilled capabilities, contained movements, non-existent relationships between fellow creatures, an inadequate and disrespectful environment, and so on. The ethics of care cannot support such breeding. These living conditions are, however, inherent to factory farming. The concepts of animal welfare or humane treatment are irreconcilable with an animal production that only takes into account medical problems if they affect production. This is why welfare in animal production is incompatible with the position of the ethics of care (Engster 2006).

9.4. Another view

9.4.1. *Breaking out of the circle of ethical justifications...*

An additional difficulty found in veterinary ethics is that the animals encountered, such as harmful animals, farm animals, pets, sports animals and experimental animals, do not all have the same status. This gives the impression that each of the ethics covered refers to a given viewpoint of veterinary practice... Clearly, there is a kind of *compartmentalization* in people's minds: we compartmentalize our relationships between what is allowed and what is not, for instance, causing suffering or killing is prohibited, but we can kill to eat; causing suffering is prohibited, but we experiment on animals; we live with our dogs and cats, and we take care of their well-being, but we accept battery farming. As Diamond (1995a) points out, this compartmentalization *allows us* to eat animals, to let scientists experiment on animals and so on. It is a compartmentalization of the *because*, where justification has the power to suppress my words...:

> The focus is *still* on "evaluations", "judgments" and explicit moral reasoning to conclusion that something is worthwhile, or a duty, or wrong, or ought to be done; our conception of what are "issues" for moral thought is still "x is wrong" versus "x is permissible" (Diamond 1995b, p. 380).

It is as if we had a form of resistance thanks to justification and argumentation, as if within moral philosophy we were looking for the cornerstone of justification. This resistance prevents us from *seeing another point of view*:

> This might mean that philosophy is inevitably sidetracked from appreciating the kind of difficulties I have in view, (that is) if philosophy does not know how to inhabit a body (does not know how to treat a wounded body as anything other than a fact) (Diamond 2011d, p. 288).

This difficulty makes it possible to turn to another form of ethical thinking, that of Wittgenstein, for whom ethics do not have a particular purpose for a specific domain. Such ethics cannot be evaluated in the same way that we might evaluate a *good antibiotic* or a *good surgical thread* in medicine. Ethics are meaningless if they imply the search for the *right* moral code:

> It is not a question of formulating a description of the right code, nor saying that it is the right code, it is "suddenly seeing" ethics differently and imbuing one's life with it. It is not a theoretical position, it is a life choice (Chauviré 2019, p. 107).

Ethics approached in this way do not have an ideal of rationality that is at the root of our arguments in morality. Reality is far more entangled than the great moral theories claim (Laugier 2011). There are no universal, univocal moral concepts, but rather concepts that apply in reality, in the narratives or descriptions that we encounter in the course of our existence and that we consider important: this readiness to gather this experience (or not) is not isolated, but is contextualized with the background of a form of life:

> I have arrived at the rock-bottom of my convictions.
>
> And one might almost say that these foundation-walls are carried by the whole house (Wittgenstein 2006, section 248).

Ethical developments in Wittgensteinian philosophy, as represented by Martha Nusbaum, Stanley Cavell, Cora Diamond, Sandra Laugier and others, depart from ethics consisting of principles of moral choice or judgments. According to Wittgenstein:

> Just as logic [...] penetrates all thought, ethics has no particular subject; rather, an ethical spirit, an attitude toward the world and life, can penetrate any thought or discourse (Diamond 2011c, p. 230).

Whatever the arguments put forward to justify an ethical position, there is something *wrong* with a discourse that wants to eradicate that particular, individual experience that we may have in our own lives. For Diamond (2011b), the real subject of ethics is that of our reactions to life, the proposals we announce, the education that we receive and give, our positions in relation to our society, to discover what matters to us in this ordinary life in our relationship to other humans and animals, and so on. It is a true *inquiry* that suggests ethics, not as a foundation, but rather as an *investigation*, serving a learning process in our own history.

9.4.2. ... to improvise relationships to other animals...

Medical learning is, of course, technical and theoretical, but is also a learning that only takes place in proximity, in experience, in this *improvisation* with the animal. It is an encounter, or rather, a *summons*. The animal *calls me*:

> I (have to) *respond* to it [its life], or refuse to respond. It calls upon me; it calls me out. I have to acknowledge it (Cavell 1996, p. 141).

Improvisation is then a form of adventure in the relationship with the animal. It does not respond to a first principle, like a duty, or an *ethical code*, but rather to an attention, that of hearing the cry of the wounded (James 1897). It is not only a matter of technical learning: "Not by taking courses, but by '*experience*'," says Wittgenstein (2005, p. 318). "One does not learn a technique, but relevant judgments." Have we been careful, in our veterinary studies, where the learning is, above all, that of a medical technique, not to have blinded ourselves – in an insidious way, as in *the fable of the frog* – to an aspect of the animal, to its vulnerability?

In our life experience, our professional practice and in our readings, we can push our ethical boundaries in the adventure of our lives. It is a change of perspective that does not bring new facts but gives us a different *view* of animal care. It is these ways of seeing that allow us to discover what challenges us, to react in an *improvised* way in the attention to the other, not in the *cure*, but in what goes beyond what we know, and which pushes our own borders in our perception of the world. This particular position is situated in a background of a form of life that does not determine what ethics are, but rather allows us to reveal, to *see,* what is important to us, those social, living, moving and sensitive life-forms. We change our view of the animal, which, for it, does not change. This attitude consists of *seeing* reality not "like" something (McFetridge and McDowell 1978; Laugier 2010), but in *seeing* things as they are: seeing the vulnerability of the other, where we did not see it before:

[It] is not to behave in conformity with rules of conduct, but to see situations in a special light, as constituting reasons for acting; this perpetual capacity, once acquired, can be exercised in complex novel circumstances, not necessarily capable of being foreseen and legislated for by a codifier of the conduct required by virtue, however wise and thoughtful he might be (McDowell 1978).

McDowell emphasizes *vision* as the most important characteristic in our approach to ethics. It is not knowledge or reason that matters, but rather that the agent *sees better*.

9.4.3. ... in a singular relationship of humanity

It is important to emphasize the fact that some situations escape moral judgment, argument or justification. These situations escape moral judgment, references such as the right to life, or a rational principle recognizing the other as the object of morality. Rather, these situations reveal a *non-moral element* (Diamond 2011a), the discovery of *what matters to me* (that *me* which is each of us) in this singularity towards other humans, animals or nature. It is, for example, these singular stories that we have with *this* animal that we care for, not this medical prowess, this rare or remarkable case that remains simply a rare case or a case of extraordinary surgical prowess. In care, I do not *know* what this animal feels, I do not *know* if it feels anything, but it is in fact in *my own attitude* that *I take into account* its sufferings, its consciousness, its worries, its fear. In other words, *I* take its life into account: it is an attitude of *humanity*. This attitude in care, like this attitude, for example, in friendship, reveals the kind of beings that we are.

We must not neglect those singular stories that are also drawn from the literature, those that tell of our forms of life: characters in novels, for example, those of Dostoevsky, Tolstoy, Hugo or London, feed the experience of our own moral lives. For example, Coetzee (2002) in his novel *Disgrace* tells us – which philosophy cannot – how euthanized dog corpses in a lost shelter in South Africa are brought in and reverently placed in the crematorium by a man, an anti-hero disgraced by his society (Diamond 2011d). After reading such a book, the way *I* (and here I am not talking about a *we*) put the *dead animal* that *I* have just euthanized in a plastic bag, then in the freezer, before the cremation company comes to pick it up, took on a different meaning. It is an act that *I* often do alone, and that does not involve anyone else, that will change nothing for this animal corpse – you could say that it is just an animal corpse. There is no justification, no precept, no imperative or inherited rule. *This is how I do it.* This way of doing things can be related – far from the classical exegeses – to the following aphorism:

Once I have exhausted the justifications I have reached the bedrock, and my spade is turned. Then I am inclined to say: "This is simply what I do" (Wittgenstein 2009, section 217).

The justification stops at a certain point, and we have mentioned these justifications and these reasons in these few pages. Now is the moment when things are no longer of the order of language, discussion or justification, nor of the rule to follow. This is *how I do it*. This is *my* way of being in the world. This is not to say that I am right; it is not this way that is in question. The ethical dimension becomes this more prevalent consideration of the texture of our own experience, subject to this precarious balance, which risks falling at any moment. It can also extend to the commitment or refusal to engage at any time with other members of my political community, for example, which is at the heart of democracy.

9.5. Conclusion

What we wanted to *show* through this text, if we dare to give an image, is that ethical life is similar to a ladder that we climb – the rungs constituting different ethical theories, without ranking them in any way – which we use to climb a wall. Knowledge of the main threads of these ethical theories helps to provide the reasons and justifications for a decision. It does not matter if these theories, whether they are inherited from utilitarianism, natural law or common sense, for example, oppose or complement each other. Rather, we should emphasize that each offers a different view of the particular situation to which we must – or must not – react.

The renunciation of taking a given point of view in advance consists of being vigilant in our ability to follow conventions. The ladder is removed. Ethics are inseparable from the ability to imagine animal life, to improvise in this relational adventure with the animal. We are always balancing on our wall, ready to fall, to miss this encounter with the animal in care. Veterinary ethics is a school of life, conducive to improvisation in our ethical adventure. All it takes is to *see differently*.

9.6. References

Aristotle (2004). Éthique à Nicomaque. *Œuvres, Éthique, Politique, Rhétorique, Poétique, Métaphysique*, translated by Richard Bodéüs. Gallimard (Pléïade), Paris.

Arras, J. (2016). Theory and bioethics. In *The Stanford Encyclopedia of Philosophy (Winter 2016 Edition)*, Zalta, E.N. (ed.) [Online]. Available at: https://plato.stanford.edu/archives/win2016/entries/theory-bioethics [Accessed 17 October 2020].

Beauchamp, T.L. (2019). L'approche des "quatre principes". In *Philosophie du soin. Santé, autonomie, devoirs*, translated by Tommy-Martin, M. and Durand, G. Vrin, Paris.

Cavell, S. (1996). *Les voix de la raison : Wittgenstein, le scepticisme, la moralité et la tragédie*, translated by Laugier, S. and Balso, N. (eds). Le Seuil, Paris.

Chauviré, C. (2019). *Ludwig Wittgenstein*. Nous, Caen.

Childress, J.F. and Beauchamp, T.L. (2020). *Les principes de l'éthique biomédicale*, 2nd edition, translated by Fisbach, M. (ed.). Les Belles Lettres, Paris.

Coetzee, J.C. (2001), *Disgrâce*, translated by Lauga du Plessis, C. Le Seuil, Paris.

Conrad, J. (ed.) (1913). Préface. In *Le Nègre du "Narcisse"*, translated by d'Humières, R. Gallimard, Paris.

Devienne, P. (2020). Peut-on parler de conscience animale ? *Animal parlé, animal parlant-2, Psychiatrie Française*, L.1/2. 5–24.

Diamond, C. (ed.) (1995a). Experimenting on animals: A problem in ethics. In *The Realistic Spirit: Wittgenstein, Philosophy, and the Mind*. MIT Press, Cambridge, Massachusetts.

Diamond, C. (ed.) (1995b). Having a rough story about what moral philosophy is. In *The Realistic Spirit: Wittgenstein, Philosophy, and the Mind*. MIT Press, Cambridge, Massachusetts.

Diamond, C. (ed.) (2011a). Le cas du soldat nu. In *L'importance d'être humain, et autres essais de philosophie morale*, translated by Hallais, E. and Laugier, S. Presses Universitaires de France, Paris.

Diamond, C. (ed.) (2011b). Perdre ses concepts. In *L'importance d'être humain, et autres essais de philosophie morale*, translated by Hallais, E. and Laugier, S. Presses Universitaires de France, Paris.

Diamond, C. (ed.) (2011c). L'éthique, l'imagination et la méthode du *Tractatus* de Wittgenstein. In *L'importance d'être humain, et autres essais de philosophie morale*, translated by Hallais E. and Laugier S. Presses Universitaires de France, Paris.

Diamond, C. (ed.) (2011d). La difficulté de la réalité et la difficulté de la philosophie. In *L'importance d'être humain, et autres essais de philosophie morale*, translated by Hallais, E. and Laugier, S. Presses Universitaires de France, Paris.

Doucet, H. (2006). La bioéthique, discipline ou pratique. In *Questions d'éthique contemporaine*, Ludivine Thiaw-Po-Une (ed.). Stock, Paris.

Doucet, H. and Dion-Labriea, M. (2011). Médecine narrative et éthique narrative en Amérique du Nord : perspective historique et critique. À la recherche d'une médecine humaniste. *Ethique et santé*, 8(2), 63–68 [Online]. Available at: https://doi.org/10.1016/j.etiqe.2010.07.001 [Accessed 15 September 2020].

Emerson, R.W. (1992). Expérience. In *Statuts d'Emerson*, Cavell, S. (ed.), translated by Fournier, C. and Laugier, S. Eclat, Arles.

Engster, D. (2006). Care ethics and animal welfare. *Journal of Social Philosophy*, 37, 521–536 [Online]. Available at: https://doi.org/10.1111/j.1467-9833.2006.00355.x [Accessed 20 November 2020].

Gilligan, C. (2019). *Une voix différente. La morale a-t-elle un sexe ?* Flammarion, Paris.

Golstein, P. (2011). *Vulnérabilité et autonomie dans la pensée de Martha C. Nussbaum.* Presses Universitaires de France, Paris.

Hubscher, R. (1999). *Les maîtres des bêtes, les vétérinaires dans la société française (XVIIe–XXe siècle).* Odile Jacob, Paris.

James, W. (1897). The moral philosopher and the moral life. *The Will to Believe, and Other Essays in Popular Philosophy.* Kessinger Publishing, USA.

Kant, I. (2019). *Groundwork for the Metaphysics of Morals*, translated by Bennett, C., Saunders, J. and Stern, R. Oxford University Press, Oxford.

Kymlicka, W. and Donaldson, S. (2011). *Zoopolis. Une théorie politique des droits des animaux,* translated by Madelin, P. and Afeissa, H.-S. Alma, Paris.

Laugier, S. (2006). Care et perception, l'éthique comme attention au particulier. In *Le souci des autres, éthique et politique du care,* Paperman, P. and Laugier, S. (eds). EHESS, Paris.

Laugier, S. (2010). *Wittgenstein, le mythe de l'inexpressivité.* Vrin, Paris.

Laugier, S. (2011). Introduction. In *L'importance d'être humain, et autres essais de philosophie morale,* translated by Hallais, E. and Laugier, S. Diamond, C. (ed.). Presses Universitaires de France, Paris.

Laugier, S. (2012). Présentation. In *Ethique, littérature, vie humaine,* Laugier, S. (ed.). Presses Universitaires de France, Paris.

Loue, S. (2002). *Textbook of Research Ethics, Theory and Practice.* Kluwer Academic Publishers, New York [Online]. Available at: https://fliphtml5.com/udixo/frtn/basic. [Accessed 5 October 2020].

McDowell, J. (2009). Comment on Stanley Cavell's "Companionable Thinking". In *Philosophy and Animal Life,* Wolfe, C., Diamond, C., Cavell, S., McDowell, J., Hacking, I. (eds). Columbia University Press, New York.

McFetridge, I.G. and McDowell, J. (1978). Are moral requirements hypothetical imperatives. In *Proceedings of the Aristotelician Society,* 52(1), 13–42. [Online]. Available at: https://doi.org/10.1093/aristoteliansupp/52.1.13 [Accessed 5 June 2020].

Misrahi, R. (2006). *Le philosophe, le patient et le soignant. Ethique et progrès médical.* Empêcheurs de penser en rond, La Découverte, Paris.

Molinier, P. (2013). *Le travail du care.* La dispute. Paris.

Mullan, S. and Fawcett, A. (2017). *Veterinary Ethics: Navigating Tough Cases.* 5m Publishing, Sheffield.

Nussbaum, M. (2006). La littérature comme philosophie morale. La fêlure dans le cristal : *La coupe d'or* de Henri James. In *Ethique, littérature et vie humaine*, Laugier, S. (ed.), translated by Halais, E. and Mondon, J.-Y. PUF, Paris.

Nussbaum, M. (2010). Par-delà la "compassion" et "l'humanité". Justice pour les animaux non humains. In *Textes clés de philosophie animale. Différence, responsabilité et communauté*, Afeissa, J.-S. and Jeangène-Vilmer, J.-B. (eds). Vrin, Paris.

Nussbaum, M. (2012a). *Les capabilités : comment créer les conditions d'un monde plus juste ?* Flammarion, Paris.

Nussbaum, M. (2012b). *Upheavals of Thought. The Intelligence of Emotions.* Cambridge University Press, Cambridge.

Ogien, R. (2009). *La vie, la mort, l'État.* Grasset, Paris.

Plot, F. (2011). Ethique de la vertu et éthique du care. Quelles connexions ? In *Le souci des autres, éthique et politique du Care*, Paperman, P. and Laugier, S. (eds). EHESS, Paris.

Putnam, H. (2013). *L'éthique sans ontologie.* Cerf, Paris.

Rawls, J. (1997). *Théorie de la justice.* Le Seuil, Paris.

Rollin, B. (2006). *An Introduction to Veterinary Medical Ethics, Theory and Cases*, II. Blackwell, Ames.

Sadegh-Zadeh, K. (2012). *Handbook of Analytic Philosophy of Medicine.* Springer, Münster.

Toulmin, A.R. and Jonsen, S. (1988). *The Abuse of Casuistry: A History of Moral Reasoning.* University of California Press, Berkeley.

Tronto, J. (2009). *Un monde vulnérable. Pour une politique du Care.* La Découverte, Paris.

Wittgenstein, L. (1994). *Remarques sur la Philosophie de la Psychologie II*, translated by Granel, G. T.E.R., Mauvezin.

Wittgenstein, L. (2006). *De la certitude*, translated by Moyal-Sharrock, D. Gallimard, Paris.

Wittgenstein, L. (2009). *Philosophical Investigations*, translated by G.E.M. Anscombe, P.M.S. Hacker and Joachim Schulte. Blackwell, Oxford.

10

Pain and Fear in Fishes: Implications for the Humane Use of Fishes

Lynne U. SNEDDON

Department of Biological and Environmental Sciences,
University of Gothenburg, Sweden

10.1. The use of fishes

Humans use fishes in a variety of different contexts and in incredibly large numbers. Trillions of fishes are caught or farmed each year to provide food. In fisheries, these animals are caught in large numbers commercially using a range of injurious and destructive techniques (Sneddon and Wolfenden 2012). Concerns for the welfare of fishes during capture, landing and slaughter as well as bycatch discard where non-target animals are caught then released damaged or dead, the prevalence of ghost fishing gear and overfishing have all received media attention. When fishes are farmed in aquaculture, they are exposed to a variety of stressors such as size-grading, vaccination, crowding, transport, high stocking densities leading to high incidence of disease transmission and slaughter where they may experience fear and pain (Sneddon et al. 2012). Millions are employed as experimental models in research laboratories. Fishes are now the second most popular laboratory animal used in regulated scientific procedures so we now use more fish than rats in experiments in the United Kingdom and Europe. Experimentation may utilize methods that compromise the animal's well-being by being invasive (e.g. from a

Animal Suffering,
coordinated by Florence BURGAT and Emilie DARDENNE. © ISTE Ltd 2023.

needle prick through to major surgery such as heart cryodamage) or causing fear when the situation they face is uncontrollable or inescapable (Sneddon 2013; Sneddon et al. 2016; Sloman et al. 2019). Fishes are also used for recreational purposes in sport or for individual enjoyment of fishing. In this case, the fish are caught using hooks, which cause tissue damage and give rise to pain, held in "play" where the fisher reals the fish in, landed in air causing suffocation and either killed or released. Catching fish, therefore, potentially results in pain and fear (Cooke and Sneddon 2007). Some 4,000 species are held in public aquaria, and fishes are the most numerous pets held in home aquaria or ponds. Public exhibits are regulated and may require regular veterinary inspection. However, some species are wild caught or transported from commercial breeding facilities. The extent to which fish welfare is compromised while being kept as a companion animal is not fully understood, but there is scope for a range of issues to arise in keeping fish in indoor aquaria or in outdoor ponds (Sneddon and Wolfenden 2019). Considering the wide range of contexts in which fish are used or held in captivity, humans have a complicated relationship with fish. Recent scientific studies have demonstrated the capacity for pain and fear in fishes, which may lead to suffering (Ashley and Sneddon 2007; Sneddon 2013, 2015, 2019).

From both an ethical and moral perspective, humans should treat animals well when under their care. This is especially important if any situations we subject animals to may cause negative emotional states such as pain and fear. Thus, we must ensure good welfare by avoiding, minimizing or alleviating painful or fearful scenarios. It is vital to understand what animals are capable of experiencing suffering when making decisions about which animals to include in legislation aimed at protecting animals. The crucial deciding factor is typically whether the animal can suffer. Therefore, scientific studies demonstrating that fishes are capable of experiencing pain or fear provide convincing evidence for their protection. Causing poor welfare to an animal in order to study it may seem in opposition to the idea of maintaining good welfare; however, the industries that use fishes are powerful lobbying groups that can oppose additional legal or regulatory protection. Therefore, in order to convince governments, regulatory bodies and the general public that fishes should be included in welfare legislation, we have to clearly demonstrate that pain and fear elicit negative responses indicative of suffering. This chapter shall present the research findings and biology of pain and fear in fishes that make a compelling case for the capacity to experience negative affective states. This has important implications for how we treat fish, and here a case is made for more ethical and humane management of this important animal group.

10.2. Pain in fish

Concepts of animal welfare have traditionally been applied to species which are considered to have the ability to experience pain, fear and suffering and as such have been associated with species with an apparently higher level of cognition when compared to fish. While scientific debate still continues as to whether fishes have the neural capacity for awareness, fear and pain (Rose 2002; Key 2016; Sneddon et al. 2014; Merker 2016; Sneddon 2015; Sneddon and Leach 2016), there can be no doubt that practices in aquaculture, commercial and recreational fishing, and scientific research do provide potentially painful and fearful situations (Conte 2004; Ashley 2007; Cooke and Sneddon 2007; Sneddon and Wolfenden 2012; Sneddon 2015). It is unlikely that animals with a brain structure different from humans would experience anything like the emotions that humans feel when experiencing pain and fear. However, if an animal experiences suffering or discomfort, the nature of the pain or fear they perceive is no less important.

Nociception is the detection of potentially injurious stimuli and is usually accompanied by an immediate reflex withdrawal response away from the noxious stimulus. Crucial to survival in all animals, nociception in humans can give rise to pain, which is defined as "an unpleasant sensory and emotional experience associated with, or resembling that associated with, actual or potential tissue damage" (IASP 2020). A note has been added to this definition: "Verbal description is only one of several behaviors to express pain; inability to communicate does not negate the possibility that a human or a non-human animal experiences pain". Humans of course can self-report pain, and this is the main means of assessing pain. However, since we cannot communicate directly with animals, an alternate definition of pain has been proposed whereby whole-animal responses to pain differ from innocuous stimuli and long-term motivational change is observed that is consistent with exhibiting discomfort, promoting healing and avoiding the noxious event in the future (Sneddon et al. 2014). Although all animal groups are thought to possess nociceptors, much of the research on nociception has focused on understanding human pain. As such, there is a wealth of information regarding nociception in mammalian systems (Sneddon et al. 2014). More recently, non-mammalian vertebrates, amphibian reptilian and avian models, have been extensively studied (review in Sneddon et al. 2014). In comparison, nociception and pain are relatively underexplored in fishes. However, contemporary studies have addressed these important questions and have not only identified and described the properties of peripheral receptors that preferentially detect noxious, injurious stimuli (nociceptors) in fish (Sneddon 2002, 2003a; Ashley et al. 2006, 2007; Mettam et al. 2012) and shown specific changes in brain activity (Dunlop and Laming 2005; Nordgreen et al. 2007; Reilly et al. 2008a; Sneddon 2011a), but also scrutinized the behavioral responses to a potentially painful event (Sneddon et al. 2003a, 2003b, Sneddon 2003b; Dunlop et al. 2006; Reilly et al. 2008b; Roques et al. 2010; Mettam et al. 2011; Maximino 2011; Alves et al. 2013; Thomson et al. 2019, 2020), all of which are ameliorated by effective analgesia or pain-relief (Sneddon 2003b, 2012; Newby et al. 2009; Nordgreen et al. 2009; Mettam et al. 2011; Deakin et al. 2019a, 2019b).

The current definition of animal pain provides two clear concepts, which can be tested to determine whether fishes can be considered capable of experiencing pain (Sneddon et al. 2014). The first states that whole animal responses to painful stimulation must differ from non-painful stimuli. Animals must have the neural mechanisms to detect injurious stimuli via nociceptors. The information from nociceptors should be conveyed to the central nervous system for processing in brain areas that innervate motivation, emotions and learning. Stress physiology may be apparent since pain is inherently stressful. Behavioral responses during pain should not be simple, instantaneous reflexes but should be more prolonged including protective behaviors and avoidance of the painful event. Any adverse reactions should be reduced by the use of analgesics or pain-relieving drugs. The second key concept defining the pain experience is that the animal should alter future behavioral decisions upon this negative painful experience such that the animal's motivation is altered. Examples of this include the animal seeking analgesia or paying a cost to accessing pain-relief, or the animals may incur a cost to avoid pain and learn to avoid pain in the future. The animal's attention should be dominated by pain if it is important and may perform other tasks poorly, or behave inappropriately. Sneddon et al. (2014) propose that these criteria should not be considered in isolation but that specific animal groups must fulfill both sets to be considered capable of experiencing pain. The premise behind this second concept focuses on the fact that pain is a negative experience and as such it should drive changes in motivation, decision-making and changes in preferences and should result in avoidance learning. If pain were not an adverse experience, then animals would not learn or alter their behavior and would continue to engage with damaging stimuli resulting in injury, compromised health and possibly mortality. Thus, it is adaptive for animals to experience pain. Each of these areas shall be taken in turn to assess how well fishes fulfill these criteria.

10.2.1. *Whole animal responses to pain*

Electrophysiology and neuroanatomical approaches have characterized nociceptors (receptors that detect painful stimuli) in a teleost or bony fish, the rainbow trout (*Oncorhynchus mykiss*), for the first time (Sneddon 2002, 2003a).

Previous studies found possible nociceptors in a jawless fish, the lamprey (Matthews and Wicklegren 1978), but other studies have failed to find nociceptors in elasmobranchs (sharks, skates and rays), where there is a lack of C fibers, which are one type of nociceptor in mammals (e.g. Snow et al. 1996). When compared to mammalian models, the electrophysiological properties of these trout nociceptors are similar (Sneddon 2004, 2012, 2018). The only differences found so far are that trout nociceptors are not responsive to cold temperatures (<4°C) (Ashley et al. 2007); it would be adaptive for the trout nociceptors to be unresponsive to cold since this species can encounter very low temperatures naturally. Neural tract tracing studies have delineated the fish neuroanatomical pathways from peripheral areas to the brain which are highly conserved when compared with mammals (Sneddon 2004). Higher brain areas are active during noxious stimulation in fishes (e.g. gene expression in forebrain, midbrain and hindbrain of common carp, *Cyprinus carpio*, and rainbow trout, Reilly et al. 2008a; electrical activity in all brain areas in Atlantic salmon (*Salmo salar*), Nordgreen et al. 2007; goldfish (*Carassius auratus*) and rainbow trout, Dunlop and Laming 2005; activity using functional magnetic resonance imaging (fMRI) in common carp, Sneddon 2011); thus, CNS activity differs from non-painful stimuli and is not restricted to the nociceptive reflex centers in the hindbrain and spinal cord (Rose 2002). Since the whole brain is involved, these may underlie the prolonged changes in behavior described below. Finally, a range of analgesic drugs are effective in amending the pain-related changes in behavior and physiology seen in painfully treated fishes (Sneddon 2003b; Sneddon et al. 2003a; Mettam et al. 2011; review in Sneddon 2012) demonstrating that molecular responses are also conserved (review in Malafoglia et al. 2013). Thus, the pain neural apparatus in fishes is similar to the mammalian system.

Changes in behavioral and physiological responses to potentially painful stimuli suggest a negative affective component to pain. Common carp withdraw from electrical stimulation with responses reduced after anesthesia was administered, yet this did not affect motor activity (Chervova and Lapshin 2011). Fish learn to avoid electric shock, a painful stimulus, usually in one or a few trials (e.g. Yoshida and Hirano 2010). This avoidance behavior persists for up to three days (Dunlop et al. 2006), but fish will enter the shock zone to obtain food after three days of food deprivation (Millsopp and Laming 2008). When given potentially painful stimuli, fishes show prolonged, complicated responses (review in Sneddon 2009, 2015). Opercular beat rate (ventilation of the gills) increases by more than a stress response in rainbow trout and zebrafish (*Danio rerio*). Increased plasma cortisol, a stress hormone, has been recorded in rainbow trout (Sneddon 2003b; Ashley et al. 2009) and Mozambique tilapia (*Oreochromis niloticus*, Roques et al. 2012). Behavior is also altered; for example, a reduction in swimming is observed after painful treatment (Sneddon 2003b; Reilly et al. 2008b; Correia et al. 2011; Roques et al.

2012). Guarding behavior (i.e. avoiding using an area into which a painful stimulus has been administered) is seen in trout which avoid eating for up to three hours after a painful injection to the lips (Sneddon 2003b); sham-handled (anesthetized only) and saline-injected controls resume feeding after 80 minutes as do acid-injected fish when treated with morphine.

Species specific behavioral responses to pain vary between mammalian species (Flecknell et al. 2007), and these species-specific responses have been observed in fishes. Piauçu (*Leporinus macrocephalus*) injected with formalin and Nile tilapia that have had the tail fin clipped increase swimming (Roques et al. 2010; Alves et al. 2013). In contrast, Mozambique tilapia subject to electric shock and Atlantic salmon experiencing abdominal peritonitis due to vaccination decreased swimming (Bjørge et al. 2011; Roques et al. 2012). In addition, rainbow trout and zebrafish reduce activity when experiencing pain (review in Sneddon 2019), which has been observed in adult trout and zebrafish as well as very young larval zebrafish at less than five days post fertilization (Deakin et al. 2019a, 2019b; Lopez-Luna et al. 2017a, 2017b, 2017c, 2017d; Thomson et al. 2019, 2020) These disparate responses demonstrate that pain behavioral indicators will have to be characterized on a species-by-species basis and to different types of pain. Pain-related changes in behavior last from three hours up to two days in some cases; thus, they are not simple instantaneous nociceptive reflexes (Sneddon 2003b; Bjørge et al. 2011; Deakin et al. 2019a, 2019b).

When potentially painful events are applied to fishes, anomalous, novel behaviors such as tail beating in zebrafish are elicited. These zebrafish have been injected with mild acetic acid in close proximity to the tail fin and perform vigorous tail fin wafting, yet swimming and activity are both reduced (Maximino 2011; Schroeder and Sneddon 2017). Anomalous behaviors only observed in response to noxious chemical injection were described as rocking to and fro on the substrate by trout and carp, and rubbing of the injection site by trout and goldfish (Sneddon 2003; Sneddon et al. 2003b; Reilly et al. 2008b; Newby et al. 2009). These responses have only been recorded in fish given a painful treatment and not observed in sham-handled controls (anesthetized but no pain), saline-injected fish (non-painful), nor reported in toxicological studies. These anomalous behaviors are, therefore, a direct result of the painful treatment, and studies have shown that they are reduced by pain-relieving drugs (Sneddon 2003a; Mettam et al. 2011).

Learned avoidance studies have done much to improve our knowledge of pain and associated fear in animals, and this is discussed in detail below. Studies have shown that goldfish are able to learn to avoid noxious, potentially painful stimuli such as electric shock (Portavella et al. 2002, 2004). When morphine (an analgesic) was administered, the voltage required to elicit this response was significantly higher. Beyond this, MIF-1 and naloxone (opiate antagonists) were found to block the effects of morphine decreasing the voltage required to elicit a response. These antagonists have shown similar effects on morphine action in mammals (Ehrensing et al. 1982). Fishes can be conditioned to associate a noxious stimulus with a neutral stimulus such as a colored light, and the fish subsequently perform avoidance behavior in response to this neutral stimulus alone. Learned avoidance of a stimulus associated with a noxious experience has also been observed in other fish species (Overmier and Hollis 1983, 1990) including common carp, Cyprinus carpio, and pike, Esox lucius, avoiding hooks in angling trials (Beukema 1970a, 1970b).

10.2.2. *Motivational alterations*

Testing whether fishes show profound long-term changes in motivation and decision-making suggests that the pain experience had a substantial effect that alters future behavior. Although it is challenging to test this concept, contemporary studies have addressed this. Analgesic self-administration paradigms where food or water is laced with a painkiller and animals can self-select the drugged water or food to reduce their pain (e.g. Pham et al. 2010) are not feasible as fishes do not feed when in pain (Sneddon 2009). However, assessing whether the fishes will pay a cost to accessing pain-relief is possible. If the experience of pain is negative, then fish should pay in either additional effort or forgo access to a resource or favorable area to obtain pain-relief. Zebrafish when given the choice between an unfavorable bare, brightly lit chamber and a favorable less brightly lit, enriched chamber with a stimulus shoal and enrichment choose to spend the majority of their time in the enriched chamber on consecutive occasions. When these fish are given a painful treatment, acid injection or saline as a non-painful treatment, they still spend most of their time in the favorable enriched chamber. However, zebrafish that are painfully treated lose their preference for the favorable area and spend most of their time in the unfavorable chamber when an analgesic, lidocaine, is dissolved in the water of this chamber (Sneddon 2012). Controls that were given access to the lidocaine-dosed unfavorable chamber did not lose their preference and spent most of their time in the favored chamber; this demonstrates that it is neither an addictive nor a sedative effect of lidocaine that resulted in painfully treated zebrafish spending most of their time in an unfavorable area where lidocaine would relieve their pain. Thus, zebrafish seek to reduce their pain by forgoing the opportunity to be in a favorable area and to access analgesia in the unfavorable chamber.

Pain is an attention-dominating state; thus, if pain is important to an animal, then they should perform poorly on competing tasks or ignore them. Rainbow trout will ignore novel objects rather than show neophobia when in pain; however, avoidance is shown if morphine is given to the fish (Sneddon et al. 2003a). Anti-predator behavior such as seeking shelter and escape behavior are dramatically reduced when rainbow trout are noxiously stimulated (Ashley et al. 2009). Socially subordinate trout with high plasma cortisol concentrations exhibit almost no signs of pain, possibly due to endogenous analgesia (Ashley et al. 2009). Combined, these results demonstrate that pain takes priority over competing stimuli and that central mechanisms may be activated to reduce pain. When considering all of the empirical evidence together, these studies show that teleost fishes do fulfill the criteria for animal pain as proposed by Sneddon et al. (2014).

10.3. Fear in fish

Similarly to nociception and pain, fear serves a function that is fundamental to survival. Fear is the activation of a defensive behavioral system that protects animals or humans against potentially dangerous environmental threats (Fendt and Fanselow 1999). In higher vertebrates, these behavioral mechanisms are often accompanied by a range of autonomic changes (Le Doux 2000), such as increased heart rate (Black and Toledo 1972), endogenous analgesia (Bolles and Fanselow 1980) and the release of several hormones such as cortisol (Tomie et al. 2002). In humans, these responses are correlated with the subjective state of fear (Bradley et al. 1993; Jones 1997). Therefore, when investigating fear in animals, it is these behavioral and physiological responses that are measured. Three main criteria can be used to assess the validity of animal (largely rodent) models of human pain (Fendt and Fanselow 1999), and as such, these criteria may also provide insight when considering fear in other animals. However, note that they are anthropomorphic and human-centered. First, the systems that control fear response should be similar (have a common neuronal basis) to those neural systems that mediate human fear and anxiety. A variety of clearly threatening stimuli should generate a consistent set of behaviors that protect the individual against the threat. Finally, drugs that modulate human fear and anxiety should show similar effects in the animal. These criteria will be considered in turn to assess the potential of fear in fish.

10.3.1. Neural substrate of fear

As with pain, the neural machinery required to detect and react to fear-causing stimuli must be comparable with the mammalian brain circuitry. Fear is generally sensed as an external threat to the whole animal. For example, the predator test is a standard fear paradigm in experiments where an animal is exposed to the sight, odor or some other cue of a predator that elicits a fight or flight response (e.g. alarm substance in fishes, Silva et al. 2015; Quadros et al. 2016). Thus, fear stimuli are psychological threats to the survival of the whole animal and fear motivates the animal to make an appropriate defensive response such as freezing, hiding or fleeing. Fear can either be innate or unlearned whereby the stimulus elicits a fear response without the animal previously being exposed to the stimulus (e.g. the predator test) or fear can be learned, and in many experimental studies, animals are provided with a non-threatening cue or conditioned stimulus (CS) such as an innocuous light or sound paired with the presentation of a fear causing stimulus such as chasing or confinement (unconditioned stimulus; US) a few seconds later. After repeated trials of the CS–US the animal learns to respond to the CS or innocuous cue by showing a fear response in the absence of the actual fear stimulus. Rodent models have been employed in such paradigms investigating the neuronal circuitry and the mammalian amygdala and hippocampal regions are particularly important in mediating emotions especially fear learning and memory. Experiments in fishes have shown comparable behaviors, cognitive mechanisms and brain areas that are homologous to the fear circuitry in mammals (Gorissen et al. 2015; Nathan et al. 2015; Perathoner et al. 2016). For example, the dorsomedial telencephalon in the forebrain area of goldfish has identical functions in fear conditioning to the amygdala of mammals mediating fear responses and learning, whereas the goldfish dorsolateral telencephalon is homologous to the mammalian hippocampus involved in spatial learning and retrieval of memories (Portavella et al. 2002; Perathoner et al. 2016).

Lesion or electrical stimulation of the dorsomedial pallium (Dm; telencephalon) has been shown to affect aggressive behavior in fishes (Marino-Neto and Sabbatini 1983; Bradford 1995), and ablation of the telencephalon of fishes produces deficits in spatial and associative learning (Salas et al. 1996a, 1996b, Lopez et al. 2000a, 2000b). Through similar lesioning studies, Portavella et al. (2002, 2004) have studied the specific contribution of the Dm and dorsolateral pallium (Dl) to different types of learning and memory. Results from this work suggest that the Dm may be involved in emotional learning and the Dl may be involved in spatial or temporal learning. Similar studies in mammals have shown that lesions to the amygdala impair emotional conditioning (Lorenzini et al. 1991; Aggelton 1992; Eichenbaum et al. 1992; Killcross et al. 1997) while lesions to the hippocampus produce deficits in spatial and associative learning (Eichenbaum et al. 1992; Kesner 1998 in Portavella et al. 2002; Olton et al. 1987). Therefore, Dm and Dl areas of the fish telencephalon share functional similarities with the amygdala and hippocampus, respectively, in mammals.

The mammalian habenula (Hb) is in evolutionary terms a highly conserved diencephalic brain structure subdivided into medial and lateral regions (MHb and LHb, respectively). The LHb sends efferent neurons to monoaminergic neurons and has been implicated in the control of aversive learning and emotional behaviors. The MHb projects to the interpeduncular nucleus (IPN) and regulates fear responses. The zebrafish dorsal habenula (dHb) also connects with the IPN and is equivalent to the mammalian medial habenula. Anatomically, the habenula system in zebrafish is similar and studies have sought to address its function by silencing this system during fear responses. Genetic inactivation of the dHb resulted in zebrafish that froze rather than exhibiting the normal flight response to a conditioned fear stimulus, suggesting that the dHb-IPN pathway is important for controlling fear responses (Agetsuma et al. 2010). Activity in the medial habenula also influences the response to alarm substance, which elicits fear and anti-predator behaviors in zebrafish (Ogawa et al. 2014). Together, the above indicates a common neuronal basis for the fear response control systems of fishes and higher vertebrates.

10.3.2. Consistent suite of fear responses

Fear responses should generate a coherent set of behavioral and physiological reactions. Measurements of startling, freezing and other defensive behaviors can be coupled with physiological parameters such as heart rate and release of stress hormones, for example, cortisol. Studies in fishes have demonstrated a consistent response to threatening stimuli such as avoidance of novel objects; freezing to reduce conspicuousness; escape or fleeing behaviors; thigmotaxis, where the fish swims next to tank walls avoiding open, central areas; sinking to depth; fast start swimming and diving responses; and anti-predator behaviors (Maximino et al. 2010). Many rodent tests of fear and anxiety are now routinely applied to fish species such as open field, novel object, classical conditioning, avoidance learning, predator cues and scototaxis (preference for darker areas). Combined with studies on pain, fear responses can be evaluated as to whether pain or fear is more important. In rainbow trout, fish show a classic anti-predator response to alarm substance by performing increased escape responses and also hiding under cover. When trout were given a pain stimulus, they did not perform correct fear responses and did not increase their use of cover nor perform escape reactions, demonstrating in this context pain was imperative (Ashley et al. 2009).

Learned response experiments also enable experimenters to assess and measure consistent behavioral and physiological responses to fearful stimuli. Studies on fear conditioning in mammals often measure levels of freezing and startle behavior (Fendt and Fanselow 1999). In fishes, a number of different behavioral responses to potentially threatening stimuli have been described and include escape responses such as fast starts (Domenici and Blake 1997; Chandroo et al. 2004; Yue et al. 2004) or erratic movement (Cantalupo et al. 1995; Bisazza et al. 1998), as well as freezing and sinking in the water (Berejikian et al. 1999, 2003). Such behaviors may serve to protect the individual from the threat, and a number of studies have illustrated that these behaviors can be shown in response to an US through learned association with a CS. Many fish species release chemical alarm substances when injured. These are thought to act as warning signals, as conspecifics show an innate behavioral fright response to these chemicals (Smith 1992; Lebedeva et al. 1994; Brown and Smith 1997; Berejikian et al. 1999). For example, Crucian carp, *Carassius carassius L*, exposed to skin extract from conspecifics killed by decapitation showed significantly reduced feeding behavior and increased alarm behaviors when compared to fish exposed to a control substance (physiological saline) and the neutral amino acid L-alanine (Hamdani et al. 2000). These alarm behaviors included dashing movements, vigorous movements in the aquarium substrate and fast swimming towards hiding places, remaining there for an extended period. These behaviors are thought to be associated with predator evasion (Hamdani et al. 2000). Pearl dace, *Semotilus margarita*, show a clear behavioral response to alarm substance and a simultaneous increase in plasma concentrations of cortisol and glucose, indicating a stress response (Rehnberg et al. 1987). Nile tilapia similarly displays decreased feeding, erratic swimming and a physiological stress response to alarm substance (Carretero Sanches et al. 2015).

Learned avoidance studies not only show that a consistent suite of behaviors are produced in response to fearful stimuli; they also provide evidence that the displayed behavior is not merely a reflex response. Learning to avoid an aversive stimulus in the future implies a cognitive process of recognizing that the behavioral response will lead to the desired effect of avoidance (Yue et al. 2004). Mosquitofish, *Girardinus falcatus*, perform a fast start escape response to a simulated predator (Cantalupo et al. 1995). In this experiment, the predator was only presented when the fish swam across the median portion of the tank. Interestingly, with repeated exposure, the fish began to avoid this particular portion of the tank. If the fish happened to swim in the tank center, it tended to perform an erratic zigzag movement (Bisazza et al. 1998; Chandroo et al. 2004; Yue et al. 2004). It has been suggested that this apparent learned association of the predator threat with a particular spatial area may require involvement of brain areas homologous to the hippocampus, as the spatial aspects of fearful stimuli are processed by the hippocampus and transmitted to the amygdala in associative learning in higher vertebrates (Maren 2001; Chandroo et al. 2004). The avoidance or zigzag escape strategy prevented the predator stimulation or removed the fish from the previously perceived negative stimulus, and therefore, it has been suggested that the fish could anticipate this frightening stimulus and the escape response was in part motivated by an affective state of fear (Chandroo et al. 2004; Yue et al. 2004).

Studies using conditioned place preference (CPP) and conditioned place avoidance (CPA) can provide insight into the positive and negative valence or quality of a stimulus to an animal. In CPP, animals are given a reward in a specific place and the animals develop a preference to be in this area. Thus, zebrafish fed in one chamber as opposed to another will spend the majority of their time in the positively rewarded chamber, thus developing a preference for this area (Wong et al. 2014). However, if a negative event, in this case different anesthetic drugs, is presented to the fish in the positive chamber, the zebrafish then delay return to the previously preferred chamber or actually avoid it (i.e. CPA). The length of delay in returning or avoidance can provide a gauge as to how negative the experience was so can determine how aversive the anesthetic drugs are (Wong et al. 2014). This approach was employed to test the response to a positive reward, food and a presumed negative event, net chasing, in gilthead sea bream. Fish exposed to the food reward spent significantly more time in the rewarded area, whereas those individuals subject to net chasing avoided the area (Millot et al. 2014).

10.3.3. *Impact of anti-anxiety drugs*

The final key criterion that animals must fulfill is demonstrating that anti-anxiety drugs reduce any fear responses such as those described above. Many agents are used to decrease fear and anxiety including benzodiazepines, opioids, cholinergic and serotonergic agents. Benzodiazepines are a major class of drugs used to treat human anxiety disorders and have been shown to reduce fear in mammalian models. Benzodiazepines act by enhancing the action of a neurotransmitter, GABA (gamma-aminobutyric acid), which has an inhibitory influence and thus exerts a sedatory effect. Benzodiazepines, such as diazepam, act at specific sites in the brain and modulate these changes in anxiety and fear behavior. However, there has been far less research into these mechanisms and anxiety-like states in other species. Binding sites for benzodiazepines have been found in the brains of fishes, and several experiments have shown that they reduce fear responses in zebrafish (Review in Stewart et al. 2011). These sites in the fish brain are found in the same areas that are found in mammals (Nielsen et al. 1978; Hebebrand et al. 1988; Rehnberg et al. 1989), and administration of the benzodiazepine drug chlordiazepoxide has been shown to reduce attacking in agonistic encounters between male Siamese fighting fish, *Betta splendans*, without inducing noticeable toxic or sedative effects (Figler et al. 1975). Studies on fathead minnows treated with chlordiazepoxide provide evidence to suggest that the benzodiazepine receptors in the central nervous system of fish may serve to modify behavior in anxiety-like states in similar ways to those seen in higher vertebrates (Rehnberg et al. 1989). When exposed to an alarm substance, the control minnows displayed a behavioral alarm response, and when a chemical feeding stimulus was released into the water while the fish were still in an alarmed state, these fish showed low levels of exploratory behavior. However, when fish were exposed to high, but non-sedative, levels of chlordiazepoxide, they did not show the fright response to the alarm substance and displayed vigorous exploration when presented with the chemical feeding stimulus (Rehnberg et al. 1989). Rodents that have been administered benzodiazepines show similar changes in exploratory behavior (Crawley 1985; Rehnberg et al. 1989). Piracetam, a derivative of GABA, is prescribed to reduce clinical anxiety in humans. Chronic administration of piracetam also reduces fear behavior in zebrafish where fish spend more time in a white area in a scototaxic (light versus dark chamber) test (Grossman et al. 2011). The opioidergic system has a key role in the modulation of human and animal fear. Fishes possess a functional opioidergic system, including both opioid peptides and their receptors akin to the mammalian system. Opioid administration in zebrafish in a fear test reduced the amount of erratic, flight swimming (Stewart et al. 2011). Serotonergic mechanisms are not only implicated in depression but also animal anxiety. Selective serotonin reuptake inhibitors (SSRIs) are potent modulators of brain serotonin, and many of these drugs have been employed in mammalian studies seeking to reduce fear. Zebrafish have a well-developed serotonergic system, but this is not anatomically or genetically identical; however, many fish serotonin receptors have similar expression patterns, binding and physiological properties compared with mammals. As with rodent and human clinical studies on the use of SSRIs, clear anxiolytic action or diminished fear responses of chronic fluoxetine has been recorded in zebrafish. The cholinergic system relates to the sympathetic and parasympathetic nerve fibers or neurons in which acetylcholine (ACh) is the neurotransmitter liberated at a synapse. Cholinergic receptors are of two types: nicotinic receptors, which are situated in striated muscles, and muscarinic receptors, which are situated in parasympathetically innervated structures. Low choline levels have been related to high anxiety in humans; therefore, attention is now turning to the cholinergic system as a new target for reducing fear. Zebrafish administered with nicotine (nicotinic-cholinergic agonist) were more active and spent less time at the bottom compared with untreated fish who displayed a classic fear response of freezing and remaining on the bottom of the tank in a novel tank test (Stewart et al. 2011). Thus, the neurobiological mechanisms of fear and the impact of selective drugs to reduce fear in humans and mammals are also apparent in fishes.

10.4. Implications in the use of fishes

Any procedure that humans subject fishes to that is tissue damaging or is perceived as a challenge to survival has the potential to cause pain and fear in fishes, thereby compromising their welfare. Fishes do appear to fulfill the criteria for experiencing pain as defined by Sneddon et al. (2014). Studies have confirmed that agnathans and teleosts possess nociceptors and the physiological and anatomical properties of these nociceptors are similar to those seen in higher vertebrates. The fish groups do possess the brain areas and pathways leading to higher brain centers that are necessary for pain to occur in other vertebrate models and that brain activity occurs in forebrain and midbrain areas rather than being restricted to reflex centers. Analgesics have been shown to reduce behavioral response to noxious stimuli, and learned avoidance to injurious stimuli has been demonstrated in those fish species tested. In a number of teleost species, profound physiological and behavioral changes are apparent while the fishes endure a painful event and these responses were shown over a prolonged period of time rather than instantaneous reflex responses. This indirect evidence would suggest pain rather than a nociceptive reflex. When assessing the motivational state of fear, researchers have investigated the behavioral and physiological changes that accompany fear in fishes in comparison to humans. These include the existence of a common neuronal mechanism that controls the fear response, consistent behavioral and physiological responses to a variety of clearly threatening stimuli and the ability of anti-anxiety drugs to reduce fear. Based on these criteria, it would seem that fishes experience fear.

If we accept that fishes are capable of experiencing some form of pain and fear, then we have to accept that their well-being is impaired when we subject them to any tissue damaging or fear-causing event. We have a complicated relationship with fish as we use them as an important foodstuff, an experimental model, essential species within our conservation efforts and a source of entertainment in angling, public exhibits and scuba diving or for companionship as pets (Sneddon 2013). The precautionary principle dictates that we give animals the benefit of the doubt as to their internal experience of negative states such as pain or fear; thus, by adopting this, we should apply ethical, welfare-friendly thinking to how we use fish. This does not preclude us from using fish, but we should do so as humanely as possible in order to improve their health and welfare. If animals fulfill all criteria for pain as proposed by Sneddon et al. (2014), then they should be treated in a manner that enables the avoidance or reduction of pain. The evidence for pain and fear in teleost fishes is substantial; therefore, this should inform ethical decision-making when considering the welfare of fish.

Improving existing procedures in aquaculture, fisheries, angling, experimentation, public exhibits and the ornamental animal industry is vital. Humane methods for animal slaughter are based on the principle that the animal is killed quickly with minimum fear and pain. However, aquaculture and recreational angling slaughter methods have been developed not to minimize stress but to achieve product quality control, efficiency and processor safety (Conte 2004). Methods vary and include electrical stunning followed by decapitation, blunt trauma to the cranium and percussive stunning using captive bolt. A variety of injuries, stress reactions and mortalities occur during capture and release of fishes by hook and line (Chopin and Arimoto 1995) and the use of a variety of nets in both commercial (Thompson et al. 1971) and recreational fishing (Steeger et al. 1994; Pottinger 1997; Cooke and Hogle 2000; Barthel et al. 2003; Cooke and Sneddon 2007) can also cause abrasion injuries leaving open lesions that are readily infected with bacteria and fungi (Barthel et al. 2003). Damage also occurs when fish collide with commercial trawling nets or gear, evident in injuries to jaws and vertebral column (Miyashita et al. 2000), and skin injuries are sustained when escaping from trawl cod ends and through trawl nets (Suuronen et al. 1996; Olla et al. 1997; Reviews in Metcalfe 2009; Sneddon and Wolfenden 2012). Consumers are willing to pay more for better welfare in terrestrial farm animals, for example, free range produce. This also applies to fishes, where consumers are asking where the fish are caught from and the method used. Poor management of fisheries has led to unsustainable fishing practices and population crashes of key species (Sneddon and Wolfenden 2012) as well as death of non-target animals or by-catch such as birds, cetaceans, turtles and so on. Aggressive behavior is a well-known problem in aquaculture where injuries to dorsal, pectoral and caudal fins, eyes and opercula are common and can have a range of effects on feeding behavior and growth through to infections and even mortality (Abbott and Dill 1985; Turnbull 1992; Turnbull et al. 1998; Greaves and Tuene 2001; Ashley 2007). Many finfish are subject to tagging procedures, in particular fin clipping as well as other invasive methods, which is known to be painful and tagging does elicit a physiological stress response (Sharpe et al. 1998; Sloman et al. 2019). Therefore, enhancing the well-being of fishes will undoubtedly benefit the aquaculture, fisheries and ornamental fish trades by yielding a better economic return.

The European Directive (Directive 2010/63/EU) concerns the welfare of protected experimental animals including fishes which are already included in the regulations of many countries. Little is known regarding the welfare of fishes in comparison with mammalian laboratory models (Sloman et al. 2019). Research is specifically required on appropriate analgesic protocols for fishes as well as housing since some anesthetics may be aversive (Wong et al. 2014). When experimental procedures cause tissue damage and the objectives of the research are not the study of pain, appropriate pain-relief should be administered to minimize any pain since a range of analgesics prevent behavioral responses to pain in fishes (review in Sloman et al. 2019). Improved welfare in the laboratory can yield more valid, reliable results from experimental studies. Research in rodents has demonstrated that individuals held under better welfare conditions give higher-quality data with reduced intraspecific variation (Singhal et al. 2014).

Although approached separately in this chapter, pain and fear are by no means exclusive of one another. This is well illustrated by a study using rainbow trout. When compared to controls, noxiously stimulated trout did not show an appropriate fear response to a fear-causing stimulus (Sneddon et al. 2003b). Theories on attention propose that that there is a limited capacity or pool of attention and that pain may prioritize, or "soak up", a large amount of this pool, leaving little capacity for competing stimuli (Kuhajda et al. 2002). This would suggest that the consequences of nociception may involve higher processing. In the trout, the noxious experience may have dominated attention and, therefore, normal responses to the fearful stimulus were not seen. Little work has been conducted on other species, but common carp do show similar anomalous behaviors while enduring acetic acid injection as given to the trout (Reilly et al. 2004). Many clinical studies have shown that humans do not perform as well on other tasks when in pain (Kuhajda et al. 2002). A reduction in the normal fear response in any animal would serve to reduce the functions of that response, namely threat or predator avoidance. Theoretically, there is, therefore, the possibility that a noxious stimulus may be indirectly damaging to a fish by reducing predator vigilance. This remains to be tested; however, Ryer (2002) has shown that walleye pollock, *Theragra chalcogramma*, exposed to a simulated trawl-stressor were less likely to avoid a predator and were consumed in greater numbers by a predator when compared to controls.

10.5. Conclusion

It is clear that we must take an ethical approach to the welfare of fishes, and since there is significant evidence to suggest their well-being is adversely affected by potentially painful and fearful situations, it is our moral responsibility to reduce any possible suffering and discomfort. A plethora of studies are now being conducted that are aimed at improving our equipment and methods to make procedures less invasive for the fish and improve welfare. In theory, if we improve well-being, productivity is enhanced and a better economic return can be made as well as producing disease-free healthy individuals; therefore, it is in our interest to consider fish welfare issues from an ethical, moral economic and public health perspective.

10.6. References

Abbott, J.C. and Dill, L.M. (1985). Patterns of aggressive attack in juvenile steelhead trout (Salmo-Gairdneri). *Canadian Journal of Fisheries and Aquatic Sciences*, 42, 1702–1706.

Agetsuma, M., Aizawa, H., Aoki, T., Nakayama, R., Takahoko, M., Goto, M., Sassa, T., Amo, R., Shiraki, T., Kawakami, K. et al. (2010). The habenula is crucial for experience-dependent modification of fear responses in zebrafish. *Nature Neuroscience*, 13, 1354–1356.

Alves, F.L., Barbosa Júnior, A., Hoffmann, A. (2013). Antinociception in piauçu fish induced by exposure to the conspecific alarm substance. *Physiology and Behavior*, 110–111, 58–62.

Ashley, P.J. (2007). Fish welfare: Current issues in aquaculture. *Applied Animal Behaviour Science*, 104, 199–235.

Ashley P.J. and Sneddon L.U. (2008). Pain and fear in fish. In *Fish Welfare*, Branson, E.J (ed.). Blackwell Publishing, Oxford.

Ashley. P.J., Sneddon, L.U., McCrohan, C.R. (2006). Properties of corneal receptors in a teleost fish. *Neuroscience Letters*, 410, 165–168.

Ashley, P.J., Sneddon, L.U., McCrohan, C.R. (2007). Nociception in fish: Stimulus–response properties of receptors on the head of trout *Oncorhynchus mykiss*. *Brain Research*, 1166, 47–54.

Ashley, P.J., Ringrose, S., Edwards, K.L., McCrohan, C.R., Sneddon, L.U. (2009). Effect of noxious stimulation upon antipredator responses and dominance status in rainbow trout. *Animal Behaviour*, 77, 403–410.

Barthel, B.L., Cooke, S.J., Suski, C.D., Philipp, D.P. (2003). Effects of landing net mesh type on injury and mortality in a freshwater recreational fishery. *Fisheries Research*, 63, 275–282.

Berejikian, B.A., Smith, R.J.F., Tezak, E.P., Schroder, S.L., Knudsen, C.M. (1999). Chemical alarm signals and complex hatchery rearing habitats affect antipredator behavior and survival of chinook salmon (*Oncorhynchus tshawytscha*) juveniles. *Canadian Journal of Fisheries and Aquatic Sciences*, 56, 830–838.

Berejikian, B.A., Tezak, E.P., LaRae, A.L. (2003). Innate and enhanced predator recognition in hatchery-reared chinook salmon. *Environmental Biology of Fishes*, 67, 241–251.

Beukema, J.J. (1970a). Angling experiments with carp (*Cyprinus carpio* L.) II. Decreased catchability through one trial learning A. *Netherlands Journal of Zoology*, 19, 81–92.

Beukema, J.J. (1970b). Acquired hook avoidance in the pike *Esox lucius* L. fished with artificial and natural baits. *Journal of Fish Biology*, 2, 155–160.

Bisazza, A., Rogers, L.J., Vallortigara, G. (1998). The origins of cerebral asymmetry: A review of evidence of behavioural and brain lateralization in fishes, reptiles and amphibians. *Neuroscience and Biobehavioral Reviews*, 22, 411–426.

Black, A.H. and de Toledo, L. (1972). The relationship among classically conditioned responses: Heart rate and skeletal behavior. In *Classical Conditioning II. Current Theory and Research*, Black, A.H. and Prokasy, W.F. (eds). Appleton, New York.

Bolles, R.C. and Fanselow, M.S. (1980). A perceptual-defensive-recuperative model of fear and pain. *Behavioral and Brain Sciences*, 3, 291–301.

Bradford, M.R. (1995). Comparative aspects of forebrain organization in the ray-finned fishes – Touchstones or not. *Brain Behavior and Evolution*, 46, 259–274.

Bradley, M.M., Lang, P.J., Cuthbert, B.N. (1993). Emotion, novelty, and the startle reflex – Habituation in humans. *Behavioral Neuroscience*, 107, 970–980.

Brown, G.E. and Smith R.J.F. (1997). Conspecific skin extracts elicit antipredator responses in juvenile rainbow trout (*Oncorhynchus mykiss*). *Canadian Journal of Zoology*, 75, 11, 1916–1922.

Brown, G.E. and Smith, R.J.F. (1998). Acquired predator recognition in juvenile rainbow trout (*Oncorhynchus mykiss*): Conditioning hatchery-reared fish to recognize chemical cues of a predator. *Canadian Journal of Fisheries and Aquatic Sciences*, 55(3), 611–617.

Cantalupo, C., Bisazza, A., Vallortigara, G. (1995). Lateralization of predator-evasion response in a teleost fish (*Girardinus falcatus*). *Neuropsychologia*, 33, 1637–1646.

Carretero Sanches, F.H., Miyai, C.A., Pinho-Neto, C.F., Barreto, R.E. (2015). Stress responses to chemical alarm cues in Nile tilapia. *Physiology and Behavior*, 149, 8–13.

Chandroo, K.P., Duncan, I.J.H., Moccia, R.D. (2004). Can fish suffer? Perspectives on sentience, pain, fear and stress. *Applied Animal Behaviour Science*, 86, 225–250.

Chopin, F.S. and Arimoto, T. (1995). The condition of fish escaping from fishing gears – A review. *Fisheries Research*, 21, 315–327.

Conte, F.S. (2004). Stress and the welfare of cultured fish. *Applied Animal Behaviour Science*, 86, 205–223.

Cooke, S.J. and Hogle, W.J. (2000). Effects of retention gear on the injury and short-term mortality of adult smallmouth bass. *North American Journal of Fisheries Management*, 20, 1033–1039.

Cooke, S.J. and Sneddon, L.U. (2007). Animal welfare perspectives on recreational angling. *Applied Animal Behaviour Science*, 104, 176–198.

Crawley, J.N. (1985). Exploratory behavior models of anxiety in mice. *Neuroscience and Biobehavioral Reviews*, 9, 37–44.

Deakin, A.G., Buckley, J., AlZu'bi, H.S., Cossins, A.R., Spencer, J.W., Al'Nuaimy, W., Young, I.S., Sneddon, L.U. (2019a). Automated monitoring of behaviour in zebrafish after invasive procedures. *Scientific Reports*, 9, 9042.

Deakin, A.G., Spencer, J.W., Cossins, A.R.C., Young, I.S., Sneddon, L.U. (2019b). Welfare challenges influence the complexity of movement: Fractal analysis of behaviour in zebrafish. *Fishes*, 4, 8.

Domenici, P. and Blake, R.W. (1997). The kinematics and performance of fish fast-start swimming. *Journal of Experimental Biology*, 200, 1165–1178.

Dunlop, R. and Laming, P. (2005). Mechanoreceptive and nociceptive responses in the central nervous system of goldfish (*Carassius auratus*) and trout (*Oncorhynchus mykiss*). *Journal of Pain*, 6, 561–568.

Dunlop, R., Millsopp, S., Laming, P. (2006). Avoidance learning in goldfish (*Carassius auratus*) and trout (*Oncorhynchus mykiss*) and implications for pain perception. *Applied Animal Behaviour Science*, 97, 255–271.

Ehrensing, R.H., Michell, G.F., Kastin, A.J. (1982). Similar antagonism of morphine analgesia by Mif-1 and naloxone in *Carassius auratus*. *Pharmacology Biochemistry and Behavior*, 17, 757–761.

Eichenbaum, H., Otto, T., Cohen, N.J. (1992). The hippocampus – What does it do? *Behavioral and Neural Biology*, 57, 2–36.

Fendt, M. and Fanselow, M.S. (1999). The neuroanatomical and neurochemical basis of conditioned fear. *Neuroscience and Biobehavioral Reviews*, 23, 743–760.

Figler, M.H., Klein, R.M., Thompson, C.S. (1975). Chlordiazepoxide (librium)-induced changes in intraspecific attack and selected non-agonistic behaviors in male Siamese fighting fish. *Psychopharmacologia*, 42, 139–145.

Gorissen, M., Manuel, R., Pelgrim, T.N.M., Mes, W., de Wolf, M.J.S., Zethof, J., Flik, G., van den Bos, R. (2015) Differences in inhibitory avoidance, cortisol and brain gene expression in TL and AB zebrafish. *Genes, Brain and Behavior*, 14, 428–438.

Greaves, K. and Tuene, S. (2001). The form and context of aggressive behaviour in farmed Atlantic halibut (*Hippoglossus hippoglossus* L.). *Aquaculture*, 193, 139–147.

Grossman, L., Stewart, A., Gaikwad, S., Utterback, E., Wu, N., DiLeo, J., Frank, K., Hart, P., Howard, H., Kalueff, A.V. (2011). Effects of piracetam on behavior and memory in adult zebrafish. *Brain Research Bulletin*, 85, 58–63.

Hamdani, E.H., Stabell, O.B., Alexander, G., Doving, K.B. (2000). Alarm reaction in the crucian carp is mediated by the medial bundle of the medial olfactory tract. *Chemical Senses*, 25, 103–109.

Hebebrand, J., Friedl, W., Reichelt, R., Schmitz, E., Moller, P., Propping, P. (1988). The shark Gaba-Benzodiazepine receptor – Further evidence for a not so late phylogenetic appearance of the benzodiazepine receptor. *Brain Research*, 446, 251–261.

IASP (2020). IASP announces revised definition of pain [Online]. Available at: https://www.iasp-pain.org/PublicationsNews/NewsDetail.aspx?ItemNumber=10475 [Accessed 1 March 2021].

Jones, R.B. (1997). Fear and distress. In *Animal Welfare*, Appleby, M.C. and Hughes, B.O. (eds). CAB International University Press, Cambridge.

Kesner, R.P. (1998). Neural mediation of memory for time: Role of the hippocampus and medial prefrontal cortex. *Psychol. Bull. Rev.*, 5, 585–596.

Key, B. (2016). Why fish do not feel pain. *Animal Sentience*, 3 [Online]. Available at: http://animalstudiesrepository.org/animsent/vol1/iss3/1/.

Killcross, S., Robbins, T.W., Everitt, B.J. (1997). Different types of fear-conditioned behaviour mediated by separate nuclei within amygdala. *Nature*, 388, 377–380.

Kuhajda, M.C., Thorn, B.E., Klinger, M.R., Rubin, N.J. (2002). The effect of headache pain on attention (encoding) and memory (recognition). *Pain*, 97, 213–221.

Le Doux, J.E. (2000). Emotion circuits in the brain. *Annual Review of Neuroscience*, 23, 155–184.

Lebedeva, N.Y., Vosilene, M.A.Y., Golovkina, R.V. (1994). Aspects of stress in rainbow trout, *Salmo gairdneri*, release of chemical alarm signals. *Journal of Ichthyology*, 33, 66–74.

Lopez, J.C., Bingman, V.P., Rodriguez, F., Gomez, Y., Salas, C. (2000a). Dissociation of place and cue learning by telencephalic ablation in goldfish. *Behavioral Neuroscience*, 114, 687–699.

Lopez, J.C., Broglio, C., Rodriguez, F., Thinus-Blanc, C., Salas, C. (2000b). Reversal learning deficit in a spatial task but not in a cued one after telencephalic ablation in goldfish. *Behavioural Brain Research*, 109, 91–98.

Lopez-Luna, J., Al-Jubouri, Q., Al-Nuaimy, W., Sneddon L.U. (2017a). Activity reduced by noxious chemical stimulation is ameliorated by immersion in analgesic drugs in zebrafish. *J. Exp. Biol.*, 220, 1451–1458.

Lopez-Luna, J., Al-Jubouri, Q., Al-Nuaimy, W., Sneddon L.U. (2017b). Impact of analgesic drugs on the behavioural responses of larval zebrafish to potentially noxious temperatures. *Appl. Anim. Behav. Sci.*, 188, 97–105.

Lopez-Luna, J., Al-Jubouri, Q., Al-Nuaimy, W., Sneddon, L.U. (2017c). Impact of stress, fear and anxiety on the nociceptive responses of larval zebrafish. *PLoS One*, 12(8): e0181010.

Lopez-Luna, J., Canty, M.N., Al-Jubouri, Q., Al-Nuaimy, W., Sneddon, L.U. (2017d). Behavioural responses of fish larvae modulated by analgesic drugs after a stress exposure. *Appl. Anim. Behav. Sci.*, 195, 115–120.

Lorenzini, A., Bucherelli, C., Falchini, S., Giachetti, A., Tassoni, G. (1991). Inhibition of conditioned freezing after selective lesions of the amygdala in the rat. *International Journal of Psychophysiology*, 11(1), 15–15.

Malafoglia, V., Bryant, B., Raffaeli, W., Giordano, A., Bellipanni, G. (2013). The zebrafish as a model for nociception studies. *Journal of Cellular Physiology*, 228, 1956–1966.

Maximino, C. (2011). Modulation of nociceptive-like behavior in zebrafish (*Danio rerio*) by environmental stressors. *Psychology and Neuroscience*, 4, 149–155.

Maximino, C., Marques de Brito, T., Dias. C.A., Gouveia Jr., A., Morato, S. (2010). Scototaxis as anxiety-like behavior in fish. *Nature Protocols*, 5, 209–216.

Maren, S. (2001). Neurobiology of Pavlovian fear conditioning. *Annual Review of Neuroscience*, 24, 897–931.

Marino-Neto, J. and Sabbatini, R.M. (1983). Discrete telencephalic lesions accelerate the habituation rate of behavioural arousal responses in Siamese fighting fish (*Betta splendens*). *Brazilian Journal of Biological Research*, 16, 271–278.

Matthews, G. and Wickelgren W.O. (1978). Trigeminal sensory neurons of the sea lamprey. *Journal of Comparative Physiology A*, 123, 329–333.

Merker, B.H. (2016). The line drawn on pain still holds. *Animal Sentience*, 90 [Online]. Available at: http://animalstudiesrepository.org/animsent/vol1/iss3/46/.

Metcalfe, J.D. (2009). Welfare in wild-capture marine fisheries. *Journal of Fish Biology*, 75, 2855–2861.

Mettam, J.M., Oulton, L.J., McCrohan, C.R., Sneddon, L.U. (2011). The efficacy of three types of analgesic drug in reducing pain in the rainbow trout, *Oncorhynchus mykiss*. *Applied Animal Behaviour Science*, 133, 265–274.

Mettam J.J., McCrohan C.R., Sneddon L.U. (2012). Characterisation of chemosensory trigeminal receptors in the rainbow trout (*Oncorhynchus mykiss*): Responses to irritants and carbon dioxide. *Journal of Experimental Biology*, 215, 685–693.

Millot, S., Cerqueira, M., Castanheira, M.F., Øverli, O., Martins, C.I.M., Oliveira, R.F. (2014). Use of conditioned place preference/avoidance tests to assess affective states in fish. *Applied Animal Behaviour Science*, 154, 104–111.

Millsopp, S. and Laming, P. (2008). Trade-offs between feeding and shock avoidance in goldfish (*Carassius auratus*). *Applied Animal Behaviour Science*, 113, 247–254.

Miyashita, S., Sawada, Y., Hattori, N., Nakatsukasa, H., Okada, T., Murata, O., Kumai, H. (2000). Mortality of blue fin tuna *Thunnus thynnus* due to trauma caused by collision during grow out culture. *Journal of the World Aquaculture Society*, 31, 632–639.

Nathan, F.M., Ogawa, S., Pahar, I.S. (2015). Kisspeptin1 modulate odorant evoked fear response in two serotonin receptor subtypes (5-HT$_{1A}$ and 5-HT$_2$) in zebrafish. *Journal of Neurochemistry*, 133, 870–878.

Newby, N.C., Wilkie, M.P., Stevens, E.D. (2009). Morphine uptake, disposition, and analgesic efficacy in the common goldfish (*Carassius auratus*). *Canadian Journal of Zoology*, 87, 388–399.

Nielsen, M., Braestrup, C., Squires, R.F. (1978). Evidence for a late evolutionary appearance of brain specific benzodiazepine receptors – Investigation of 18 vertebrate and 5 invertebrate species. *Brain Research*, 141, 342–346.

Nordgreen, J., Horsberg, T.E., Ranheim, B., Chen, A.C.N. (2007). Somatosensory evoked potentials in the telencephalon of Atlantic salmon (*Salmo salar*) following galvanic stimulation of the tail. *Journal of Comparative Physiology Part A*, 193, 1235–1242.

Nordgreen, J., Garner, J.P., Janczak, A.M., Ranheim, B., Muir, W.M., Horsberg, T.E. (2009). Thermonociception in fish: Effects of two different doses of morphine on thermal threshold and post-test behaviour in goldfish (*Carassius auratus*). *Applied Animal Behaviour Science*, 119, 101–107.

Ogawa, S., Nathan, F.M., Parhar, I.S. (2014). Habenular kisspeptin modulates fear in the zebrafish. *Proceedings of the National Academy of Sciences of the United States of America*, 111, 3841–3846.

Olla, B.L., Davis, M.W., Schreck, C.B. (1997). Effects of simulated trawling on sablefish and walleye pollock: The role of light intensity, net velocity and towing duration. *Journal of Fish Biology*, 50, 1181–1194.

Olton, D.S., Meck, W.H., Church, R.M. (1987). Separation of hippocampal and amygdaloid involvement in temporal memory dysfunctions. *Brain Research*, 404, 180–188.

Overmier, J.B. and Hollis, K.L. (1983). The teleostean telencephalon in learning. In *Fish Neurobiology, Vol. 2: Higher Brain Areas and Functions*, Davis, R.E. and Northcutt, R.G. (eds). University of Michigan Press, Ann Arbor.

Overmier, J.B. and Hollis, K.L. (1990). Fish in the think tank: Learning, memory and integrated behaviour. In *Neurobiology of Comparative Cognition*, Kesner, R.P. and Olson, D.S. (eds). Lawrence Erlbaum, Hillsdales.

Perathoner, S., Cordero-Maldonado, M.L., Crawford, A.D. (2016). Potential of zebrafish as a model for exploring the role of the amygdala in emotional memory and motivational behaviour. *Journal of Neuroscience Research*, 94, 445–462.

Portavella, M., Vargas, J.P., Torres, B., Salas, C. (2002). The effects of telencephalic pallial lesions on spatial, temporal, and emotional learning in goldfish. *Brain Research Bulletin*, 57, 397–399.

Portavella, M., Torres, B., Salas, C., Papini, M.R. (2004). Lesions of the medial pallium, but not of the lateral pallium, disrupt spaced-trial avoidance learning in goldfish (*Carassius auratus*). *Neuroscience Letters*, 362, 75–78.

Pottinger, T.G. (1997). Changes in water quality within anglers' keepnets during the confinement of fish. *Fisheries Management Ecology*, 4, 341–354.

Quadros, V.A., Silveira, A., Giuliani, G.S., Didonet, F., Silveira, A.S., Nunes, M.E., Silva, T.O., Loro, V.L., Rosemberg, D.B. (2016). Strain- and context-dependent behavioural responses of acute alarm substance exposure in zebrafish. *Behavioural Processes*, 122, 1–11.

Rehnberg, B.G., Smith, R.J.F., Sloley, B.D. (1987). The reaction of pearl dace (Pisces, Cyprinidae) to alarm substance – Time course of behavior, brain amines, and stress physiology. *Canadian Journal of Zoology – Revue Canadienne De Zoologie*, 65, 2916–2921.

Rehnberg, B.G., Bates, E.H., Smith, R.J.F., Sloley, B.D., Richardson, J.S. (1989). Brain benzodiazepine receptors in fathead minnows and the behavioral-response to alarm pheromone. *Pharmacology Biochemistry and Behavior*, 33, 435–442.

Reilly, S.C., Cossins, A.R., Quinn, J.P., Sneddon, L.U. (2004). Discovering genes: The use of microarrays and laser capture microdissection in pain research. *Brain Research Reviews*, 46(2), 225–333.

Reilly, S.C., Quinn, J.P., Cossins, A.R., Sneddon, L.U. (2008a). Novel candidate genes identified in the brain during nociception in common carp (*Cyprinus carpio*) and rainbow trout (*Oncorhynchus mykiss*). *Neuroscience Letters*, 437, 135–138.

Reilly, S.C., Quinn, J.P., Cossins, A.R., Sneddon, L.U. (2008b). Behavioural analysis of a nociceptive event in fish: Comparisons between three species demonstrate specific responses. *Applied Animal Behaviour Science*, 114, 248–259.

Roques, J.A.C., Abbink, W., Geurds, F., van de Vis, H., Flik, G. (2010). Tailfin clipping, a painful procedure: Studies on Nile tilapia and common carp. *Physiology and Behavior*, 101, 533–540.

Roques, J.A.C., Abbink, W., Chereau, G., Fourneyron, A., Spanings, T., Burggraaf, D., van de Bos, R., van de Vis, H., Flik, G. (2012). Physiological and behavioral responses to an electrical stimulus in Mozambique tilapia (*Oreochromis mossambicus*). *Fish Physiology and Biochemistry*, 38, 1019–1028.

Rose, J.D. (2002). The neurobehavioral nature of fishes and the question of awareness and pain. *Reviews in Fisheries Science*, 10, 1–38.

Ryer, C.H. (2002). Trawl stress and escapee vulnerability to predation in juvenile walleye pollock: Is there an unobserved by-catch of behaviourally impaired escapees? *Marine Ecology – Progress Series*, 232, 269–279.

Salas, C., Broglio, C., Rodriguez, F., Lopez, J.C., Portavella, M., Torres, B. (1996a). Telencephalic ablation in goldfish impairs performance in a "spatial constancy" problem but not in a cued one. *Behavioural Brain Research*, 79, 193–200.

Salas, C., Rodriguez, F., Vargas, J.P., Duran, E., Torres, B. (1996b). Spatial learning and memory deficits after telencephalic ablation in goldfish trained in place and turn maze procedures. *Behavioral Neuroscience*, 110, 965–980.

Schroeder, P.G. and Sneddon L.U. (2017). Exploring the efficacy of immersion analgesics in zebrafish using an integrative approach. *Applied Animal Behaviour Science*, 187, 93–102.

Sharpe, C.S., Thompson, D.A., Blankenship, H.L., Schreck, C.B. (1998). Effects of routine handling and tagging procedures on physiological stress responses in juvenile Chinook salmon. *Progressive Fish-Culturist*, 60, 81–87.

Silva, P.I.M., Martins, C.I.M., Khan, U.W., Gjøen, H.M., Øverli, Ø., Höglund, E. (2015). Stress and fear responses in the teleost pallium. *Physiology & Behavior*, 141, 17–22.

Singhal, G., Jaehne, E.J., Corrigan, F., Baune, B.T. (2014). Cellular and molecular mechanisms of immunomodulation in the brain through environmental enrichment. *Frontiers in Cellular Neuroscience*, doi: 10.3389/fncel.2014.00097.

Sloman, K.A., Bouyoucos, I.A., Brooks, I.J., Sneddon, L.U. (2019). Ethical considerations in fish research. *Journal of Fish Biology*, 94, 556–577.

Smith, R.J.F. (1992). Alarm signals in fishes. *Reviews in Fish Biology and Fisheries*, 2, 33–63.

Sneddon, L.U. (2002). Anatomical and electrophysiological analysis of the trigeminal nerve in a teleost fish, *Oncorhynchus mykiss*. *Neuroscience Letters*, 319, 167–171.

Sneddon, L.U. (2003a). The evidence for pain in fish: The use of morphine as an analgesic. *Applied Animal Behaviour Science*, 83, 153–162.

Sneddon, L.U. (2003b). Trigeminal somatosensory innervation of the head of a teleost fish with particular reference to nociception. *Brain Research*, 972, 44–52.

Sneddon, L.U. (2004). Evolution of nociception in vertebrates: Comparative analysis of lower vertebrates. *Brain Research Reviews*, 46, 2, 123–130.

Sneddon, L.U. (2009). Pain perception in fish: Indicators and endpoints. *ILAR Journal*, 50, 338–342.

Sneddon, L.U. (2011a). Pain perception in fish: Evidence and implications for the use of fish. *Journal of Consciousness Studies*, 18, 209–229.

Sneddon, L.U. (2011b). Cognition and welfare. In *Fish Cognition and Behavior*, 2nd edition, Brown, C., Laland, K., Krause, J. (eds). Wiley-Blackwell, Oxford.

Sneddon, L.U. (2012). Clinical anaesthesia and analgesia in fish. *Journal of Exotic Pet Medicine*, 21, 32–43.

Sneddon, L.U. (2013). Do painful sensations and fear exist in fish? In *Animal Suffering: From Science to Law, International Symposium*, Van der Kemp, T.A. and Lachance, M. (eds). Carswell, Toronto.

Sneddon, L.U. (2015). Pain in aquatic animals. *Journal of Experimental Biology*, 218, 967–976.

Sneddon, L.U. (2018). Comparative physiology of nociception and pain. *Physiology*, 33, 63–73.

Sneddon L.U. (2019). Evolution of nociception and pain: Evidence from fish models. *Phil. Trans. Roy. Soc. Lond. B*, 374, 20190290.

Sneddon, L.U. and Leach, M.C. (2016). Anthropomorphic denial of fish pain. *Animal Sentience 2016.035* [Online]. Available at: http://animalstudiesrepository.org/animsent/vol1/iss3/28/.

Sneddon, L.U. and Wolfenden, D.C.C. (2012). How are large-scale fisheries affect fish: Pain perception in fish? In *Sea the Truth: Essays on Overfishing, Climate Change and Pollution*, Soeters, K. and Nicolaas, G. (eds). Pierson Foundation, Amsterdam.

Sneddon, L.U. and Wolfenden, D.C.C. (2019). Ornamental fish (Actinopterygii). In *UFAW Companion Animal Handbook*, Yeates, J. (ed.). Wiley Blackwell, Oxford.

Sneddon, L.U., Braithwaite, V.A., Gentle, M.J. (2003a). Do fishes have nociceptors? Evidence for the evolution of a vertebrate sensory system. *Proceedings of the Royal Society of London Series B: Biological Sciences*, 270, 1115–1121.

Sneddon, L.U., Braithwaite, V.A., Gentle, M.J. (2003b). Novel object test: Examining nociception and fear in the rainbow trout. *Journal of Pain*, 4, 431–440.

Sneddon, L.U., Elwood, R.W., Adamo, S., Leach, M.C. (2014). Defining and assessing pain in animals. *Animal Behaviour*, 97, 201–212.

Sneddon, L.U., Wolfenden, D.C.C., Thomson, J.S. (2016). Stress management and welfare. In *Biology of Stress in Fish*, Schreck, C., Tort, L., Farrell, A., Brauner, C. (eds). Academic Press, Cambridge.

Snow, P.J., Renshaw, G.M.C., Hamlin, K.E. (1996). Localization of enkephalin immunoreactivity in the spinal cord of the long-tailed ray *Himantura fai*. *Journal of Comparative Neurology*, 367, 264–273.

Steeger, T.M., Grizzle, J.M., Weathers, K., Newman, M. (1994). Bacterial diseases and mortality of angler-caught largemouth bass released after tournaments on Walter F. George reservoir, Alabama/Georgia. *North American Journal of Fisheries Management*, 14, 435–441.

Stewart, A., Wu, N., Cachat, J., Hart, P., Gaikwad, S., Wong, K., Utterback, E., Gilder, T., Kyzar, E., Newman, A. et al. (2011). Pharmacological modulation of anxiety-like phenotypes in adult zebrafish behavioral models. *Progress in Neuro-Psychopharmacology, Biology and Psychiatry*, 35, 1421–1431.

Suuronen, P., Erickson, D.L., Orrensalo, A. (1996). Mortality of herring escaping from pelagic trawl cod ends. *Fisheries Research*, 25, 305–321.

Teles, M.C., Dahlbom, S.J., Winberg, S., Oliveira, R.F. (2013). Social modulation of brain monoamine levels in zebrafish. *Behavioural Brain Research*, 253, 17–24.

Thompson, R.B., Hunter, C.J., Patten, B.G. (1971). Studies of live and dead salmon that unmesh from gill nets. International North Pacific Fish Community Annual Report, 108–112.

Thomson J.S., Al-Temeemy A.A., Isted H., Spencer J.W., Sneddon L.U. (2019). Assessment of behaviour in groups of zebrafish (*Danio rerio*) using an intelligent software monitoring tool, the Chromatic Fish Analyser. *J. Neurosci. Meths.*, 328, 108433.

Thomson, J.S., Deakin, A.G., Cossins, A.R., Spencer, J.W., Young, I.S., Sneddon, L.U. (2020). Acute and chronic stress prevents responses to pain in zebrafish: Evidence for stress-induced analgesia. *Journal of Experimental Biology*, 223, jeb224527.

Tomie, A., Silberman, Y., Williams, K., Pohorecky, L.A. (2002). Pavlovian autoshaping procedures increase plasma corticosterone levels in rats. *Pharmacology Biochemistry and Behavior*, 72, 507–513.

Turnbull, J.F. (1992). Studies on dorsal fin rot in farmed Atlantic salmon (*Salmo salar* L.) parr. PhD Thesis, University of Stirling.

Turnbull, J.F., Adams, C.E., Richards, R.H., Robertson, D.A. (1998). Attack site and resultant damage during aggressive encounters in Atlantic salmon (*Salmo salar* L.) parr. *Aquaculture*, 159, 345–353.

Wong, D., von Keyserlingk, M.A.G., Richards, J.G., Weary, D.M. (2014). Conditioned place avoidance of zebrafish (*Danio rerio*) to three chemicals used for euthanasia and anaesthesia. *PLoS ONE*, 9, e88030.

Yue, S., Moccia, R.D., Duncan, I.J.H. (2004). Investigating fear in domestic rainbow trout, *Oncorhynchus mykiss*, using an avoidance learning task. *Applied Animal Behaviour Science*, 87, 343–354.

11

Welfare, Sentience and Pain: Concepts, Ethics and Attitudes

Donald M. Broom

St Catharine's College and Department of Veterinary Medicine,
University of Cambridge, UK

11.1. Welfare

Animal welfare science has developed rapidly during the last 30 years (Broom 2011). Much of the work has concerned how individuals cope with problems. Substantial challenges to animal functioning include those resulting from (i) pathogens, (ii) tissue damage, (iii) attack or threat of attack by a conspecific or predator, (iv) other social competition, (v) complexity of information processing in a situation where an individual receives excessive stimulation, (vi) lack of key stimuli such as a teat for a young mammal or social contact cues, (vii) lack of overall stimulation and (viii) inability to control interactions with the environment (Broom 2021). Potentially damaging challenges may come from the environment outside the body or from within it. Systems that respond to or prepare for challenges are coping systems and coping means having control of mental and bodily stability (Broom and Johnson 1993, 2019). Coping requires the functioning of the nervous system, including the brain, so is limited to animals.

Systems for attempting to cope with challenges may respond to short- or long-term problems, or sometimes to both. The various types of responses are interdependent and most involve the brain. Some coping systems include feelings as a part of their functioning, for example, pain, fear and the various kinds of pleasure, all of which are adaptive (Broom 1998; Fraser 2008). The welfare of an individual is its state as regards its attempts to cope with its environment (Broom 1986), and this includes feelings and health. Welfare is a characteristic of an individual animal at a certain time. The state of the individual can be assessed, so welfare will vary on a range from very good to very poor. This meaning of welfare is widely used by animal welfare scientists and is close to the usage, dating back 400 years, of how well an individual fares or goes through life. However, it does not mean a service or other resource given to an individual such as handouts to the poor (Broom and Johnson 2019). Welfare scientists all agree that animal welfare is measurable and hence is a scientific concept (Fraser 2008), and that welfare involves mental aspects. Hence, research on welfare involves measurements of brain function and its consequences for behavior and physiology. The OIE (World Organization for Animal Health 2011) followed this definition when writing about what is meant by animal welfare although some of the explanatory wording in the 2011 document was not precise. Animal welfare indicators give information about positive and negative feelings and other coping mechanisms such as those that affect health. Welfare research also includes studies of what individuals need and the strength of their positive and negative preferences. It is important to consider the needs of each kind of animal, as proposed by Thorpe (1965). A need is a requirement, which is part of the basic biology of an animal, to obtain a particular resource or respond to a particular environmental or bodily stimulus. The need itself is in the brain. It allows the effective functioning of the animal.

While feelings comprise part of the mechanisms used by individuals to cope with their environment, some mechanisms do not involve feelings, for example, some of those that are used to cope with pathology. A feeling is a brain construct involving at least perceptual awareness, which is associated with a life regulating system, is recognizable by the individual when it recurs and may change behavior or act as a reinforcer in learning (Broom 1998). Emotions are similar to feelings but physiologically describable (Broom 2007). Rolls (2005) considered feelings to be the subjective consequences of emotions involving consciousness or awareness. Emotion can be defined as follows: an emotion is a physiologically describable component of a feeling characterized by electrical and neurochemical activity in particular regions of the brain, autonomic nervous system activity, hormone release and peripheral consequences including behavior. Other attempts to define or describe emotion are discussed by Paul and Mendl (2018). The physiological and behavioral basis are discussed further by Boissy et al. (2007), Broom (2014) and Broom and Johnson (2019).

The many measures of welfare include those of physiology, behavior, pathology, injury and mortality rate. These measures overlap with those of stress effects. Stress is an environmental effect on an individual, which overtaxes its control systems and results in adverse consequences and eventually reduced fitness (Broom and Johnson 1993, modified after Broom 1988). This definition is used to clarify the meaning of a word that is often used colloquially, and sometimes by scientists, in an imprecise way. First, when most people refer to "stress" they imply a negative effect on the individual, so it is not logical to suggest that stress can be beneficial. Second, those who equate stress with hypothalamic–pituitary–adrenocortical axis activity render the word redundant, and such use is considered unscientific and unnecessary by most scientists working in the area. A third meaning that has been ascribed to stress makes it largely synonymous with stimulation. If every impact of the environment on an organism were called stress, then the term would have no value.

Fraser (1999) pointed out that when members of the public talk about animal welfare, their ideas often include the functioning of the animals, the feelings of the animals and the naturalness of the environment. The feelings, referred to by Fraser and others, are encompassed by the above definition of welfare as they are important components of coping mechanisms and of biological functioning. Rollin (1989, 1995) said that "animals should be able to lead reasonably natural lives", and both Rollin and Fraser (Fraser et al. 1997; Fraser 1999, 2008) refer to the importance of understanding animal needs. However, neither of these authors said that naturalness contributes to a definition of welfare or should be part of welfare assessment. Other authors have described naturalness as a component of welfare and when Appleby and Hughes (1997) explain what welfare is, their diagram has naturalness as a circle partly overlapping with two other circles labeled function and feelings. The state of an individual trying to cope with its environment will necessarily depend on its biological functioning or, put another way, on its nature. Natural conditions have affected the needs of the animal and the evolution of coping mechanisms in the species. Gygax and Hillman (2019) also say this: "Natural behaviour in this sense involves reaching adequate goal states for all persistent or recurring wants that arise in a given environment." The environment provided should fulfill the needs of the animal but does not have to be the same as the environment in the wild. Indeed, conditions in the wild may result in starvation, disease and predation, with consequent very poor welfare (Yeates 2018). The concept and definition of welfare does not include naturalness, so the overlapping circles diagram is incorrect for this reason, and also because feelings are a part of function so should not be a separate circle. For systems involving the use of non-human animals, welfare is a key part of sustainability. A system or procedure is sustainable if it is acceptable now and its expected future effects are acceptable, in particular in relation to resource availability, consequences of functioning and morality of action (Broom 2014, modified after Broom 2001, 2010).

Investigation of the needs of each kind of animal is important for understanding animal welfare (Thorpe 1965; Broom 2021). Needs may be fulfilled by physiology or behavior, but the need itself is not physiological or behavioral (Toates and Jensen 1991; Broom 1996, 2008). Needs can be identified using studies of motivation or by assessing the welfare of individuals whose needs are not satisfied (Hughes and Duncan 1988a, 1988b; Dawkins 1990; Broom and Johnson 2019). Studies of motivation can start from a known resource, or a known action by the animal, and assessing the causal factors that influence decision-making. The needs of animals of a certain species will generally be the same, but there will be some interindividual variation depending on experience during development. The means of fulfilling needs will vary depending on the environment at that time and the capabilities and experience of the individual. Individuals often develop one or more strategies for achieving objectives. An animal may need to perform a certain behavior, as an essential part of its control systems, and may be seriously affected if unable to carry out the activity, even in the presence of the ultimate objective of the activity. For example, pigs need to root in soil or some similar substratum or to chew deformable material (Hutson 1989; Chou et al. 2020) and hens need to dust-bathe (Vestergaard 1980). Strength-of-preference studies tell us about needs and the terminology used in motivational strength estimation is that developed for micro-economics (Matthews and Ladewig 1994; Fraser and Matthews 1997; Kirkden et al. 2003).

The idea of providing for "the five freedoms", first suggested in the Brambell Report in 1965, was not quite in line with Thorpe's concept of needs. The list of freedoms provides a general guideline for non-specialists, but the rather general idea of freedoms is now replaced by the more scientific concept of needs. A longer list of domains is better than five freedoms but not as precise as to focus on the species and consider the needs of such animals. Considering the scientific evidence for needs is the starting point for reviews of the welfare of a species or group of closely related species. A list of needs has been the first step in Council of Europe recommendations and EU scientific reports on animal welfare for over 20 years.

11.2. One health, one welfare, one biology

The terms health and welfare apply to many kinds of animals. The One Health concept makes it clear that health means exactly the same for non-human animals as it does for humans. One Health is a worldwide strategy that encourages interdisciplinary collaboration and communication in relation to all aspects of health care for humans and non-human animals. It also promotes viewing the individual human, or other animal, in relation to all interactions with the environment. A resolution promoting the similarity of human and non-human animal health and the great potential for collaboration between the human medical and veterinary researchers and practitioners was adopted in 2007 by the American Medical Association and the American Veterinary Medical Association. The concept is further explained by Monath et al. (2010) and Karesh (2014).

There are similarities in physiological, immunological and clinical research on stress and welfare in humans and a range of other species (Broom 2001), so human psychiatry and medicine can learn from farm animal and other welfare research. Also, animal welfare scientists should use more information from human research on related topics. Progress has been slowed by the attitude that human biology is different from the biology of other animals. However, there is only one biology (Tarazona et al. 2020; Broom 2021). The one welfare approach emphasizes that the concept of welfare is identical when applied to humans or non-human animals (Colonius and Early 2013; Garcia Pinillos et al. 2015, 2016, 2018; Broom 2017). This approach is being incorporated into the teaching of animal welfare (McGreevy et al. 2020). There is now much evidence showing that, when the welfare of individual humans or non-humans is poor, there is increased susceptibility to disease. A key deduction from this is that improving welfare generally reduces disease. The similarities in disease and in other causes of poor welfare in humans and other species mean that those with a medical background and those with a veterinary or other biological background benefit from exchanging information. An example of this described by Daigle (2018) is the similarity between post-partum problems in pigs and humans. In order to use this approach effectively and provide good care for people and good care for animals used by people, all should be considered as individuals. While this statement is unsurprising to many practitioners and researchers, some still have the idea that herd treatment is always sufficient and individuals do not matter.

If concepts such as biology, health, welfare, stress, pain, etc. have the same meaning for all animals, including humans, so should other words, such as euthanasia. Euthanasia means killing an individual for the benefit of that individual and in a humane way (Broom 2007b, 2017a). Killing a pet or laboratory animal that is no longer wanted should be humane, which means carried out in such a way that welfare is good to a certain high degree, but is not euthanasia.

11.3. Sentience

The brain is the site of mechanisms underlying the behavior of animals and of most coping systems involved in welfare. Perception, cognition, awareness and feelings are located in the brain, and the brain receives input from sensory receptors and initiates muscular responses, glandular responses and other bodily changes.

Organs of the body, such as the heart, influence brain function, but all thoughts and feelings are in the brain. They are not in the heart or any other part of the body. No emotions are in the heart and it is incorrect and misleading to say "I knew in my heart" or, when referring to a feeling, "My heart tells me...". Since all analysis, thought and emotional parts of brain functioning are interlinked, it is not useful for the concept of mind to be considered separately from the brain (Panksepp 1998, 2005; Broom 2003, 2014; Le Doux 2012). All of what people call the mind is in the brain.

At a certain stage of the development of individual humans, and of other complex animals, they become aware of themselves (De Grazia 1996) and of interactions that they have with their environment. Some of this awareness occurs at an early stage, such as when the individual learns to avoid a painful action like chewing their own foot. At a point in growth of a fetus, embryo or young individual, the ability to experience happiness, and other pleasurable states, and pain, fear, grief and other aversive states is initiated. This is the point where the individual becomes sentient. Kirkwood (2006) proposed that to have sentience, the individual must have the capacity to feel, thus implying a level of awareness and cognitive ability rather than just the sense of touch. Sentience means having the capacity to have feelings. In order to have feelings, a certain level of awareness and cognitive ability is necessary. Kirkwood also said "to be sentient is to have a feeling of something", but sentience does not mean actually having the feelings because an individual can be sentient when it is not having feelings. The abilities needed to have the capacity for feelings are described by Broom (2014, slightly modified after Broom 2006). A sentient being is one that, in order to have feelings, has some ability: to evaluate the actions of others in relation to itself and third parties, to remember some of its own actions and their consequences, to assess risks and benefits and to have some degree of awareness.

Each year, scientific papers provide new information about the cognitive and emotional functioning of a wide range of animals. It is now known that very many non-human species recognize individuals of their own and other species, that pigs, magpies and perhaps cleaner wrasse fish can use information from mirrors, that parrots, crows and bees can count and that young cows show emotional responses to having learned something new (Broom 2014; Kohda et al. 2019). There are many similarities between the level of human cognitive ability and the levels of ability of some non-human species (Trestman 2015; Broom and Johnson 2019). The differences in cognitive ability between humans and other vertebrate animals are in degree, and it is difficult to find any category of cognition that is not shared by humans and some other species.

The opinion of most people about which individuals of our own and other species are sentient has become broader over time, encompassing initially just a subset of humans, and then: some mammals kept as companions; animals that seemed most similar to humans such as monkeys; the larger mammals; all mammals; all warm-blooded animals; all vertebrates; and now some invertebrates in addition. Some members of the general public have taken note of evidence for sentience from biologists concerning the abilities and functioning of the animals. Complex organization of life and capability for sophisticated learning and awareness are respected and ill-treatment of the animals is then less likely. However, there is also a view of animals solely in relation to their effects on, or perceived value to, humans with little concern for them as individuals. When sentience is considered, laws are more likely to protect the animals as individual beings not just as property, and to protect them better.

11.4. Pain

Pain is an aversive sensation and feeling associated with actual or potential tissue damage. Pain results in poor welfare and is not limited to humans or mammals. Melzack and Dennis (1980) said, "The nervous systems of all vertebrates are organized in fundamentally the same way", and "the experience of pain is often inferred from the behaviours of mammals, and it is not unreasonable to attribute pain experience to birds, amphibia and fish" (and presumably reptiles). Mechanisms involved in pain detection and processing are reviewed for fish and other animals by Sneddon (2019, see also this volume). It is often said that non-human animals cannot tell you when they are in pain or how bad it is. However, in human pain studies, self-reporting on a scale from no pain to very severe pain can be unreliable because people lie or deceive themselves. Direct measurement, such as a facial expression scale, can be more accurate than human reporting (Broom 2001), so guides to pain assessment in humans now include chapters on direct measurement methods (Turk and Melzack 2011).

Pain receptors are called nociceptors, but the distinction between nociception and pain seems to be a relic of attempts to emphasize the differences between humans and other animals. Sneddon (2019) says, "All animals are considered capable of nociception, which is the detection of potentially injurious stimuli, and is usually accompanied by a nocifensive withdrawal reflex away from that stimulus. For pain, however, the animal must demonstrate a change in future behavioral decisions and motivational changes." The term reflex is sufficient for this distinction. In sentient animals where almost all reactions to output from nociceptors involve learning and other high-level brain activity, the separation of pain and nociception is not helpful.

For other sensory systems, such as visual and auditory, the simpler and more complex aspects are not given different names. Pain perception can exist without the involvement of pain receptors, as can visual or auditory perceptions exist without their receptors being involved. Wall (1992) said that the concept of pain was "confused by the pseudoscience surrounding the word nociception". "Nociception" can be used for the activation of sensory pain receptors. The term "nociception" should not otherwise be used to separate systems in some animals from systems in others. The pain system should be considered as a whole (Broom 2001e, 2014; Broom and Johnson 2019).

Pain assessment (Sneddon et al. 2014) includes many methods, and some are used for many years: for example, the tail-flick response of rats (since 1941), the jaw-opening response (since 1964), limb withdrawal (since 1975) and self-mutilation (for much longer, Dubner 1994). However, severe pain can exist without any detectable behavioral change. A major response of rabbits that are in pain is inactivity (Leach et al. 2009). Thresholds for the elicitation of pain responses vary with species and individuals (Morton and Griffiths 1985; Rutherford 2002). We should consider which behavioral pain responses are adaptive for each species. Species that live socially and help one another when attacked by a predator use distress signals such as loud vocalizations when pain is felt. However, in species that can very seldom collaborate in defense, such as small antelopes or sheep, survival is better if they do not show obvious responses to pain. Predators may select apparently weak individuals to attack, and vocalizations when injured might attract predators rather than conferring any benefit, so these prey animals usually do not vocalize when injured. Sheep often make no sound during the mulesing operation during which they are held upside down in a holding frame while a 15 cm-diameter area of skin around the anogenital apertures is removed using scissors. Sheep have all of the normal mammalian pain system, and they produce high levels of cortisol and beta-endorphin after the mutilation (Shutt et al. 1987) so they are in pain during and after mulesing, even if not vocalizing. A further example is of female monkeys, which are normally very noisy but quiet when giving birth and presumably in pain but avoiding attracting predators. Cows with calving difficulties are quiet but show tail-raising behavior, an indicator of localized pain (Barrier et al. 2012). Animals like humans, dogs or pigs often vocalize when in pain, as this may elicit help from group members. The pitch and loudness of the sound can be measured. Pain in rats can be quantified (Flecknell 2001), as they change the amount of locomotion and adopt specific postures.

Vertebrate animals all have very similar pain receptors, neurotransmitters and central nervous pathways to the brain (Cameron et al. 1990; Broom 2021). Naturally occurring opioids are widespread, and the same analgesics are effective in a wide range of species (Nasr et al. 2012). However, within different groups of fish, there is variation in the region of the brain where pain analysis occurs. It should not be assumed that analysis will be in the same area as in humans or that, because an area that has a pain analysis function in humans is small or absent in other vertebrates, the function itself does not occur.

When tissue is removed from an animal, neuromas may form, which often continue to be painful throughout life. Neuromas are produced when the beak of birds is trimmed and when the tails of dogs or pigs are cut off (Gentle 1986; Simonsen et al. 1991; Sandercock et al. 2016). After docking the tail of a pig, pain-associated genes are expressed for at least four months (Sandercock et al. 2019). After a surgical operation, behavior associated with pain can be quantified, for example in rabbits: full-body flexing, tight huddling, hind-leg shuffling, staggering, drawing back, eyelids closed and facial grimace (Farnworth et al. 2011; Keating et al. 2012; Banchi et al. 2020). Facial grimace scales have been developed for mice, rats, rabbits, horses and sheep (Leach et al. 2012; Dalla Costa et al. 2014; Gleerup et al. 2015; McLennan et al. 2016, 2019; Meyer et al. 2020). Pain scoring systems have also been used in assessing the severity of pain during disease in cattle, such as foot-and-mouth disease or lumpy skin disease (El Shoukary et al. 2019). A scale of behavioral measures of pain helps in the diagnosis of colic and other disorders of horses (Maskato et al. 2020).

11.5. Welfare and moral actions

An important aspect of moral behavior is to consider the welfare of other individuals, whether they are human or non-human. Scientific evidence about welfare should be taken into account in doing this. Welfare is a quality of all animals but not of non-living objects, plants or other organisms that do not have a nervous system. In recent years, legislation and codes of practice about the welfare of animals used by people and about human welfare have been developed. Animal welfare is thought of as a key component of the sustainability of systems and products involving animals. All components should be considered when evaluating sustainability and product quality. It is not acceptable for a small group of people to benefit greatly from an activity if that activity has significant negative consequences for other people, other animals, or other organisms and environments. Humans are too human-centered. One example of this thinking is that diseases are not considered to be of importance, for example, whether or not money should be spent on investigating them, unless they affect humans. Decisions about whether or not an action is justified often hinge on impacts on people and their jobs and not on the amount of harm the action would cause to non-human animals. The importance of freedom for humans is extolled but freedom for other animals is given little value. The effects of an activity on the rest of the world, not just on humans, should be taken into account before it is initiated or continued (Broom 2021).

What are the most urgent animal welfare problems? They are those where the magnitude of poor welfare, duration times intensity, is high and large numbers of individual animals are affected (Broom 2017b). When the magnitude of poor welfare is considered, the greatest animal welfare issue in the world is a severe problem of the most numerous species used by humans: pain and suffering caused by leg problems in broiler chickens. Other important world animal welfare issues are: poor housing of pigs, poor conditions for farmed fish and genetic selection resulting in lameness, mastitis and reproductive disorders in dairy cows. Considering wild animals, taking animals from the wild for the pet trade and allowing cats to injure and kill birds, mammals and reptiles are major world problems.

The ideas that the resources of the world only exist so that humans can use them, that evolution has occurred to produce humans, that humans are special in some way and that humans are more important than other animals are biologically indefensible. A large change in human thinking is needed if the current destruction of the planet is not to continue and ultimately end in human extinction. The discussions about one biology, sentience and other topics raise a further fundamental question: who are we? As argued by Broom (2003), referring also to Singer (1981) and Banner (1999), those included as part of "us" expanded during human history from family and friends, to tribe, to nation or racial group or religious group, to all humans, and to some other animals in addition. The concepts of "we" and "us" should include, not just all humans but all sentient animals (Broom and Johnson 2019; Broom 2020). In order to change attitudes towards non-human animals and to improve welfare, biologically incorrect usage of words should not continue. There is a need to change the use of some words in every language. Examples of change that should occur (modified after Broom 2021) are as follows:

Biology, health, welfare, stress, pain, sentient, euthanasia and many other terms should be used in the same way whether the subject is human or non-human.

Animal should always include all animals: humans, other mammals, birds, fish, insects, etc. and should not be used to imply not human. Hence, it is not correct to say "humans and animals", as if humans were not animals; it is better to say "humans and other animals". Animal and the names of particular animals such as pig, bitch, cow, monkey, donkey, goose, snake, toad, shark, etc. should not be used as terms of abuse.

Although all characteristics of organisms depend on genetic information, since no characteristic of any organism develops without environmental effects, nothing is entirely genetically determined and the words instinctive and innate, which imply absence of environmental input, should not be used.

Behavior, cognition, knowledge, feelings and many other life processes are controlled by the brain. Although other organs and systems in the body can have an influence on brain function, it is not correct to say: I know in my heart, my heart tells me, I feel it in my heart or I feel it in my gut. There is no scientific evidence that there is a separate system called mind which is different from the brain, so differentiation of mind and brain is not logical.

When a system or process is described as sustainable, all the components of sustainability, one of which is the welfare of individuals, should be taken into account.

11.6. References

Appleby, M.C. and Hughes, B.O. (eds) (1997). *Animal Welfare*. CABI, Wallingford.

Banchi, P., Quaranta, G., Ricci, A., Mauthe von Degerfeld, M. (2020). Reliability and construct validity of a composite pain scale for rabbit (CANCRS) in a clinical environment. *PloS One* 15, p.e0221377. doi.org/10.1371/journal.pone.0221377.

Banner, M. (1999). *Christian Ethics and Contemporary Moral Problems*. Cambridge University Press, Cambridge.

Barrier, A.C., Haskell, M.J., Macrae, A.I., Dwyer, C.M. (2012). Parturition progress and behaviours in dairy cows with calving difficulty. *Appl. Anim. Behav. Sci.*, 139, 209–217.

Boissy, A., Manteuffel, G., Jensen, M.B., Moe, R.O., Spruijt, B., Keeling L.J., Winckler, C., Forkman, B., Dimitrov, I., Langbein, J. et al. (2007). Assessment of positive emotions in animals to improve their welfare. *Physiol. Behav.*, 92, 375–397.

Broom, D.M. (1986). Indicators of poor welfare. *Br. Vet. J.*, 142, 524–526.

Broom, D.M. (1988). Les concepts de stress et de bien-être. *Rec. Méd. Vét.*, 164, 715–722.

Broom, D.M. (1996). Scientific research on veal calf welfare. *Veal Perspectives to the Year 2000. Proceedings of International Symposium*, Le Mans, France, 147–153. Fédération de la Vitellerie Francaise, Paris.

Broom, D.M. (1998). Welfare, stress and the evolution of feelings. *Adv. Study Behav.*, 27, 371–403.

Broom, D.M. (2001). Evolution of pain. In *Pain: Its Nature and Management in Man and Animals. Roy. Soc. Med. Int. Congr. Symp. Ser.*, Soulsby, E.J.L. and Morton, D. (eds), 246, 17–25.

Broom, D.M. (2003). *The Evolution of Morality and Religion.* Cambridge University Press, Cambridge.

Broom, D.M. (2006). The evolution of morality. *Applied Animal Behaviour Science*, 100, 20–28.

Broom, D.M. (2007a). Cognitive ability and sentience: Which aquatic animals should be protected? *Diseases Aquat. Organisms*, 75, 99–108.

Broom, D.M. (2007b). Quality of life means welfare: How is it related to other concepts and assessed? *Anim. Welfare*, 16 suppl, 45–53.

Broom, D.M. (2008). Consequences of biological engineering for resource allocation and welfare. In *Resource Allocation Theory Applied to Farm Animal Production*, Rauw, W.M. (ed.). CABI, Wallingford.

Broom, D.M. (2010). Animal welfare: An aspect of care, sustainability, and food quality required by the public. *J. Vet. Med. Educ.*, 37, 83–88.

Broom, D.M. (2014). *Sentience and Animal Welfare.* CABI, Wallingford.

Broom, D.M. (2017). *Animal Welfare in the European Union.* European Parliament Policy Department, Citizen's Rights and Constitutional Affairs, Brussels, 75. doi: 10-2861/891355.

Broom, D.M. (2020). The necessity of human attitude change and methods of avoiding pandemics. *Anim. Sentience*, 369, 3.

Broom, D.M. (2021). *Domestic Animal Behaviour and Welfare*, 6th edition. CABI, Wallingford.

Broom, D.M. and Johnson, K.G. (1993). *Stress and Animal Welfare.* Chapman and Hall, London.

Broom, D.M. and Johnson, K.G. (2019). *Stress and Animal Welfare: Key Issues in the Biology of Humans and Other Animals*, 2nd edition. Springer Nature, Cham.

Cameron, A.A., Plenderleith, M.B., Snow, P.J. (1990). Organization of the spinal cord in four species of elasmobranch fish: Cytoarchitecture and distribution of serotonin and selected neuropeptides. *J. Comp. Neurol.*, 297, 201–218.

Chou, J.Y., D'Eath, R.B., Sandercock, D.A., O'Driscoll, K. (2020). Enrichment use in finishing pigs and its relationship with damaging behaviours: Comparing three wood species and a rubber floor toy. *Appl. Anim. Behav. Sci.*, 104944. doi.org/10.1016/j.applanim.2020.104944.

Colonius, T.J. and Earley, R.W. (2013). One welfare: A call to develop a broader framework of thought and action. *J. Amer. Vet. Med. Ass.*, 242, 309–310.

Daigle, C. (2018). Parallels between postpartum disorders in humans and preweaning piglet mortality in sows. *Animals*, 8, 22. doi.org/10.3390/ani8020022.

Dalla Costa, E., Minero, M., Lebelt, D., Stucke, D., Canali, E., Leach, M.C. (2014). Development of the horse grimace scale (HGS) as a pain assessment tool in horses undergoing routine castration. *PLoS One* 9, e92281.doi:10.1371/journal.pone.0092281.

Dawkins, M.S. (1990). From an animal's point of view: Motivation, fitness and animal welfare. *Behav. Brain Sci.*, 13, 1–31.

De Grazia, D. (1996). *Taking Animals Seriously*. Cambridge University Press, Cambridge.

Dubner, R. (1994). Methods of assessing pain in animals. In *Textbook of Pain*, 3rd edition. Wall, P.D. and Melzack, R. (eds). Churchill Livingstone, Edinburgh.

El Shoukary, R., Nasr Eldin, N., Osman, A. (2019). Change in behavior, blood parameters and pain score in response to different treatment strategies in bull infected with FMD or LSD. *SVU-Int. J. Vet. Sci.*, 2, 82–107. doi: 10.21608/svu.2019.6807.1004.

Farnworth, M.J., Walker, J.K., Schweizer, K.A., Chuang, C.-L., Guild, S.-J., Barrett, C.J., Leach, M.C., Waran, N.K. (2011). Potential behavioural indicators of post-operative pain in male laboratory rabbits following abdominal surgery. *Anim. Welfare*, 20, 225–237.

Flecknell, P. (2001). Recognition and assessment of pain in animals. In *Pain: Its Nature and Management in Man and Animals*. *Roy. Soc. Med. Int. Cong. Symp. Ser*. Soulsby, L. and Norton, D. (eds), 246, 63–68.

Fraser, D. (2008). *Understanding Animal Welfare: The Science in Its Cultural Context*. Wiley Blackwell, Chichester.

Fraser, D. and Matthews, L.R. (1997). Preference and motivation testing. In *Animal Welfare*, Appleby, M.C. and Hughes, B.O. (eds). CAB International, Wallingford.

Fraser, D., Weary, D.M., Pajor, E.A., Milligan, B.N. (1997). The scientific conception of animal welfare that reflects ethical concerns. *Anim. Welfare*, 6, 187–205.

García Pinillos, R. (2018). *One Welfare: A Framework to Improve Animal Welfare and Human Well-Being*. CABI, Wallingford.

García Pinillos, R., Appleby, M.C., Scott-Park, F., Smith, C.W. (2015). One welfare. *Vet. Rec.*, *179*, 629–630.

Gentle, M.J. (1986). Neuroma formation following partial beak amputation (beak-trimming) in the chicken. *Res. Vet. Sci.*, 41, 383–385.

García Pinillos, R., Appleby, M., Manteca, X., Scott-Park, F., Smith, C., Velarde, A. (2016). One welfare – A platform for improving human and animal welfare. *Vet. Rec.*, 179, 412–413. doi:10.1136/vr.i5470.

Gleerup, K.B., Forkman, B., Lindegaard, C., Andersen, P.H. (2015). An equine pain face. *Vet. Anaesth. Analg.*, 42, 103–114. doi:10.1111/vaa.12212.

Gygax, L. and Hillman, E. (2019). "Naturalness" and its relation to animal welfare from an ethological perspective. *Agriculture*, 8, 136. doi.org/10.3390/agriculture8090136.

Hughes, B.O. and Duncan, I.J.H. (1988a). Behavioural needs: Can they be explained in terms of motivational models? *Appl. Anim. Behav. Sci.*, 20, 352–355.

Hughes, B.O. and Duncan, I.J.H. (1988b). The notion of ethological "need", models of motivation and animal welfare. *Anim. Behav.*, 36, 1696–1707.

Hutson, G.D. (1989). Operant tests of access to earth as a reinforcement for weaner piglets. *Anim. Prod.*, 48, 561–569.

Karesh, W.B. (ed.) (2014). *One Health. O.I.E. Scientific and Technical Review*. O.I.E, Paris.

Keating, S.C., Thomas, A.A., Flecknell, P.A., Leach, M.C. (2012). Evaluation of EMLA cream for preventing pain during tattooing of rabbits: Changes in physiological, behavioural and facial expression responses. *PloS One*, 7, e44437, 11.

Kirkden, R.D., Edwards, J.S.S., Broom, D.M. (2003). A theoretical comparison of the consumer surplus and the elasticities of demand as measures of motivational strength. *Anim. Behav.*, 65, 157–178.

Kirkwood, J.K. (2006) The distribution of the capacity for sentience in the animal kingdom. In *Animals, Ethics and Trade: The Challenge of Animal Sentience*, Turner, J. and D'Silva, J. (eds). Compassion in World Farming Trust, Petersfield.

Kohda, M., Hotta, T., Takeyama, T., Awata, S., Tanaka, H., Asai, J.Y., Jordan, A.L. (2019). If a fish can pass the mark test, what are the implications for consciousness and self-awareness testing in animals? *PLoS Biol.*, 17(2), e3000021. doi: 10.1371/journal. pbio.3000021.

Le Doux, J. (2012). Rethinking the emotional brain. *Neuron*, 73, 653–676. doi.org/10.1016/j. neuron.2012.02.004.

Leach, M.C., Allweiler, S., Richardson, C., Roughan, J.V., Narbe, R., Flecknell, P.A. (2009). Behavioural effects of ovariohysterectomy and oral administration of meloxicam in laboratory housed rabbits. *Res. Vet. Sci.*, 87, 336–347.

Leach, M.C., Klaus, K., Miller, A.L., di Perrotolo, M.S., Sotocinal, S.G., Flecknell, P.A. (2012). The assessment of post-vasectomy pain in mice using behaviour and the mouse grimace scale. *PloS ONE*, 7, e35656.

Maskato, Y., Dugdale, A.H., Singer, E.R., Kelmer, G., Sutton, G.A. (2020). Prospective feasibility and revalidation of the equine acute abdominal pain scale (EAAPS) in clinical cases of colic in horses. *Animals*, 10, 2242. doi.org/10.3390/ani10122242.

Matthews, L.R. and Ladewig, J. (1994). Environmental requirements of pigs measured by behavioural demand functions. *Anim. Behav.*, 47, 713–719.

McGreevy, P.D., Fawcett, A., Johnson, J., Freire, R., Collins, T., Degeling, C., Fisher, A.D., Hazel, S.J., Hood, J., Lloyd, J.K. et al. (2020). Review of the online one welfare portal: Shared curriculum resources for veterinary undergraduate learning and teaching in animal welfare and ethics. *Animals*, 10, 1341. doi:10.3390/ani10081341.

McLennan, K.M., Rebelo, C.J.B., Corke, M.J., Holmes, M.A., Leach, M.C., Constantino Casas, F. (2016). Development of a facial expression scale using footrot and mastitis as models of pain in sheep. *Appl. Anim. Behav. Sci.*, 176, 19–26. doi: 10.1016/j.applanim. 2016.01.007.

McLennan, K.M., Miller, A.L., Dalla Costa, E., Stucke, D., Corke, M.J., Broom, D.M., Leach, M.C. (2019). Conceptual and methodological issues relating to pain assessment in animals: The development and utilisation of pain facial expression scales. *Appl. Anim. Behav. Sci.*, 217, 1–15. doi.org/10.1016/j.applanim.2019.06.001.

Meyer, N., Kröger, M., Thümmler, J., Tietze, L., Palme, R., Touma, C. (2020). Impact of three commonly used blood sampling techniques on the welfare of laboratory mice: Taking the animal's perspective. *PloS One*, 15, p.e0238895. doi.org/10.1371/journal.pone.0238895.

Monath, T.P., Kahn, L.H., Kaplan, B. (2010). One health perspective. *ILAR J.*, 51, 193–198.

Morton, D.B. and Griffiths, P.H.M. (1985). Guidelines on the recognition of pain, distress and discomfort in experimental animals and an hypothesis for assessment. *Vet. Rec.*, 116, 431–436.

Nasr, M.A.F., Nicol, C.J., Murrell, J.C. (2012). Do laying hens with keel bone fractures experience pain? *PloS One*, 7, e42420, 6.

Panksepp, J. (1998). *Affective Neuroscience*. Oxford University Press, New York.

Panksepp, J. (2005). Affective consciousness: Core emotional feelings in animals and humans. *Consciousness Cognition*, 14, 30–80.

Paul, E.S. and Mendl, M.T. (2018). Animal emotion: Descriptive and prescriptive definitions and their implications for a comparative perspective. *Appl. Anim. Behav. Sci.*, 205, 202–209. doi.org/10.1016/j.applanim.2018.01.008.

Rollin, B.E. (1989). *The Unheeded Cry: Animal Consciousness, Animal Pain and Science*. Oxford University Press, Oxford.

Rolls, E.T. (2005). *Emotion Explained*. Oxford University Press, Oxford.

Rutherford, K.M.D. (2002) Assessing pain in animals. *Animal Welfare*, 11, 31–53.

Sandercock, D.A., Smith, S.H., Di Giminiani, P., Edwards, S.A. (2016). Histopathological characterization of tail injury and traumatic neuroma development after tail docking in piglets. *J. Comp. Pathol.*, 155, 40–49. doi.org/10.1016/j.jcpa.2016.05.003.

Sandercock, D.A., Barnett, M.W., Coe, J.E., Downing, A.C., Nirmal, A.J., Di Giminiani, P., Edwards, S.A., Freeman, T.C. (2019). Transcriptomics analysis of porcine caudal dorsal root ganglia in tail amputated pigs shows long-term effects on many pain-associated genes. *Frontiers Vet. Sci.*, 6, 314. doi.org/10.3389/fvets.2019.00314.

Shutt, D.A., Fell, L.R., Cornell, R., Bell, A.K., Wallace, C.A., Smith, A.I. (1987). Stress-induced changes in plasma concentrations of immunoreactive β-endorphin and cortisol in response to routine surgical procedures in lambs. *Aust. J. Biol. Sci.*, 40, 97–103.

Simonsen, H.B., Klinken, L., Bindseil, E. (1991). Histopathology of intact and docked pigtails. *Br. Vet. J.*, 147, 407–412.

Singer, P. (1981). *The Expanding Circle: Ethics and Sociobiology*. Farrar, Strauss and Giroux, New York.

Sneddon, L.U. (2019). Evolution of nociception and pain: Evidence from fish models. *Phil. Trans. Roy. Soc. B*, 374(1785), 20190290. doi.org/10.1098/rstb.2019.0290.

Sneddon, L.U., Elwood, R.W., Adamo, S., Leach, M.C. (2014). Defining and assessing pain in animals. *Anim. Behav.*, 97, 201–212. doi:10.1016/j.anbehav.2014. 09.007.

Thorpe, W.H. (1965). The assessment of pain and distress in animals. Appendix III in Report of the Technical Committee to Enquire into the Welfare of Animals Kept Under Intensive Husbandry Conditions, F.W.R. Brambell (chairman). HMSO, London.

Toates, F. and Jensen, P. (1991). Ethological and psychological models of motivation-towards a synthesis. In *Farm Animals to Animats*, Meyer, J.A. and Wilson, S. (eds). MIT Press, Cambridge.

Trestman, M. (2015). Clever Hans, Alex the Parrot, and Kanzi: What can exceptional animal learning teach us about human cognitive evolution? *Biol. Theory*, 10, 86–99. doi-org.ezp. lib.cam.ac.uk/10.1007/s13752-014-0199-2.

Vestergaard, K. (1980). The regulation of dustbathing and other behaviour patterns in the laying hen: A Lorenzian approach. In *The Laying Hen and its Environment*, Moss, R. (eds). Martinus Nijhoff, The Hague.

Wall, P.D. (1992). Defining "pain in animals". In *Animal Pain*, Short, C.E. and van Poznak, A. (eds). Churchill Livingstone, New York.

World Organization for Animal Health (2011). *Terrestrial Animal Health Code*. OIE, Paris.

Yeates, J. (2018). Naturalness and animal welfare. *Animals*, 8, 53–70. doi:10.3390/ani8040053.

Conclusion

Animal Suffering, Multiple Paradigms Revealed

Emilie D**ARDENNE**

Equipe d'accueil Anglophonie, Communauté,
Ecriture (ACE), Université de Rennes 2, France

This interdisciplinary work on the animal condition in all its painful aspects, the ethics that frame it and the policies that govern it, has shown the diversity, the intensity, even the intensification of the exploitation of other animals. These applications have multiple aims: dietary, medical, experimental, scenographic, ornamental and emotional.

The works presented have highlighted the profound paradoxes that characterize them, including: the mass confinement of animals in intensive farms, confinement accompanied by a declared concern for their welfare; the recognition of animals as sentient beings in law, but the maintenance of a status corresponding to that of movable property; and in the same country, an animal (dog, rabbit) seen as both a pet and an animal destined for slaughter, whose flesh will be consumed after it has been violently put to death. The paradoxes identified are coupled with tensions: one which opposes the commodification and singularization of the living, and one which contrasts their objectification and their individualization. The moral paradigms that frame the way we think about the suffering of non-human animals and our obligations towards them are competing and changing. To take just a few examples, we can cite the fact that in Korea, commensality is morally more important than the consideration of the suffering of dogs, and, in France, the trans-categorical status of the rabbit or the horse, which gives these animals a fluid perception ranging from pet animals to be protected to livestock that it is normal to consume. It is also worth mentioning that the notion of animal welfare is subject to vague guidelines that are determined by divergent assessments across Europe. There is a great divide between what official discourse tries to institute in varying degrees and the animal condition observed in real life.

At the semantic level, these paradoxes and tensions are translated, as we have seen, by hypallagic or oxymoronic expressions, which either represent shifts in meaning or associate opposites, creating distorting effects or acting as revealing signs. We find them in these pages: the desire to offer a "freer captivity" to zoo animals (Pouillard, Chapter 1); Korean dogs as "suffering commodities" (Dugnoille, Chapter 3); the fact that "welfare accompanies suffering" in European regulations (Marchadier, Chapter 4); or the expression "happy meat", which refers to the eating of the bodies of livestock that have been well treated during their lives and have been slaughtered painlessly (Višak, Chapter 7). The language used makes a mockery of the suffering of other animals. It expresses the real or symbolic violence exerted on them, or, in a deeper sense, translates the absence of consideration of their experiences: in the context of zoos, the aim of "enriching" the environment of a "captive" animal would be to improve its "well-being" (Pouillard, Chapter 1); in veterinary medicine, the words "misery", "distress" and "vulnerability" are reduced to neurophysiological processes. It is a question of "stress" and "nociception" (Devienne, Chapter 9). The communications of the animal production sector conceal painful and murderous practices under a soothing vocabulary. Thus, the mass killing of chickens and pigs by clubbing, gassing or asphyxiation following the closure of American slaughterhouses at the beginning of the Covid-19 epidemic was described as "mass depopulation". The tendency to disregard singular animals, from their experiences and from their individual suffering is clearly apparent, calling into question the objectivity of our representations of their sufferings.

The investigation carried out over the course of these pages has shown, once again, that the notion of animal welfare is misleading in its uses, because it is not used as the opposite of ill-being, but constitutes an instrument for measuring the physical and psychological state of an animal in its relationship with its environment. The linguist Catherine Kerbrat-Orecchioni, in her book *Nous et les autres animaux*, even evokes in its connection a "characterized lexical imposture" (Kerbrat-Orecchioni 2021, p. 492). The phrase is indeed used to evoke the levels of discomfort endured by animals in laboratories, slaughterhouses and intensive farms. Moreover, while in the European Union's regulatory texts the notion of animal welfare covers the suffering of animals with a modest veil, the very principle of inflicting pain on them, holding them captive and killing them is so firmly established that the implementation of acts that are harmful or traumatic for them is supervised, and therefore authorized.

Among the other salient conclusions reached by this collective work is the observation that the commodification of other animals, a phenomenon that underlies much of the suffering they endure under human tutelage, can only be understood and studied in correlation with other facts and processes: colonialism, globalization, urbanization, industrialization, transportation development, mass consumption, the humanistic paradigm (the belief that human beings are at the center of representations and constitute the highest value), cultural imperialism, ethnocentrism and the advent of a post-domestic society. It was therefore fruitful to approach the problem in a systemic way, using an interdisciplinary approach. The blocking factors for the consideration of animal suffering must thus also be considered globally.

How did our society come to question the nature, extent and consideration of animal suffering? The reappraisal of moral sentience, insofar as it is most evident in the capacity to feel the pain of others, and physical sentience, as sensoriality, dates back to the 18th century. However, the greater interest in other animals, in anthropozoological relations, and in the role and status of non-humans in human societies as an academic movement is recent. This shift has been called the "animal turn" in the humanities and social sciences. It is well represented in the contributions gathered here. We find markers of this animal turn in law, moral philosophy, history, semiotics and ethology, where an accumulation of scientific studies has shown that animals can have a subjectivity, a psychological individuality and a culture. It is in the wake of this that the animal rights and animal welfare terminology was enriched at the end of the 20th century around the notions of sentience, speciesism, the animal rights movement and animal liberation. The science of animal welfare – an expression that must be dissociated from the ideological use made of it in zootechnics or elsewhere – has also developed in the last 30 years and has contributed to the awareness of non-human sentience. This discipline is concerned with how individuals cope with problems. There are two consensuses among scientists in this field: 1) to the extent that animal welfare is measurable (by studying physiology, behavior, pathology, injury, stress-related effects and mortality rates), it is a scientific concept; 2) welfare must include mental aspects. This science, which is important for the understanding of animal suffering at a biological level, has contributed to the definition of sentience: a sentient being is one who, in order to have feelings, possesses certain capacities. Sentient beings are able to evaluate the actions of others in relation to themselves or to third parties, to remember some of their own actions and their consequences, and to evaluate risks and benefits. They also have a certain degree of awareness (Broom, Chapter 11). It is also in the wake of this that disciplines are now opening up to these considerations, as is currently the case in economics (Espinosa, Chapter 6).

At the epistemological level, we have seen that, among the disciplines that are concerned with the damage suffered by animals, some are reductionist; in other words, they consider beings as bodies made up of organs. This is the case with veterinary medicine – because of the object of this discipline, and even while it is not, in principle, closed to a broader approach – and with zootechnics, which chooses a reductionist approach in order to found and justify its practice. Zootechnics perceives livestock as machines "providing services and products" and machines "constructed according to a certain plan: they are comprised of determined elements, of organs, as defined by both anatomy and mechanics" (Baudement). Within this framework, individuals are sets that can be reduced in varying degrees to the sum of the elements that comprise them. This positivist attitude has contributed to the fact that animal suffering is not taken into account. Although the reductionism of yesteryear is no longer systematic, the positivist paradigm of these sciences has not disappeared (Devienne, Chapter 9), and with it, the representation of animals, not as complex individuals but as aggregates of mechanisms and simple elements, has persisted. This representation was reinforced by the interventionist paradigm, crystallized at the end of the 19th century, which led to the consideration of animals as elements of a species, then as sums of genes, rather than as individuals (Pouillard, Chapter 1).

In addition, there are the productivist and anthropocentric paradigms. The question of the productivist paradigm, in its Western form, touches on several domains, from the captive management of wild animals to the development of zootechnics in the 19th century, from the intensification of meat production in the 20th century to European ambitions for animal protection, ambitions that were dashed by the productivist rationality of the late 20th century. The anthropocentric paradigm, for its part, has nourished the supposed need to make animals suffer in order to satisfy human needs. This suffering is not situational (to protect oneself from the aggressiveness of animals), but structural (to dominate animals), and derives neither from circumstances nor from nature, but from an ethico-cultural system (Marchadier, Chapter 4). Seen through the anthropocentric lens, the uses of non-human animals always see the scientific, food and recreational objectives of the experimentation or breeding procedures taking precedence over the interests of the animals. Regulatory texts contribute to their interests being placed on the back burner and to arrangements being possible to circumvent the regulations, so that unorthodox operations and painful practices are authorized, or even encouraged (Marchadier, Chapter 4; Obriet, Chapter 5). Whether alive, captive or dead, animals always seem to be considered as being at the service of humans. The anthropocentrism of a large section of modern and contemporary human societies is powerfully revealed in the contributions gathered here.

Yet many of these societies have reached a stage in their development where they may decide to break away from the aberrant relationship they have with other animals. Going back in time, and even more recently in some parts of the world, groups were or are forced to eat animal flesh in order to survive. They had to or continue to consume highly concentrated forms of food, including animal products. Today, however, it is hardly a question of survival: feeding on animal flesh is no longer essential, at least for the majority of human groups. Advances in nutrition have made it possible to balance a plant-based diet, so why continue to maintain a productivist and proprietary vision of livestock?

In the last century, the advent of a culture that the American psychologist Melanie Joy describes as "carnist" (Joy) led to profound changes in the systems of meat production, emphasizing the productivity of bodies. This underlines, in passing, the popular misconception that ancient times were crueler to animals than the contemporary period. This common assumption is disqualified in several of these contributions, since: 1) if we consider the number of animals suffering under human guardianship, it is false, since there are infinitely more animals bred and killed today than there were in the past, and they are now bred under sometimes very dense conditions of confinement (Li, Chapter 2; Sneddon, Chapter 10; Broom, Chapter 11). Besides, large-scale animal experimentation is also a recent phenomenon (Obriet, Chapter 5); 2) as an asset to the household, some animals were once treated as precious resources (Li, Chapter 2), whereas today, in industrial production, they acquire a collective identity that prevents individual consideration of their interests and pathologies (Devienne, Chapter 9); 3) transportation without rest, food or water was not as long as it is today, when it is common for animals raised on one continent or in one region to be transported to another continent or to a distant region to be killed (Li, Chapter 2).

Among the other preconceived notions that are challenged in this volume, there is also the idea that economics is the main obstacle to taking the interests of non-humans into account. Romain Espinosa shows, on the contrary, that economics is capable of integrating animals into discussions of societal choices. Another example is the idyllic perception of the life of free animals, an idealized and anthropocentric vision according to which wild animals would live happy lives so long as no harm is done to them (Horta, Chapter 8). Another is that fish are not sentient and have very short memories. Lynne Sneddon (Chapter 10) responds that the current definition of animal pain provides two clear concepts that can be tested to determine whether fish are capable of feeling pain: 1) the animal's responses to painful stimulation must differ from non-painful stimuli; animals must possess the neural mechanisms to detect painful stimuli via nociceptors; 2) after a painful experience, the animal must change its future behavioral decisions, so that its motivation is altered by the experience. Many studies show that fish possess nervous system receptors that respond to pain in a similar way to mammals. However, while it is recognized, as the many studies cited in this contribution invite us to do, that fish are capable of feeling pain and fear, we must also recognize that their welfare is degraded when we cause damage to their tissues or put them through frightening events.

These chapters also highlight some of the worst practices in terms of the pain and distress endured by animals, such as: very poor welfare levels for industrially farmed pigs, chickens and fish (Broom, Chapter 11; Li, Chapter 2), painful and lethal uses of billions of fish (Sneddon, Chapter 10), dogs frightened and beaten or hanged to death (Dugnoille, Chapter 3), mutilation, water control and the brutal killing of laboratory animals in France: cervical dislocation, decapitation, electric stunning (Obriet, Chapter 5) and the immense suffering endured by wild animals, especially for the numerous offspring of certain species, offspring that often die young after experiencing starvation, injury, predators and disease (Horta, Chapter 8). With regard to animals living under human guardianship, pigs seem particularly to be victims of cruel acts (Li Chapter 2; Marchadier, Chapter 4), in China as in Europe: animals buried alive, forcibly watered or made witnesses to the killing of other pigs, pigs undergoing caudectomies, teeth grinding and castrations. As Fabien Marchadier (Chapter 4) points out, these practices are not prohibited by the European regulations intended to protect animals, but rather they are authorized so long as they are carried out *according to a certain protocol.* Donald Broom (Chapter 11) points out that some of these operations can cause long-term pain: piglet tail docking, for example, causes measurable pain for more than four months. In addition to the number of animals, the intensity of the pain is of concern. In animal experimentation, two cursors can contribute to these measures: 1) the number of animals involved in procedures classified as "severe"; 2) the number of animals reused in multiple procedures, reuse being encouraged by public authorities as a means of reducing the total number of animals used (Obriet, Chapter 5). It should also be noted that, aporetically, the experiments conducted by researchers to establish animal sentience are based precisely on procedures that are painful, traumatic, frightening or lethal for the individuals, for example, the procedure that shows that carp species in contact with extracts from the bodies of fellow carp killed by decapitation significantly modify their feeding behavior and display alarming behaviors, such as rapid movements and attempts to hide (Sneddon, Chapter 10).

As an absolute counter-model to factors contributing to reducing traumatic or painful experiences for animals, factory farming appears in the course of the texts as a contemporary aberration, a sort of pinnacle of the irrational exploitation of non-human animals, a murderous, mass and destructive exploitation of the environment, the climate, human health and, of course, generating intense and prolonged suffering. Intensive farming is the subject of much attention, as emphasized in many of the texts collected in this volume.

In the face of the damage suffered, some solutions or approaches have been proposed or evaluated: reduction in the consumption of animal products (Višak, Chapter 7; Li, Chapter 2); the revision and extension of the scope of legal norms (Marchadier, Chapter 4; Obriet, Chapter 5); a more precise definition of animal welfare (Broom, Chapter 11); heavier and more systematically enforced penalties for infringements (Marchadier, Chapter 4); increased attention to language and culture (Broom, Chapter 11; Horta, Chapter 8). In the case of wild animals, vaccination, contraception and the rescue of victims of natural disasters or animals living in urban, industrial or agricultural areas are all ways to alleviate suffering. Since a society's overall preferences may also influence policy or economic activity, we have also seen that a society concerned with animal welfare will have an interest in limiting animal husbandry when it is carried out in poor conditions. The Twenty Measures for Animals project reports that there is a willingness to pay more for animal welfare among consumers of animal products. The strongest of the Twenty Measures are the ban on slaughter without stunning and the sterilization and identification of pets. In France, the cruelest practices of factory farming – the use of carbon dioxide to gas pigs and the keeping of chickens in cages – are also subject to a higher willingness to pay (Espinosa, Chapter 6).

Other avenues are being pursued by animal rights organizations that echo some of the approaches considered by the contributors to this volume:

– caring for abandoned or abused animals (animal placed in homes or shelters);

– changing individual and collective behavior (through awareness-raising and promotion of plant-based food);

– actions taken by whistleblowers (field investigations, videos made public);

– political activity towards systemic change, which includes expert or relational lobbying, petitions, institutional communication, referendum proposals and European citizen initiatives;

– legal instruments (legal recourse, attempts to modify animal law, proposal for legal personification);

– collaborating with the agribusiness sector;

– developing educational approaches.

Finally, we note the existence of several political groups, established since the beginning of the 21st century, dedicated to the improvement of the animal condition: the Dutch *Partij voor de Dieren* (2002), the Spanish *Partido Animalista Contra el Maltrato Animal* (2003), the Australian *Animal Justice Party* (2010), the Turkish *Hayvan Partisi* (2011) and the French *Parti Animaliste* (2016), among many others.

While animal suffering, although scientifically established, still struggles to be considered for its own sake, as is evident from the reading of this volume, the correlations between it and climate change, the multiplication of zoonoses, the ecological crisis, and human illnesses linked to the consumption of animal products will perhaps render it less insignificant. We can hope so, in order that the countless beings, whether terrestrial or aquatic, wild or domesticated, that endure suffering are taken into account for what they are: sentient and conscious individuals who value their own lives.

C.1. References

Baudement, É. (1862). *Les races bovines au Concours universel agricole de Paris, en 1856, études zootechniques publiées par ordre de S. Exc. Le ministre de l'Agriculture, du Commerce et des Travaux publics*, Introduction et atlas. Imprimerie impériale, Paris.

Joy, M. (2011). *Why We Love Dogs, Eat Pigs, and Wear Cows. An Introduction to Carnism*. Conari Press, San Francisco.

Kerbrat-Orecchioni, C. (2021). *Nous et les autres animaux*, Labyrinthes, Paris.

List of Authors

Donald M. BROOM
St Catherine's College and
Department of Veterinary Medicine
University of Cambridge
UK

Florence BURGAT
Archives Husserl
Ecole Normale Supérieure
Paris
France

Emilie DARDENNE
Equipe d'accueil Anglophonie,
Communauté, Ecriture (ACE)
Université de Rennes 2
France

Philippe DEVIENNE
Practicing Veterinarian and
Doctor of Philosophy
Vincennes
France

Julien DUGNOILLE
University of Exeter
UK

Romain ESPINOSA
Centre international de recherche sur
l'environnement et le développement
(CIRED)
CNRS
Paris
France

Oscar HORTA
University of Santiago de Compostela
Spain

Peter J. LI
University of Houston-Downtown
USA

Fabien MARCHADIER
Equipe de recherche en droit privé
(ERDP)
Université de Poitiers
France

Muriel OBRIET
Association Transcience
Paris
France

Violette POUILLARD
LARHA
CNRS
Lyon
France
and
Ghent University
Belgium

Lynne U. SNEDDON
Department of Biological and
Environmental Sciences
University of Gothenburg
Sweden

Tatjana VIŠAK
Department of Philosophy and
Business Ethics
University of Mannheim
Germany

Index

Printed and bound by CPI Group (UK) Ltd, Croydon, CR0 4YY

13/08/2023

03246013-0001